HOW TRUMP GOVERNS

How Trump Governs

An Assessment and Prognosis

Michael A. Genovese

CAMBRIA
PRESS

Amherst, New York

Requests for permission should be directed to
permissions@cambriapress.com, or mailed to:
Cambria Press
100 Corporate Parkway, Suite 128
Amherst, New York 14226, USA

Photos on front cover: Flanked by Vice President Mike Pence and Speaker
of the House Paul Ryan, President Donald Trump delivers his Joint Address
to Congress at the U.S. Capitol Building in Washington, D.C., Tuesday,
February 28, 2017. (Official White House Photo by Shealah Craighead).

Library of Congress Cataloging-in-Publication Data

Names: Genovese, Michael A., author.

Title: How Trump Governs: An assessment and prognosis /
by Michael A. Genovese, President, Global Policy
Institute at Loyola Marymount University.

Description: Amherst, New York : Cambria Press, 2017.
| Includes bibliographical references and index.

Identifiers: LCCN 2017035559|
ISBN 9781604979886 (alk. paper) |
ISBN 1604979887 (alk. paper)

Subjects: LCSH: Trump, Donald, 1946- | United States--Politics and
government--2017---Decision making. | United States--Foreign
relations--2017---Decision making. | Presidents--United States--Biography.

Classification: LCC E912 .G46 2017 |
DDC 973.933092--dc23
LC record available at https://lccn.loc.gov/2017035559

To Gaby
Yesterday, Today, and Tomorrow

TABLE OF CONTENTS

LIST OF FIGURES

LIST OF TABLES

ACKNOWLEDGEMENTS

The craft of writing a book is a solitary, lonely act. Many hours spent alone, just you, the pen and paper (or computer). The great sports writer Red Barber once said that: "Writing is easy. You just sit down and open a vein."*

If writing is a lonely job, producing a book is a cooperative effort. It involves typists, researchers, editors, proofreaders, copy editors, publishers, and a slew of other important people along the way. It also involves a supportive family.

My wife has given me, over the years, a very special gift that other scholars will recognize as vitally important: guilt-free writing time. She was understanding and supportive on those days she suggested a movie, but I said, "I'm sorry, I need to..." or when she'd say "Can we put up the Christmas lights this weekend?" and I'd say, "How about next weekend, this weekend I have a deadline?" How did I get so lucky?

My team of administrative assistants and researchers at the Global Policy Institute at Loyola Marymount University, and at the LMU Institute for Leadership Studies, were dedicated, hardworking, patient with me, considerate, and ever diligent. And so to John Pickhaver, Hector Blanes

Pomares, Ashley Oshiro, Breanne Schneider, Sabrina Leung, and Jeremy Selland, my deepest thanks.

And of course, my publisher and editors at Cambria Press—especially Toni Tan and David Armstrong—were kind, professional, and constantly supportive. What a pleasure it is working with such wonderful and capable people.

* See Red Barber and Robert W. Creamer, *Rhubarb in the Catbird Seat* (Lincoln: Bison Books, 1997).

How Trump Governs

CHAPTER 1

INTRODUCTION

This is a book about presidential power and politics. It will present the reader with an evaluative template with which to measure and assess the early leadership of the president, Donald J. Trump. A president's term lasts for four years, so our goal is to look not only at the early actions of the Trump Administration but also their prospects for the future.

The presidency has become the political epicenter of the American system. It was not designed for that. When invented 230 years ago, the office was set up to be limited in power and bound up in a separation-of-powers system.

Over the years, as American power rose, presidential power grew.[1] But the most significant burst of presidential power occurred with the Great Depression of 1929, when the federal government assumed greater responsibility for economic prosperity and when a large bureaucratic state was created under the executive branch; World War II with the centralization of power to the executive; the Cold War when the National Security State was created, largely under the control of the executive branch; and later the rise of the post-9/11 antiterrorist state—these all contributed to a swelling of the presidency.

The rise of the U.S. as the dominant, or hegemonic, post–World War II international power and as the largest and most powerful economic force on the globe, and the cultural penetration allowed for by technological changes contributed both to the rise of American power and the rise of presidential power. For better or worse, the United States has been transformed into a presidential nation. Today, the presidency is at the center of both American and international policies.[2]

A NEW PRESIDENT AND NEW HOPE

Every new presidency is a time of hope. Fresh ideas, new people, new policies all give us reason to hope that tomorrow will be better than today.[3]

With every new president who comes to the White House, I tell my students that—whether I voted for them or not—I hope that the new president is a great success. While I do have my partisan leanings, the success of a president from any party means success for America. And when things are going well for my country, things go well for me. My job is more secure, my retirement savings grow, my neighbor's kid can get a job out of college, we can pay for both guns and butter. Peace and prosperity, justice and security—it is the gold standard for governing, and I wish that for each president and for my country.

But invariably hope fades, problems persist, some solutions backfire, the laws of unintended consequences hit you, and your popularity drops as your troubles rise. We expect—and hope for—too much of our presidents. They do not have the powers to meet our high demands. We thus set them up for disappointment or failure.

HOW TRUMP GOT ELECTED[4]

Donald Trump had been threatening to run for president since the 1980s. Most people believed it was merely another way for Trump to get media attention, and his many presidential overtures were dismissed out of hand. But in 2016, Trump actually took the plunge. No one gave him a chance.

THE PRIMARIES

In the Republican primaries, sixteen prominent party leaders (and Trump) sought the nomination. The prohibitive favorite was Jeb Bush, the son of one president, the brother of another, and the former governor of Florida. Donald Trump went into full attack mode and focused all his early fire on Bush.

On January 1, 2015, it looked like "The Jeb and Hillary Show." For Hillary Clinton, a Joe Biden run might be a problem, but the tragic death of his son on March 30, 2015, seemed to take the fire out of Biden. Beyond that, the Democrats' bench was very thin. A few non-threatening candidates—Jim Webb, former Senator from Virginia; Lincoln Chafee, former governor of Rhode Island; Martin O'Malley, former Maryland governor; and Bernie Sanders, an Independent (not even a Democrat) Senator from Vermont and self- proclaimed Democratic-Socialist. It was a group of nonstarters, and Clinton probably felt safe.

But Clinton had baggage: Bill, her controversial ex-president husband, ongoing questions about her e-mails while serving as secretary of state, the baggage of Benghazi, millions of dollars in speaking fees to Wall Street groups, and a "Clinton fatigue" all proved to be death by a thousand cuts. Plus, Hillary's campaign seemed flat and lifeless. There was no driving message, no passion.

And then Bernie Sanders exploded on the scene. The 74-year-old leftist of Jewish descent caught fire. 2016 was another angry-voter election, and Sanders captured the mood of the angry voters in the Democratic Party. What were Democrats angry about? The 1%, income inequality, Wall Street. Economic fears turned to anger, then to passion, and Sanders was their voice.

On the Republican side, Jeb Bush initially seemed like he would clinch the GOP nomination. After all, he had the money, the support of the establishment (which worked both ways for him), and an air of inevitability that might chase challengers away.

And then The Donald happened. Trump captured the angry voters on the right. And what were Republicans angry about? They felt let down by the Republican establishment which they felt betrayed them and made deals with Big Government politicians. They were angry at President Barack Obama ("not one of us") and felt "they" were taking over. They were upset that everyone else was benefitting from the economic recovery, they were mad at immigrants, Muslims, and "them." Donald Trump channeled their anger, amplified it, and gave voice to it. Responding to the surprising rise of Trump, Bush at first discounted Trump, then pursued a tortoise-and-hare approach, and when that too did not dislodge Trump as leader of the pack, he tried—unsuccessfully—to be an attack dog. Nothing worked. Jeb was one of the early Republican dropouts.

Trump appealed to the average citizen and was loathed by the Republican donor class. His "affluenza" became an asset, as he played the part of celebrity demagogue flying above politics as usual. Reality television was now at center stage in American electoral politics and seemed to be changing the rules of engagement. The consensus was that celebrity status was replacing experience as a prime requirement for anyone hoping to attract the average voter.

The standards and values of reality television—the exaggerated feuds, the personal vilification, and the deleted expletives—have invaded the political realm. And it is a form of social decay. It is good manners that allow citizens to argue without coming to blows, and even to find productive compromise. In most everyday circumstances, manners matter more than laws. Good manners involve an affirmation that we, all of us, are part of the same community, and that everyone is due a certain minimal amount of respect. Poor manners, in contrast, can indicate the dehumanization of individuals and groups. The boor is often the bigot.[5]

Texas Senator Ted Cruz responded to Trump's implying that Cruz's father might be implicated in the JFK assassination with an all-out attack on Trump. Defending his father, Cruz went on to call Trump "a pathological liar, utterly amoral," and as "narcissistic." He further said that Trump was a man "for whom morality does not exist," that Trump is "terrified of strong women," and that he, Trump, openly bragged about how "great it is to commit adultery." Cruz wasn't finished. He mocked Trump's statement that conquering "venereal disease was his personal Vietnam,"[6] and that Trump was a "serial philanderer and boasts about it." Did anyone care or was Trump the celebrity with Teflon coating, a celebrity who just might be the next president of the United States? In the long primary season, Trump attracted large crowds and his attack style led rival after rival to fall.

Trump won the Indiana primary, and then on May 4, 2017, the following day, Cruz dropped out. The next day, John Kasich, Governor of Ohio, too dropped out. There was no stopping Trump now, but could he unite the party? Could he reduce his high "negatives"? Could he appeal to women? Could he win?

It was down to two. Trump versus Clinton. A flamboyant, politically inexperienced billionaire, who during the primaries came across as racist, sexist, and bullying, against a very politically experienced but flat campaigner. In a year of anti-Washington sentiment, could the novice outsider appeal to angry voters—and were there enough—to win the election?

Trump and Clinton had secured the nominations, but the irony is that both candidates had astronomically high negative ratings. A RoperCenter poll from April found Trump to have the highest "strongly unfavorable" rating of any candidate since 1980.[7] Hillary Clinton had the second highest negative rating. It was shaping up to be a brutal contest between two of the most disliked figures in American politics. And if things got down and dirty, it was advantage Trump. The Donald won the Republican primaries by attacking his opponents viciously. During the primaries Trump likened opponent Ben Carson to a pedophile,[8] implied that Ted Cruz's wife was ugly,[9] cited the *National Enquirer* as his source linking Ted Cruz's father to the Kennedy assassination,[10] and the list goes on and on.

According to the conventional wisdom, after securing the party nomination, a candidate should:

1) solidify the base,
2) try to expand from the base,
3) select key battleground states that had to be won in order to gain victory in the general election.

But Trump was anything but conventional.

Both Clinton and Trump began their campaigns with high unfavorable ratings, and the campaigns reinforced and amplified these negative views. Clinton and Trump did not rise in favorability as their campaigns progressed, they became even more *unpopular*. By election time, Clinton had an over 40% unfavorable rating while Trump registered over 50%.[11]

For Trump, the endorsements were not coming in. Mitt Romney, the party's nominee in the previous election, refused to endorse him, as did Republican Senator Lindsey Graham and Ben Sasse. House Speaker Paul Ryan said he was just not ready to endorse. Jeb Bush said he wouldn't vote for Trump.

Securing the nomination was difficult enough for Donald Trump, but putting the party back together was probably harder. Several prominent Republicans, including George H. W. Bush, George W. Bush and Romney, refused to support Trump. This marked the first time since 1912, when Teddy Roosevelt refused to endorse (and even ran against) William Howard Taft, that a party's previous nominee refused to endorse the current nominee. Some prominent Republicans even went as far as to search for an independent/Republican "third-party" candidate to oppose Trump. With party unity in jeopardy, down-ticket Republicans (i.e., those running for Senate or Congress) worried Trump might take them down with him.

In early June, as a triumphant Trump tried to unite the Republicans behind his candidacy, the thin-skinned candidate got into trouble with leaders in his own party when on several occasions he ventured off message and then began attacking the federal judge hearing a lawsuit (alleging fraud) against Trump University. Trump asserted that because the judge was Mexican (he was actually born in Indiana), there was a conflict of interest; he said that the judge would inherently be unable to be fair to him and that the judge should therefore recuse himself from the case. Trump repeated his attack on several different occasions and, even when given the opportunity to retract these remarks, refused to back down.[12]

Illinois Republican Senator Mark Kirk then withdrew his endorsement of Trump. South Carolina Republican Senator Lindsey Graham announced he would not vote for Trump, and House Majority Paul Ryan called Trump's attack on the judge "the textbook definition of a racist."[13] Republicans were quickly abandoning the seemingly sinking Trump ship. Could Trump put a plug in this crack?

And what would Bernie Sanders do? As the primary season approached the end line, Sanders kept insisting he would take his case all the way to the convention. But with the race already sewn up in early June, prolonging the race seemed fruitless and dangerous. Clinton needed Sanders's young voters, but they wouldn't let go of their hopes of Sanders becoming the Democratic candidate. Might Sanders be the 2016 version of Ralph Nader? (In 2000 Nader had drained enough votes from Al Gore in Florida to deliver the presidency to George W. Bush.)

The June 7 Super Tuesday primaries put Hillary Clinton over the top. She had more than enough committed delegates to be widely seen as the Democratic Party's presumptive nominee. It was a historic night. Eight years earlier the United States elected an African American president.

Now, for the first time, a woman would receive the nomination for president from one of the two major parties.

The race was on: Donald Trump versus Hillary Clinton. Everyone expected the race to be down and dirty, and it was.

Trump gained attention—and votes—by bashing Mexicans (calling them "rapists and criminals"), calling for a travel ban for people from several mostly Muslim countries, trashing a war hero (John McCain), insulting a "gold star" family, making a series of misogynistic remarks, and insulting a handicapped reporter. Every insult, instead of disqualifying Trump, made him *more* popular with Republican voters.

Jeb Bush was caught by surprise—gentlemen just don't behave the way Trump was behaving—and his mumbling, fumbling, tepid response to Trump's full-throttled attacks made Bush look weak and helpless. He dropped out early.

Then, one by one, Trump shot down frontrunner after frontrunner until he was the last man standing. To the surprise of the Republican establishment, the populist Trump succeeded in a hostile takeover of the Republican Party.

THE REPUBLICAN CONVENTION

In the week prior to the Republican Convention, Donald Trump made a particularly public display of his vice-presidential "dating-game" selection process, with several key possibilities traveling to Indiana where Trump —and his children—interviewed the hopefuls.[14] In marched Mike Pence, Newt Gingrich, Chris Christie, and others to audition before the Trump family and be put through the "pass-the-children" test, demonstrating just how important Trump's children were in the campaign. There were no women or minorities invited to the auditions.

In the end, Trump made the "safe" choice: Mike Pence, Indiana Governor and former House member. Trump was still having trouble solidifying the conservative wing of the Republican Party, and Pence, a fiscal and social conservative, was to help reassure conservatives that yes, Trump is "one of us."

In his July 16 public announcement that Mike Pence would be his vice-presidential nominee, Trump repeatedly got off message. His script was a promotion of Pence, and yet Trump kept drifting from script to talk about himself.[15] Was this a Trump weakness, or a Trump strength? Was his imperial ego the reason for his rise, or would it be the cause of his downfall?

In presenting his new VP choice to the public, Trump spent 29 minutes talking about himself before introducing Pence.[16] Contrast this with past Republican VP announcements: George W. Bush spoke for seven minutes, then turned things over to Dick Cheney;[17] Mitt Romney spoke for 8 ½ minutes before turning things over to Paul Ryan.[18]

The Republican Convention began on Monday, July 18, 2016, in Cleveland, Ohio. John Kasich, the state's Republican governor and Trump's former primary rival, refused to even attend the convention[19] (only 33% of the party's fifty-four U.S. Senators showed up at the convention;[20] with Arizona's Jeff Flake saying "I've got to mow my lawn,"[21] and Nebraska's Ben Sasse telling reporters he would be taking his children to "watch some dumpster fires across the state"[22]). The dump-Trump forces made a desperate last-ditch effort to stop the presumptive nominee, but that fizzled and faded by the end of day one.

From a distance, the convention looked like a sea of white. The delegates were a fairly old and an almost-exclusively white crowd. According to *Fusion*, of the Democratic Party's 4,766 delegates, 2,887 delegates were women, 1,182 were African American, 747 Latinos, 633 LGBT, 292 Asian, and 147 were Native American.[23] By contrast, of the 2,472 at the Republican Party Convention, eighteen delegates (.73%) were African American.[24] The convention's version of diversity seemed to be rich, white males interacting with even richer white males. As for the glitz of star power, the A-list of Hollywood headliners speaking for Trump was led by Scott Baio[25] and Willie Robertson from the reality show *Duck Dynasty*.

At just before 4:00PM on the first day of the convention, the Republican National Committee (RNC) rushed through on voice vote only (with no debate), a rule (rule 39) that would have all but ended the dump-Trump effort. Nine states formally demanded a roll-call vote (seven is the number of states necessary to compel—by RNC rules—a roll-call vote) on the rules. But the convention chair refused.[26]

Gordon Humphrey, former Republican Senator from New Hampshire and an "anybody-but-Trump" advocate,[27] said the Republican leadership running the convention were "brownshirts" who were acting like fascists.[28] Former Virginia attorney general Ken Cuccinelli told MSNBC, "They [the RNC] cheated."[29] The dump-Trump forces failed to get the RNC to follow the rules they themselves had established. The road had been cleared for a Trump nomination. But what of party unity? After this melee, the Colorado state delegation walked out.

Monday started off with a bang as the floor fight over the convention rules failed to silence the dump-Trump supporters. But by mid-evening, the convention morphed into a dump-on-Hillary-Clinton festival as speaker after speaker attacked Clinton for everything from Benghazi to her e-mails. But the highlight of the day was a speech by Donald Trump's third wife, Melania Trump, delivered with poise, grace, and somebody else's words. That somebody else was Michelle Obama.[30]

Just hours after Melania delivered her speech to rave reviews, word got out that she had lifted portions of her convention speech from Michelle Obama's 2008 convention speech.[31] Campaign head Paul Manafort wasted no time throwing Melania under the bus as he tried to distance himself (and the speechwriter he assigned to work with Melania) from the debacle.[32]

Melania's speech was a gold-plated gift to late-night comedians and social media. The jokes flowed freely:

Melania: Not only were the accusations of plagiarism hurtful to me, but they also hurt my children Sasha and Malia.[33]

Opening of Melania's speech: "I was born a poor black child in Chicago..."[34]

Day two of the Republican Convention went much better for Trump. He was officially named the party's nominee, and the speeches by New Jersey Governor Chris Christie and Trump's eldest son Donald Trump Jr. were well received. But the plagiarism issue just wouldn't go away. The RNC and Trump campaign manager Paul Manafort insisted that there was no plagiarism. And yet on Wednesday morning the campaign announced that a Trump company employee Meredith McIver did indeed plagiarize portions of Melania's speech from a Michelle Obama 2008 speech. The campaign chaos was becoming the story of the convention. Could they put the train back on the tracks?

To make things worse, on day three of the convention it was reported that the Secret Service was investigating one of Donald Trump's advisers, Al Baldasaro, after he called for the execution of Hillary Clinton. His exact quote, "Hillary Clinton should be put in the firing line and shot for treason."[35] Thus, as the convention continued, the Trump team, appearing dazed and confused, couldn't seem to get its act together. If they couldn't run a convention, how did they expect to run a government?

Things just kept getting worse for Trump on day three of the convention, which was supposed to be Mike Pence's opportunity to present himself to the American people as the ticket's vice-presidential pick. Pence's speech was solid, but it got buried under the controversy that was Ted Cruz. Senator Cruz—still stinging from the Trump attack on Heidi Cruz, the senator's wife (intimating in a tweet that she was ugly), and on Rafael Cruz, the senator's father (suggesting in a tweet that he was somehow implicated in JFK's assassination)—refused in his prime-time convention speech to endorse Trump. Yet again, the Trump team had lost control of the narrative, got off message, and appeared incompetent.

Could Trump give his flagging convention a reboot? The final day of the Republican Convention was a filler awaiting the star's performance. Daughter Ivanka Trump introduced her father to the convention and television-viewing public, hoping—with some success—to humanize him and present the soft, fuzzy side of Trump.

When Trump himself finally took to the podium, he delivered a very long (one-hour and twenty minutes, longer than the 2012 Obama and Romney acceptance speeches combined) and a very dark, angry address. A *Los Angeles Times* article said, "It was a voice suffused with anger and steeped in resentment."[36]

Trump's convention speech was a surprisingly dark, almost apocalyptic portrayal of a country on the verge of collapse, and as he said, "I alone can fix it."[37] Arguing that the Democrats had left a legacy of "death, destruction, terrorism, and weakness," Trump promised to "liberate our citizens from the crime and terrorism and lawlessness that threatens their communities." But "beginning on January 20 of 2017, safety will be restored."[38]

Trump's speech was "I" and "me," but rarely "we." Only he, Trump said, could save America. So dark was his message that comedian Bill Maher joked that the speech was "so depressing that Melania started to plagiarize a suicide note."[39] The speech energized the crowd at the convention, but was the public ready to accept such an apocalyptic vision?

And as was the case with the previous three days of the Republican Convention, day four was also a day of damage control for the Trump campaign as Paul Manafort and other Trump spokespersons had to explain away the controversial remarks Trump made in a *New York Times* interview in which he suggested that as president, he might not honor our NATO treaty obligations to our allies.[40] Blowback from this bizarre remark found both Democrats and Republicans condemning Trump for such a foolish and dangerous statement. Even Republican Senate Majority leader Mitch McConnell was tepid in his response to Trump's flub: "I am willing to kind of chalk it up to a rookie mistake."[41] But Trump, in typical Trump fashion, stood by his remarks.

The highlight of the Republican Convention? The speeches by the Trump children—Tiffany, Donald Jr., Eric, and Ivanka (Barron, age 10, did not speak) —were uniformly excellent and gave a boost to a convention high on flubs and low on quality.

Among the many flubs and fumbles of the Republican Convention, perhaps the most worrisome was the anger, hatred, and resentment so evident in the crowd. The *Los Angeles Times* said the delegates were "reminiscent of a lynch mob" with their daily repetition of the convention mantra regarding Clinton, "Lock Her Up." It wasn't pretty, it wasn't mature, and it wasn't appropriate.[42]

THE GENERAL ELECTION

Trump's opponent in the general election was Hillary Rodham Clinton, former First Lady, former U.S. Senator from New York, and former Secretary of State in the Obama Administration. While Clinton had the experience, she was not trusted by many Americans. She seemed to some to be too political a politician, and her baggage heavily weighed her down in the general election.[43]

Trump continued his attack style that served him so well in the primaries into the general election. Ironically both Trump and Clinton had historically high "negatives." This would be more of an unpopularity contest that a popularity race

At this time, Trump trailed Hillary Clinton in the polls, and the first of three presidential debates was on the horizon.

It was generally conceded that Clinton bested Trump in all three presidential debates, and Trump seemed ill prepared for all the debates. While it is customary to blame the campaign for the candidates' shortcomings, in this case it was clear that Trump simply refused to be "handled" and failed to do his homework. Was Trump lazy? Conceited? One would have thought that for something of this potential magnitude, Trump might have spent a bit more time preparing.

Both Clinton and Trump hit hard and went negative. It was a race to see what we were against rather than what we were for. It was not our finest hour.

Throughout most of the campaign, Trump trailed Clinton in the polls. As the campaign drew to an end, virtually every pollster predicted a tight Clinton victory. But Trump's supporters were enthusiastic, angry, and staunchly anti-Clinton, whereas Clinton's supporters were only lukewarm towards the former first lady.

Trump's team believed he could win over a few blue states in the rust belt, states that the Clinton team referred to as her "blue wall," in reference to the presumed strength of her support in traditionally Democratic states. But several of those states went to Trump, giving him a surprise victory.

Clinton won the popular vote by about 3 million votes, (65,844,610 to 62,979,636, or 48.2% to 46.1%), but presidents are not elected by the people—they are elected by the Electoral College. There Trump won a 306-232 victory.[44]

It was a tight race, and in the end, Trump was the surprise, upset winner. He was able to unify the Republican Party, win over some traditionally Democratic voters in the "rust belt" that had been hit hard by the 2007–2008 recession and by globalization. He also benefitted from some voter-suppression effects in Republican states, Russia's release of hacked Democratic members' e-mails that were publicly distributed by WikiLeaks, an FBI director who kept the Clinton e-mail story on the front pages, and a lackluster campaign by Clinton.

Figure 1. 2016 Presidential Election Map (270 electoral votes to win).

Source. https://www.270towin.com/2016_Election/interactive_map.

It was an ugly, deeply disturbing, controversial presidential campaign; and in the end, real-estate mogul and reality television celebrity Donald J. Trump—our oldest elected president and the first president with no political or military experience—was elected 45th president of the United States.

Donald Trump was—to say the least—an unusual choice as president. Trump had bashed and insulted his way through a crowded Republican primary field and rode his attack/insult style all the way to the White House.

Trump's Biography

Donald John Trump was born in 1946 in Queens, New York. His father Frederick was a successful real estate developer in New York. In an effort to instill some discipline in him, his parents sent him at age thirteen to the New York Military Academy. He later attended Fordham University, then transferred to the Wharton School of Finance at the University of Pennsylvania. He graduated in 1968 with a degree in economics, then went to work in his father's business.

In 1971 Trump was given control of his father's company, which he later renamed the company the Trump Organization. He expanded the business, and over time had good years and bad, including declaring bankruptcy six times, on his way to building a billion-dollar company.

On several occasions, Trump flirted with runs for the presidency but always backed away at the eleventh hour. His public profile was raised even higher in 2004 when he starred in the reality television series *The Apprentice*. Trump championed the "birther" movement, calling into doubt whether President Barack Obama was born in the United States. Of course, Obama was born in the United States, but even when this was beyond dispute, Trump continued to get publicity out of questioning the president's birthplace.

On June 16, 2015, Trump announced his candidacy for the presidency, ran in caucuses and primaries; and on July 21, 2016, he accepted the Republican Party nomination for president.

Electing Presidents: A Functional Leadership Selection System?

American presidential elections tend to be *long, costly,* and *superficial.* And the 2016 race fulfilled that trifecta very well. It took nearly three long, often tedious years to select Donald Trump as the 45th president of the United States. In the United Kingdom it takes about six weeks.

Overall, the 2016 national elections cost billions of dollars. The race also tended towards the ridiculous as swaggering bombast trumped thoughtful policy discussions, and the pompous outmaneuvered the ponderous. The Trump media magnet pulled everyone into its wake, and serious public policy discussion was relegated to the back pages of our sadly disappearing daily newspapers.

Ours is a leadership selection process difficult to defend and harder still to explain. I often travel to teach and lecture in Europe and am frequently asked to explain the American presidential selection system to people who simply can't fathom how the most powerful nation on earth elects the most important leader on earth with such a bizarre and broken system. The Electoral College? No other nation has such a baroque electoral mechanism, and others wonder how the globe's chief proponent of democracy could employ such an odd, and as was the case in the 2000 (and again in 2016) presidential system where the candidate with the most votes (Al Gore, then Hillary Clinton) lost; what an undemocratic device for selecting its president. And money! How, they often ask, could the country that goes to war to impose democracy on other nations, allow Big Money and Corporations to "buy" its presidents? Our presidential selection system simply does not make sense to outsiders. Should it make sense to us?

Does the process attract and reward the best potential candidates, or does it repel good potential candidates from running in the first place? Does the process by which we elect presidents reward the worst of the candidates, and punish the best? And does it test the skills and temperament of would-be presidents? Is what it takes to get elected different from what it takes to govern effectively? Does this system fulfill our democratic promise? Is this the best we can do?

In elections we not only pick our leaders, we also have a national discussion on our collective future. We (the people) are supposed to tell them (elected officials) where we want the nation to be headed. We give the directions. Or do we?

A functional electoral system should:

1) produce several talented people who are seeking the office
2) test the qualities necessary to govern effectively
3) expose those qualities of character or temperament that a president should not have
4) be fair and transparent
5) present issues of substance to the voters
6) offer a clear choice regarding directions in which to take the nation

James M. Burns called our selection process the "least functional" in the world. And Adlai Stevenson II—who ran for and lost the office on two occasions (both times to Dwight D. Eisenhower)—once said that "anyone who could be elected president, didn't deserve the office." He also told the story of a woman supporter at a campaign rally who shouted out "Mr. Stevenson, all thinking people support you," to which Stevenson replied, "That's wonderful, but I need a majority." The great lawyer Clarence Darrow (1857–1938) noted that "When I was a boy, my mother told me that in America, anyone could be president—and now, looking at the two candidates, I'm inclined to believe her!" Why does hardly anyone say a good word about our presidential selection system? Is it really that broken?

In the next chapter, we will explore the meaning and consequences of the 2016 presidential election, what it means for American politics, how the election and its outcome will affect President Trump's leadership and power prospects, and we will provide a template to better understand and evaluate a new president's performance. That template will inform the remainder of the book.

Notes

1. Michael A. Genovese, *The Power of the American Presidency, 1787–2000* (New York: Oxford University Press, 2000).
2. Michael A. Genovese, *A Presidential Nation: Causes, Consequences, and Cures* (Boulder: Westview Press, 2012).
3. Valerie Bunce, *Do New Leaders Make a Difference? Executive Succession and Public Policy Under Capitalism and Socialism* (Princeton: Princeton University Press, 1981).
4. This section draws on my earlier book, *The Trumping of American Politics: The Strange Case of the 2016 Presidential Election* (Amherst, NY: Cambria Press, 2017).
5. The Viewpoint, *The Week*, April 15, 2016, 12.
6. Tribune News Services, "Cruz Refuses to be Trump's 'Servile Puppy' After Attacks on His Wife, Father," *Chicago Tribune*, July 21, 2016.
7. Roper Center, "Two Thumbs Down: 2016 Presidential Candidates Favorability," April 2016.
8. Tribune News Services, "Cruz Refuses to be Trump's 'Servile Puppy'"
9. Ibid.
10. Donovan Slack, "Trump Bizzarely Links Cruz's Father to JFK Assassination; Cruz Goes Ballistic," *USA Today*, May 3, 2016.
11. "Trump and Clinton Finish with Historically Poor Images," *Gallup Poll*, November 8, 2016.
12. Jia Tolentino, "Trump and the Truth: The 'Mexican Judge,'" *The New Yorker*, September 20, 2016.
13. Heather Caygle, "Ryan: Trump's Comments Textbook Definition of Racism," *Politico*, June 7, 2016.
14. For the impact of the Trump children in the campaign, see Lizzie Widdicombe, "First Family: The Influence of Ivanka Trump and Jared Kushner," *The New Yorker*, August 22, 2016.
15. Eric Bradner, Dana Bash, and MJ Lee, "Donald Trump Selects Mike Pence as VP," *CNN*, July 16, 2016.
16. Tessa Berenson, "Donald Trump Introduces Mike Pence as Vice President Pick," *Time*, July 16, 2016.
17. Ibid.
18. Ibid.

19. Noah Bierman, "Ohio Gov. John Kasich is Everywhere (Except the Convention), Condemning Donald Trump (Without Naming Him)," *The Los Angeles Times*, July 21, 2016.

20. Jessica Taylor, "Dumpster Fires, Fishing, and Travel: These Republicans are Sitting Out of the RNC," *NPR*, July 18, 2016.

21. Ibid.

22. Peter Sullivan, "Kasich Defends Decision to Skip Conventions," *The Hill*, July 19, 2016.

23. Collier Meyerson, "So we counted all the women and people of color at the DNC and the RNC... ," Fusion, July 27, 2016, http://fusion.net/story/330193/dnc-rnc-women-people-of-color-numbers/.

24. Ibid.

25. Scott Baio is an American actor who is best known for his role as Chachi Arcola on the sitcom *Happy Days* (1977–1984) and its spin-off *Joanie Loves Chachi* (1982–1983), as well as the title character on the sitcom *Charles in Charge* (1984–1990). See http://www.imdb.com/name/nm0000281/bio.

26. Ralph Z. Hallow, "RNC Weighs Scrapping Convention Rule Book to Head-Off Anti-Trump Maneuvers," *The Washington Times*, March 16, 2016.

27. Jason Devaney, "NH Ex-Senator Gordon Humphrey: Trump Supports 'Brownshirts,'" *Newsmax*, July 18, 2016.

28. Ibid.

29. Zeke J. Miller and Alex Altman, "Convention Floor Erupts After Never Trump Action Fails," *TIME Magazine*, July 18, 2016.

30. Anita Kelly, "Section of Melania Trump's Monday Speech Mirrors Michelle Obama's in 2008," *NPR*, July 19, 2016.

31. Ibid.

32. James Hohmann, "The Daily 202: Melania's Plagiarized Convention Speech Shows Trump's Campaign is Still Not Ready for Prime Time," *The Washington Post*, July 19, 2016

33. Gina Barreca, "Can't Give Melania Any Credit for Speech," *Hartford Courant*, July 20, 2016.

34. Ibid.

35. Connor Friedersdorf, "Trump Advisors: Hillary Clinton 'Should be Shot in a Firing Squad for Treason,'" *The Atlantic*, August 16, 2016.

36. Mark Z. Barabok and Noah Bierman, "Trump's Populist Promise," *Los Angeles Times*, May 22, 2016, B1.

37. Alex Altman, "Midnight in America: Donald Trump's Gloomy Convention Speech," *Time*, July 21, 2016.

38. Ibid.

39. Ibid.

40. The Editorial Board, "President Trump Fails NATO," *The New York Times*, May 26, 2017.

41. Jordain Garney, "McConnell: Trump's NATO Remarks a 'Rookie Mistake,'" *The Hill*, July 21, 2016.

42. Editorial, "Toxic Politics of 'Lock her up," *Los Angeles Times*, July 21, 2016, A14.

43. See Genovese, *The Trumping of American Politics*.

44. Trump ended up with 304 actual electoral votes, as two "faithless electors" decline to vote for Trump.

CHAPTER 2

WHAT CAMPAIGNS AND ELECTIONS CAN TELL US ABOUT PRESIDENTIAL EFFECTIVENESS

Elections have consequences. They tell us who is to govern and, occasionally, where we wish to go. What does the 2016 presidential election tell us about ourselves? Where we are headed? What unifies and divides us? And what does the 2016 election mean for Donald Trump's prospects for the future?

THE MEANING OF THE 2016 ELECTION[1]

November 9. Years of campaigning. Billions of dollars spent. A squalid and depressing campaign. Two highly unpopular candidates. And in the end, Donald J. Trump, a political outsider, a political novice, a change candidate, ended up the surprise, upset winner (See figure 1).

He was the least experienced person ever elected to the presidency, having no political or military background. He was also the oldest person ever elected president. His negatives were high, yet he won more electoral votes than George W. Bush won in 2000 or 2004. Who would have predicted it? How did it happen?

Turnout

It was an ugly divisive race. Did it turn off voters? No. 2016 drew about the average percentage of voters, as past elections (see table 1). Still, 58% for a presidential election is low when compared with most other democracies. On average, fewer than 60% of Americans even bother to vote in presidential elections. That number decreases significantly in mid-term elections and falls off even more in state and local elections. For a country that prides itself on being a model democracy, it may be surprising that so few of us actually bother even to vote.

Why Trump Should Have Won

The time was right for a change. Eight years of one party should have given the opposition a leg up in a "throw the bums out" political season. More of the same was hard to sell and so, Trump, as the change candidate, had an advantage. Moreover, over 70 percent of the public was unhappy with the direction in which the government/country was headed, so there too was advantage Trump. Trust in government was very low, and as the outsider who was not a professional politician, Trump did not suffer from beltway phobia.

Table 1. Voter Turnout.

Year	% Turnout
1960	62.8%
1964	61.4%
1968	60.7%
1972	55.1%
1976	53.6%
1980	52.8%
1984	53.3%
1988	50.3%
1992	55.2%
1996	49.0%
2000	50.3%
2004	55.7%
2008	57.1%
2012	54.9%
2016	58%
Average Turnout	55.1%

Source. Compiled by author.

Finally, the public—left-wing supporters for Sanders and right-wing Tea Party supporters for Trump—were in the streets demanding something new. Starting with the base support of one of the major parties and building on the discontent of the voters, Trump had all the ingredients for the electoral success; and yet even so, Hillary Clinton did win the popular vote.

WHY TRUMP ALMOST LOST

No politician has given himself more self-inflicted wounds than Trump. Has there ever been a major party nominee who shot himself in the foot more than Donald Trump? Space does not permit me to list the numerous ways in which Trump nearly self-destructed. Despite running against a weak opponent with tons of heavy baggage, Trump seemed always to find a way to draw attention away from Hillary's many weaknesses and draw the spotlight onto himself as he said one controversial thing after another. Even so, Trump still managed to pull victory out of the jaws of defeat.

WHY CLINTON SHOULD HAVE LOST

She was a poor campaigner, this had all the makings of a "change" election; Hillary was unpopular and not trusted; the Russians and the FBI gummed up the works for Hillary; and Hillary seemed perpetually under investigation. She was vulnerable, and several of the more mainstream Republican hopefuls whom Trump defeated in the primaries, almost certainly would have beaten Clinton. She was poised to lose. Clinton simply had too much negative baggage, and while she won the popular vote by over 2 percent, her undoing was the Electoral College.

WHY HILLARY COULD HAVE WON

Why? Experience, money, organization, ground game, and Trump. Hillary's political experience was vast, and especially when compared to the political outsider, she simply knew more, had done more, and could draw on a vast network of associates to help her. The Clinton money machine was also a stable pipeline of funding that allowed her early on to form an experienced and capable campaign organization that built up a first-class ground game, giving her a decided advantage over the Trump campaign. And, of course, running against Trump seemed to be the gift that just kept giving. But it was not enough.

Amid Trump's surprising victory, let us not lose sight of the historic fact that, despite her loss, a bit of history was made by the fact that a woman—for the first time ever—was the nominee for president of one of the major parties.

IT'S STILL THE ECONOMY, STUPID

Hillary Clinton was unable to retain the "blue wall" of the rust belt states in America's manufacturing section of the midwest. Workers, fearing the effects of globalization and economic change, abandoned the Democratic Party and voted for Trump in numbers sufficient to barely eke out Republican wins in Pennsylvania, Wisconsin, Michigan, and Ohio.[2] Economic uncertainty contributed mightily to the Trump victory.

Political scientists have long argued that the economy (or more accurately, our "perceptions" of the state of the economy) significantly contributes to how we vote. In a strong economy, we tend to reward the incumbent president or their party; in a down economy, we tend to blame and punish the incumbent. In 2016, following the recession of 2008, the economy was fairly strong. Unemployment was down, the stock market was up; but economic growth was a bit sluggish, the benefits of the recovery went largely to the upper class, and with globalization, modernization, and automation, certain jobs (e.g., coal) and some regions (e.g., the Rust Belt) remained hard hit. Candidate Trump did a masterful job of speaking to the anger, dislocation, and fears of these voters.

Is Demography Destiny?

Democrats have long believed that demographic changes in the American population would guarantee electoral victories in the polls. The decline of white voters and the rise of voters of color seemed to favor the Democrats, giving them an insurmountable electoral edge against the Republicans. And while voters of color did overwhelmingly vote Democratic, a sufficient number of minority voters went with Trump adding to his sizeable margin of white voters who went with the Republican ticket. Demography is not destiny; and in the future, Democrats will have to work very hard to maintain the loyalties of various minority voting groups, each of whom (e.g. African Americans and Hispanics) have different agendas.

Economic uncertainty contributed mightily to the Trump victory. Yes, demographics matter, but turnout is the key: can you get your voters activated, motivated, and willing to go out and vote? Candidate Trump energized his supporters; candidate Clinton saw some drop in turnout among key Democratic groups (e.g., African Americans) in key regions (e.g., the Rust Belt).[3]

How the Vote Unfolded

Many of the group voting patterns we expect played out in 2016, but there were several interesting wrinkles (see table 2).

The Gender Gap. Since 1980, there has been a persistent gender gap of about 8 points favoring the Democrats.[4] In 2016, that gap was 12 points.[5] Interestingly, however, more than half of the white women who voted in the presidential election voted for Trump.[6]

The Hispanic Gap. Donald Trump rose to political prominence by trashing Mexicans and immigrants. Did they make him pay a heavy price? Of the eight states with Hispanic populations larger than the national average, only Texas went to Trump.[7] Fewer than one in ten Republican voters were nonwhite.[8] The number of Hispanic eligible voters was roughly 25 million in 2016; by 2030 it will be 40 million.[9] Mitt Romney won Texas by 16 points in 2012,[10] and in 2016 Trump won the state by 9 points.[11]

Hispanics typically vote for the Democratic candidate at a 65% rate.[12] In 2016, that is the percent who went for Clinton.[13] Where was the surge of Hispanics who were angered by Trump's immigrant and Mexican bashing? In 2012, Obama got 71% of the Hispanic vote.[14] Why the drop-off in a year that should have been a huge Democratic vote?

African American Voters. African Americans have long been a stable part of the Democratic coalition, and in 2016 Hillary Clinton won 88% of African American votes—about average for a Democratic candidate.[15]

In exit polls from the election, Trump did well with those wanting "change," but Clinton was seen as having the right experience (around 90%). Those "angry" with the federal government went overwhelmingly (over 75%) for Trump.[16] And the key reason voters gave in defense of their vote was "dislike" of the other candidate," confirming that both candidates had very high unfavorable ratings.

The White Male Vote. Donald Trump did very well with white male voters. Although as a voting group, white males are in decline, they rallied behind Trump and served as the core group of his base. He got 58% of the male vote to Clinton's 41%.[17] As CNN commentator Van Jones noted, this election was a "white-lash."[18]

Millennials. Millennials helped elect Barack Obama—twice. They voted for Clinton 54% to Trump's 37%,[19] but turnout was not what Clinton expected. The 18–29 age group comprised only 19% of the voters in 2016.[20]

Table 2. 2016 Voting Blocks.

		T	H	Gap	% of Vote
Sex	Men	53	41	12T	48%
	Women	42	54	12H	52%
Race	White	58	37	21T	70%
	Black	8	88	80H	12%
	Hispanic	29	65	36H	11%
	Asian	29	65	36H	4%
Age	18-29	37	54	17H	19%
	30-44	42	50	8H	25%
	45-64	53	44	9T	40%
	65 + over	52	45	7	16
Education	HS or less	51	45	6T	18%
	Some College/ Associate Degree	52	43	9T	32
	College Grad	45	49	4H	32%
	Post Grad Study	37	58	21H	18%
Income	Under $30,000	41	53	12H	17%
	$30-49,999	42	51	9H	19%
	$50-99,999	50	46	4T	31%
	$100-199,999	48	48	0	24%
	$200,000-249,999	48	48	0	4%
	$250,000 or over	48	46	2T	6%
Urban/Rural	Over 50,000	35	59	24H	34%
	Suburbs	50	45	5T	49%
	Small City/Rural	62	34	28T	17
Married	Yes	53	43	10T	59%
	No	38	55	17H	41%
What was the most important issue in the campaign?	FP	34	60	26H	13%
	Immigration	64	33	31T	13%
	Economy	42	52	10H	52%
	Terrorism	57	39	18T	18%

Source. According to exit polls (adapted from *New York Times* November 9, 2016).

College-Educated Voters. Traditionally a part of the Republican coalition, in 2016, college graduates preferred Clinton by 4% and people with postgraduate educations went 58-37% for Clinton.[21]

The Rust Belt. From the beginning, Donald Trump believed he could win over traditionally Democratic states in the rust belt. He was right. Pennsylvania, Ohio, Michigan, and Wisconsin all went for Trump. This was a significant reason why Trump won.

Republican voters came home; Democratic voters stayed home. White working-class voters went for Trump and, astonishingly, 29% of Hispanics voted Trump.[22] The Obama coalition did not coalesce for Clinton (it truly was an Obama, not a Democratic Party, coalition). Non-college-educated women went for Trump.[23] White voters went 58% for Trump, 53% of men voted for Trump, 67% of those without a college degree went to Trump.[24] Young, black, and Hispanic voters let Clinton down with lower turnout than expected.[25] Change voters—of whom there were many, went for Trump. Angry voters—again, many—voted for Trump. A number of people voted against Clinton. The rust belt voted for Trump. Plus enthusiasm won out over organization in voter turnout as Trump's voters were more passionate and committed to their candidate than Clinton's supporters.

POLITICAL REALIGNMENT?

Do the results of the election portend significant shifts in voting trends, even a political realignment? White working-class voters (a staple of the Democratic coalition) voted for Trump, while college-educated voters (who are traditionally Republican) went for Clinton.

Political realignments, deep fundamental shifts in parties on loyalties and ideological change, occur rarely. The last true realignment occurred in 1932–1934 when Franklin D. Roosevelt and the Democrats swept into office during the Great Depression, and the Democrats became America's dominant party for roughly forty years. That realignment began to break down in the 1970s when southern states shifted from the Democratic to the Republican Party. Since then, the partisan back-and-forth has not brought on a new realignment, and heightened polarization. The country may be ripe for a new party system.

So much of Trump's populist support came from less-educated, white, working-class males who felt they were the victims of globalization. Their manufacturing jobs—a guarantee of a middle-class existence—have evaporated due to outsourcing. These are voters who suffer economic and job insecurity, having been hit hard by stagnant wages, who are sometimes mocked (for living in "flyover states"), and they resent the elites who have benefited from the recovery while they have floundered. And while the Democratic Party has traditionally been the party of the working class, in an age of globalization, many voters perceived the Democrats—especially on trade issues—to be weak on working-class issues. There is also the importance of symbolic voting, possibly because of resentment against liberals, who supposedly look down upon working-class, blue-collar voters.[26] It is ironic that Democrats were the party that has favored programs (e.g., Obamacare, minimum wage, etc.) that help those struggling economically, while the Trump administrations's initial policies have been to repeal Obamacare and maintain (and in some cases, possibly increase) tax cuts for the rich.

Clinton had a difficult time attracting these traditionally Democratic voters. These "downwardly mobile white workers" flocked to Trump. Of these voters, Robert Packer writes:

> "Working class," meanwhile, has become a euphemism. It once suggested productivity and sturdiness. Now it means downwardly mobile, poor, even pathological. A significant part of the W.W.C. has succumbed to the ills that used to be associated with the black urban "underclass": intergenerational poverty, welfare, debt, bankruptcy, out-of-wedlock births, trash entertainment, addiction, jail, social distrust, political cynicism, bad health, unhappiness, early death. The heartland towns that abandoned the Democrats in the eighties to bask in Ronald Reagan's morning sunlight;

the communities that Sarah Palin, on a 2008 campaign stop in Greensboro, North Carolina, called "the best of America. . . the real America"—those places were hollowing out, and politicians didn't seem to notice. A great inversion occurred. The dangerous, depraved cities gradually became safe for clean-living professional families who happily paid thousands of dollars to prep their kids for the gifted-and-talented test, while the region surrounding Greensboro lost tobacco, textiles, and furniture-making, in a rapid collapse around the turn of the millennium, so that OxyContin and disability and home invasions had taken root by the time Palin saluted those towns, in remarks that were a generation out of date.[27]

These voters are the most pessimistic people in the country, and they are changing our political arithmetic.[28] Republican political strategist Steve Schmidt argues that the divide in America used to be left versus right, now it is up versus down. While liberal versus conservative still matters, the real cleavage is between those who can benefit from globalization's changes and those left behind. This will only get more pressing in the coming years as automation, robotics, and driverless cars put more of the working class out of work and on unemployment. This trend suggests the rise of "Rust Belt Republican" in states like Ohio, Michigan, and even Pennsylvania.

The loyalties different groups show to a political party can be deep and long running. But coalitions aren't permanent, and at times, over various issues, a voting bloc—never totally monolithic—may migrate to the opposition party. Such, for example, is the case of the once solidly Democratic South shifting—beginning in the mid-1960s due to Lyndon B. Johnson and the Democratic Party's embrace of civil rights reform— to the Republicans, creating the solid Republican South,[29] resulting in the polarization of Congress.

One reversal does not a permanent reversal of loyalties make, but a shift of note did take place in the 2016 election that—if it endures—could spell a realignment of our party system. In this election, many working-class, blue-collar voters went for Trump. This is a group who usually voted for Democrats. On the other side of the equation, college-educated voters—a traditional part of the Republican base—went for Clinton. Is this a temporary or long-term shift? Should this trend continue, we might well be witnessing the birth of class-based politics in America.

POLITICAL SCIENTISTS PICK THE WINNERS

Many political scientists believe that campaigns matter little, candidates are only of marginal importance, and campaign strategies do little to change votes. These folks believe that larger forces—the state of the economy, the mood of the public, or levels of presidential popularity—shape election outcomes more than the candidates. Are they right?

At each presidential election, the community of vote predictors issue their predictions, and some of the more prominent ones are featured in a pre-election volume of *PS*, published by the American Political Science Association. 2016 was no exception. What did their different models predict?

The polarized party model looks at the deep divisions in the two parties. These models predicted—not very helpfully—a close race. The sluggish economic growth models "suggested a Trump victory." The public mood models also favored Trump and the Republicans. The presidential approval models predicted a close race. And the preconvention preference poll models favored Clinton and the Democrats.[30]

A summary of the forecasts did favor a Clinton victory as well as Democratic gains in the House (from between no change and a 32-seat pickup) and the Senate (from 4-7 seat pickup). Oh boy, was all this wrong! Trump won the election, and the Democrats picked up only a handful of seats in the House and could not win control of the Senate. National polls were accurate in predicting a Clinton popular vote victory, but they got the Electoral College math wrong.

One political historian, Allan Lichtman, did correctly predict Trump's win. Lichtman's prediction "isn't based on horse-race polls, shifting demographics or his own political opinions. Rather, he uses a system of true/false statements he calls the 'Keys to the White House' to determine his predicted winner."[31]

Most of the "experts" predicted a close race, but they overestimated the percent of Clinton votes (most had her just above the 50% mark). No matter which key variable was selected on which scholars based their conclusions—state of the economy, time for a change vote, unemployment rate, direction the country is going, state-by-state analysis, popularity of the sitting president, poll watchers—virtually all gave Clinton a slight edge.

EXPLAINING TRUMP'S RISE

How are we to explain/understand the rise of Trump? During the primaries, Trump either hijacked the party in a hostile takeover, or he was the logical next step for a party that had seemed to become increasingly antireason, antiscience, and antievidence.

It is true that you reap what you sow—for years, starting with the Reagan presidency, blossoming during the Bill Clinton presidency, becoming fully toxic under Speaker Newt Gingrich, condoning the hatred sometimes evident in the Tea Party movement, and going to excess in the Obama years, the Republicans created a climate and a culture in which they began consciously channeling paranoia,[32] racial animus,[33] birther conspiracies,[34] a culture of partisan hatred.[35]

The Republican Party set the table and created the conditions that made the rise of Trump possible. As Fareed Zakaria wrote:

> There have always been radicals on both sides of the political spectrum. But what is different about the conservative movement is that, since the 1990s, some of its most distinguished mainstream members have embraced the rhetoric and tactics of the extremes.

A memo put out by Newt Gingrich's political action committee that decade urged candidates to use savage rhetoric against their Democratic opponents. Some of the recommended words were "failure," "pathetic," "disgrace" and "incompetent." In the past ... Trump has called Mitt Romney a "failed candidate," Jeb Bush "pathetic," Sen. Lindsey Graham (R-S.C.) "a disgrace" and Obama "totally incompetent." [36]

And Zakaria concluded his argument, noting:

Here is a much simpler explanation for Donald Trump: Republicans have fed the country ideas about decline, betrayal and treason. They have encouraged the forces of ant-intellectualism, obstructionism, and populism. They have flirted with bigotry and racism. Trump merely chose to unashamedly embrace all of it, saying plainly what they were hinting at for years. In doing so, he hit a jackpot.[27]

The Republican Party created Trump. He exploited the climate set by Republicans, but he did not create this climate. It had been building for years. Some people had real concerns and complaints; others had found in Trump a champion of their prejudices.

A populist tsunami had been building on the right for twenty years. Many Americans hurt by the recession, trapped in by low wages, stagnant jobs, and hurt by the larger forces of globalization turned against the establishment. Their genuine concerns became part of the Trump movement. But so did racist, nativist, sexist elements. Writing in *Atlantic.com*, conservative David Frum wrote:

Trump has appealed to white identity more explicitly than any national political figure since George Wallace. But whereas Wallace was marginalized first within the Democratic Party, and then within national politics, Trump has increasingly been accommodated. Yes, Trump was often fiercely denounced by rivals and insiders in the earlier part of the campaign. But since effectively securing the nomination, that criticism had quieted. Trump is running not to be president of all Americans, but to be the clan leader of white Americans. Those white Americans who respond to his message head his abusive comments, not as evidence of his unfitness for office, but as proof of his commitment to their tribe. [37]

In 2016, the Republican mainstream ended up coming home to Trump after initially being suspicious of their party's nominee. Roughly 90% of Republicans ended up voting for Trump.

TRUMP'S IMPACT IN THE REPUBLICAN PARTY

So what awaits the Republican Party in a Trump era? A civil war? Reconciliation? Divorce of the Trumpkins from the establishment? A return to (ab)normalcy? Capture by the radical fringe?

Trump exposed deep fissures between the Republican establishment and the grassroot populists who flocked to Trump. Those cleavages will not disappear, but do they spell doom for the party?

It would be hard to fully purge the Trumpkins from the party. Trump's supporters have already been placed in key positions in the Republican National Committee, they comprise a key voting bloc within the party, their views are legitimized by the Fox News and talk radio voices on the right, they staff key positions in the Trump administration, and as the postelection period shows, they are here to stay.

What impact would Trump have on the long-term interests of the Republican Party? Was he a "stain" that could be washed away, or a "tattoo" that would be a permanent mark?

Populism is sometimes popular, until it gets elected. Then the illiberal tendencies often clash with the American tradition of liberal democracy. The search for a strongman savior to solve our problems may seem attractive in difficult times, but rarely has the strongman been the solution to our problems and usually ends up as a problem to be solved.

Has Donald Trump energized or damaged the Republican Party? Part of the answer to that question depends on whether Trumpism takes hold in the party. Trump, the individual may be an aberration, a one-off, impossible to replicate and therefore a one-time-only candidate.

Should the GOP return to its pre-Trump positions of small government, free trade, low tax, and entitlement cut, or should it grow the base by opening the party to nonwhite groups, welcoming them into the fold? Or can a Trump presidency secure a new governing coalition for the Republicans?

Trump has exploited the rift in society of the ins versus the outs, the haves versus the have-nots, the educated versus less educated, urban versus rural, the elite versus the downtrodden. Trump's followers are not monolithic. One part of his coalition is made up of those who were battered and bruised by the recession of 2007–2008. Deeply hurt by the recession, globalization, and the loss of manufacturing jobs, they were stymied by income stagnation and left with little hope. These angry voters have a legitimate beef with the establishment. Their incomes decline as income inequality grows; their future seems dim while a small minority become super rich. These are people who need to be listened to; they have very real problems that need to be addressed.

But there is the other part of the Trump coalition: racists, xenophobes, misogynists, nativists, those whom Hillary Clinton indelicately referred to as "deplorables."[38] Their anger and resentment over an African American (or a woman) in the White House, immigrants, and other such prejudices drove the Trump bus. And they are still out there, angry and contemptuous of society.

In 1984, Ronald Reagan won 56% of the white vote and 44 states, and he won the election in a landslide.[39] In 2012, Mitt Romney won 59% of the white vote and lost the election.[40] Moving ahead, the Republican Party simply has to broaden its appeal to minorities or it may decline electorally. But how will that change the party?

To some it was the party of Lincoln; to others, it was the party of Reagan. Today, the Republican Party is the party of Trump.

THE DEMOCRATS AFTER TRUMP'S WIN

Many Democrats will argue that 2016 is the "last white election," that by 2020 (and beyond), the electorate belongs to them.[41] But playing this waiting game (waiting for the demographics to catch up with the politics) has its dangers. It frees the Democrats to dismiss self-analysis as they simply wait for the next election.

But if they are smart, they will try to figure out how they can offer policies that attempt to reclaim the white working-class voters who were once theirs. Simply writing off the working class is tantamount to following in Republican footsteps as they write off people of color —it simply makes no sense.

The Democratic Party needs to do some serious soul-searching lest it become merely the "boutique issue party," appealing to this group and that group, but never actually standing up for ideas.

After the 1964 rout of Republican Barry Goldwater, forecasts of the death of the Republican Party were common. Four years later, they won the White House.[42] The same fears were manifested by the Democrats after 1972 nominee George McGovern got routed by Richard Nixon. Four years later, they too won the White House.[43] So reports of the death of the 2016 Democratic Party may well be premature.

RUSSIAN MEDDLING: THE OLD COLD WAR HEATS UP

Russia, under the direction of Vladimir Putin, interfered with the 2016 U.S. presidential election[44] intending to hurt Hillary Clinton and help Donald Trump.[45] That was the conclusion of virtually all the U.S. intelligence agencies, including CIA Director John Brennan, FBI Director James Comey, and Director of National Intelligence James R. Clapper.

Did this have an impact on the election? It is hard to say. Clearly, the drip-drip-drip of WikiLeaks stories by the Russians put Hillary Clinton on the defensive in the final weeks of the campaign, and these stories played into Donald Trump's narrative in his attacks against Clinton, but *how many voters were swayed by this?*

President-elect Trump and his surrogates have gone to great lengths to dismiss, question, and even ridicule the reports of Russian tampering in a U.S. election, but the evidence seems to tell a different story. The Russians got what they wanted: the defeat of Hillary Clinton and the election of Donald Trump. But did their intrusion into the process cause the result?

Both Republican and Democratic lawmakers demanded an investigation. Trump tried to deflect these efforts.

Did Russia Help Elect Donald Trump?

U.S. intelligence agencies plus the intelligence units from several NATO countries confirmed that Russia had been actively meddling in elections in Germany, Great Britain, and the United States. The goal? To break up NATO and undermine democracy. England's "Brexit" vote and the NATO bashing of candidate Donald Trump were the consequences of Mr. Putin's mischief. Putin loathed Clinton. And the bizarre bromance between Putin and Trump was for the wily Russian, merely a marriage of convenience— it suited his ends. Putin viewed Trump as a "useful fool."[46] In his national security briefings, Trump was informed of the Russian interference in the election, which seemed only to bolster Trump's impression of Putin.[47]

The Russian *DUMA* (legislature) was in session when Trump's election was announced. The hall burst out in a round of applause.[48]

Did the FBI Help Elect Donald Trump?

The FBI's unprecedented intrusion into the 2016 election kept the issue of Hillary Clinton's e-mail problem in front of the American voter, and in spite of their refusal to charge Clinton with any crime, it reinforced Trump's "crooked Hillary" narrative.[49]

Many observers were surprised that James Comey went public with information on the Clinton e-mail inquiry. Traditionally the FBI avoids any hint of being involved in a presidential campaign, and Comey's very public pronouncements on Clinton, while being all but silent on the Trump team investigation regarding Russia seemed to politicize the Clinton inquiry, while placing the FBI deep into the activities of campaign 2016.

THE BLUE WALL COMES TUMBLING DOWN

Many commentators argue that it was the collapse of the Democrats' "blue wall" that led to the defeat of Hillary Clinton.[50] The Clinton campaign believed that it had an insurance policy against a Trump surge: the states of Wisconsin, Michigan, and Pennsylvania—the blue wall that would block a Trump advance.[51]

But as the Industrial Belt morphed into the Rust Belt, and as union membership dropped (in 1964, 37% of Ohio worker were union members, by 2016 that number had dropped to 12%;[52] and much the same was true of Michigan, Pennsylvania, and Wisconsin),[53] the solidly Democratic blue wall began to crack. In 2016 it fell.

In Wisconsin, Democrats had won seven consecutive presidential contests. The same was true in Michigan. In Pennsylvania, Democratic presidents won six straight contests.[54] In Wisconsin, Clinton lost by just 27,257 votes (47.9% to 46.9%).[55] In Michigan, Clinton lost by only 11, 612 (47.6% to 47.3%).[56] And in Pennsylvania, Clinton lost by 68,236 votes (48.8% to 47.6%).[57]

DID GENDER DOOM HILLARY?

Did gender hurt Clinton? While few voters would publicly admit that the fact that Hillary Clinton was a woman might prevent them from voting for her, several studies suggest that a woman might not be as electorally acceptable to as many voters as we think. [58] It is hard to quantify this bias, but it might have had a marginal impact in Clinton's vote. And even 1% would have dramatically impacted the results of the election.

Clinton did well with women voters in general, but not with white women, a majority of whom voted for her opponent, in spite of the *Access Hollywood* tape and numerous examples of Trump insulting women.

As the first woman to run on a major party ticket for president,[59] one might have expected Clinton to get a "bump" from other women, but that was not the case. There was a gender gap, but one that mirrored gaps of the recent past.

Did Voter Suppression Matter?

Did voter suppression efforts work? A Republican "block the vote" effort to suppress votes was a part of their victory strategy.[60] It was called "Operation Ratf***ked" by Republican strategist Ben Ginsberg,[61] and it was aimed at minorities and young voters whose participation in the election they hoped to limit.

The key to this strategy was the 2013 Supreme Court decision *Shelby County v. Holder* where the Court dramatically weakened Section 5 of the Voting Rights Act (which required federal preapproval of changes in voting laws in areas with a history of discrimination). In gutting that portion of the Act, the Court opened a door to voter suppression that a number of Republican-controlled states used to limit voting access. How? Higher hurdles to voting, new ID rules, shortening the hours polls were open, reducing or eliminating same-day registration, all done in the name of reducing voter fraud that did not exist in any significant way. Most of the more restrictive states were in the East and South, while the Western states were more open or relaxed in their voting requirements. And Republican-controlled states clearly dominated in their willingness to embrace voting restrictions.[62] It was expected that these new laws could depress Latino vote, as well as the African American and the millennial vote.[63]

Several of the new voting restrictions were thrown out by state courts, but many remained.[64] Thirty-two states have some form of voter ID laws, and most of them went for Trump. Accident? You be the judge?

From 2000 to 2016, we have seen a steady rise in the number of states "requesting" ID (from under 14 in 2000 to over 30 in 2016) and the number "requiring" ID (0 in 2000 to 9 in 2016).

This effort by Republicans to limit voting was deliberate and coordinated.[65] If you have any doubts, here is the Facebook response to this effort by Todd Allbaugh, a Wisconsin staff aide to a Republican state legislature:

> You wanna know why I left the Republican Party as it exists today? Here it is; this was the last straw: I was in the closed Senate Republican Caucus when the final round of multiple Voter ID bills were being discussed. A handful of the GOP Senators were giddy about the ramifications and literally singled out the prospects of suppressing minority and college voters. Think about that for a minute. Elected officials planning and happy to help deny a fellow American's constitutional right to vote in order to increase their own chances to hang onto power.[66]

And in 2013, Don Yelton, a North Carolina Republican Party county precinct chairman, said that his state's voter ID laws would, "kick the Democrats in the butt."[67] Florida's Republican Party Chairman Jim Green admitted that his state's Voter ID law was designed to suppress Democratic votes, saying "we've got to cut down on early voting because early voting is not good for us."[68]

DID BIG MONEY MATTER IN 2016?

Citizens United and other Court decisions striking down limitations on money in the political process did open the floodgates of money into politics, but 2016 was the year when money seems *not* to have been a major factor. Donald Trump semi-self-funded his race, ran an effective Twitter-outreach campaign, and relied on an estimated billion dollars of free publicity from the media.

2016 was also the year that Bernie Sanders demonstrated that one could run a credible presidential campaign relying on a large number of small donors. Hillary Clinton ran a conventional big-money campaign, and she proved the exception in this exceptional election year. Hilary Clinton outspent Trump by a wide margin, as did outside spending groups. Clinton's team raised roughly $500 million and outside groups raised an additional $200 million for Clinton.[69] Trump raised (not counting the value of the free media he received) about $250 million and outside spending on behalf of Trump was around $75 million.[70] Clearly, money did not determine the outcome of the 2016 race.

DID MEDIA—NEW AND OLD—IMPACT THE ELECTION?

Trust in the media, especially the mainstream media, was low. Many voters, especially younger voters, got their news from social media. There was thus a new vulnerability to "fake news" which proliferated the blogosphere. Given the fact that voters felt they could not rely on standard media outlets, a door was opened for candidates—and Donald Trump masterfully used this to his advantage.[71]

There were wide variations by party membership in trust of the mainstream media. And while trust declined by both Democrats and Republicans (in 1997, about 64% of Democrats had some trust in the media, by 2016 that number dropped to 51%; for Republicans in that period, trust fell from 41% to around 14%), Republicans clearly had more negative impressions of the media.[72]

Recent campaigns have clearly been more social-media oriented, which is not surprising given that almost half of Americans say they get their news from social media "often" or "sometimes," and that number has risen with each of the past five presidential elections.[73]

PARTY POOPER

The Republicans went into the November 8 election with majorities in both the House (247 to 188) and Senate (54-44 with two Independents, Bernie Sanders and Angus King caucusing with the Democrats). As election day approached, Republicans wondered how much Donald Trump might hurt their candidates in down-ticket races. As it turns out, while the Republicans did lose seats in the House and Senate, the numbers were well within what one might normally expect.

Voting in 2016 reinforced the hyperpartisan model of voting which suggests that the parties are becoming more divided and more partisan. This creates a gulf between the two parties in which each party increasingly sees the opposition in more harsh and negative ways. Cooperation, bargaining, and compromise—so vital for a healthy, functioning democracy—becomes near impossible in such conditions.

It is common for Americans to complain about the quality of our presidential candidates, but 2016 surpassed all records. More people voted against a candidate than for one. While in 2004 a majority of Democrats said their primary motivation was to vote against George W. Bush, never before have both candidates received a higher combined "voted against" score than in 2016.[74]

THE NONPARTY PARTIES

In 2016 outsiders (nonparty members) sought to seize the party nomination in the Democratic (Bernie Sanders) and Republican (Donald Trump) parties. It is possible to do this because all one has to do to seek the nomination is register in that party (which Sanders did on the morning he filed for his candidacy) and run. If you get enough votes in the party caucuses and primaries, you get the nomination, and the party hierarchy can do little to stop you.

Bernie Sanders was an Independent Socialist until he sought the Democratic nomination. Donald Trump has changed political parties at least five times.[75] But they each strategically calculated that regardless of the party insiders, a wide-open nomination battle might be winnable. And so, leading the ticket on a major party is a prize that virtually anyone can seek. And the establishment favorite (Jeb in 2016) can be left out in the cold.

Is this a good or bad thing? It may be good because an open, dynamic nomination gives the members of the party—the rank-and-file—the opportunity to select *their* nominee, absent too much interference from the higher-ups. Thus, an outsider can capture the hearts and minds of members and truly be the representative of the members of that party.

But others see it as a bad thing because it may be the party bosses and regulars who have the long-term interests of the party in mind, can select the candidate that best represents the party itself, or who has a legitimate chance of winning the election. Party insiders *would not* have selected Sanders or Trump, yet both had fairly large, committed followings. But in both cases, their followers were deeply committed, but not necessarily representations of the larger party across the nation.

So, which is better, a wide-open race or one that is filtered through the party leadership? If "the people" had spoken, it might have been Bernie Sanders versus Donald Trump. If the party insiders had spoken, it would been Jeb Bush versus Hillary Clinton.

What kind of party system has virtually no control over who shall be the party's nominee for president? Is it even "really" a party if *anyone* can come in and, with enough votes, capture the nomination?

RURAL VERSUS URBAN

In 2016, Hillary Clinton won only 472 counties while Donald Trump won nearly 3,000.[76] That sure sounds like a landslide, but on closer inspection Clinton won dense, urban areas, while Trump won more sparsely populated rural areas. Clinton's 472 counties accounted for roughly two-thirds of the nation's total economic output.[77] Are there two Americas?

This urban-rural split characterizes a deep divide in the United States; one nation separate and unequal. The urban and coastal regions are a deep blue, the rural and heartland regions a deep red.

TRUMP'S ENEMIES LIST

Questions of Trump's character and temperament were raised again on election night when supporter (and former "The Apprentice" competitor) Omarosa Manigault went public with Donald Trump's "enemies list." Not since the days of the disgraced Richard Nixon has a president had —and used—an enemies list. "It's so great," she said, "our enemies are making themselves clear so that when we get into the White House, we know where we stand." Then, referring to a tweet by Republican Senator Lindsey Graham in which he announced he had voted for Evan McMullin, the former-Republican-turned-Independent candidate, noted that "If [Graham] felt his interests was with that candidate, God Bless him. I would never judge anybody for exercising their right to and the freedom to choose who they want. But let me just tell, Mr. Trump has a long memory and we're keeping a list."[78]

PANTS ON FIRE IN A POST-TRUTH WORLD

Can we trust politicians? Hillary Clinton is, in effect, a career politician. Donald Trump, in contrast, is anything but a politician. So who is more truthful? Who has more of what Stephen Colbert calls "truthiness?"

PolitiFact has done the heavy lifting for us on the truth meter (see tables 3 and 4).

Table 3. Donald Trump's Questionable Relationship to the Truth.

Donald Trump PolitiFact Scorecard	
True	14 (4%)
Mostly True	37 (11%)
Half True	49 (15%)
Mostly False	63 (19%)
False	111 (34%)
Pants on Fire	57 (17%)

Source. PolitiFact, http://www.politifact.com/truth-o-meter/lists/people/comparing-hillary-clinton-donald-trump-truth-o-met/

Table 4. How Does Clinton Compare with Trump Regarding Truth?

Hillary Clinton PolitiFact Scorecard	
True	72 (25%)
Mostly True	76 (26%)
Half True	69 (24%)
Mostly False	40 (14%)
False	29 (10%)
Pants on Fire	7 (2%)

Source. PolitiFact, http://www.politifact.com/truth-o-meter/lists/people/comparing-hillary-clinton-donald-trump-truth-o-met/

During the campaign, as well as early in his presidency, Donald Trump seemed sometimes to have a rather distant relationship to the truth. Be it grossly exaggerating the size of the crowd at his inauguration, to claims he won the popular vote in the election, to his obsession with the "birther" fraud, Donald Trump seems to say what conveniences or advantages himself. And given that "trust" is a key element in leadership, Trump jeopardizes his ability to govern when he dissembles.

WHO IS THE REAL TRUMP?

He ran by dividing (and attacking parts of) the nation; yet his election night speech was gracious and inclusive. Will a Trump presidency further divide us or unite us?

George W. Bush ran for president in 2000 as "a uniter, not a divider." He ended up being a very divisive president.[79] In 2008, Barack Obama said, "There is no red America, there is no blue America, there is only the United States of America." He too turned out to be a divisive president.[80] What of Trump?

Trump's defenders applaud that he is not a career politician and that he is a disruptive force in Washington D.C. But to lead, he must deal with the power brokers of the beltway. Can he be both a disruptive oppositional force and a leader who brings us together?

ANOTHER OUTSIDER

America loves outsiders. We think they are not infected with the "beltway disease" and that they will ride into town like the sheriff in an old Western movie, clean up the mess ("drain the swamp"), and fix all our problems. It is a romantic vision of a world where good triumphs over evil, and one man (yes, man) can save us. The problem is that this just isn't reality.

We've tried time and again, to bring in outsiders, but they are part of the problem, not the solution. Inexperienced outsiders have not done well in the White House. Yet the romantic attraction remains.

Since 1976, we've elected six outsiders and one insider (George H.W. Bush). You decide if the outsiders were our salvation or not (see table 5). In *The Republic*, Plato argued that leading the *polis* required years of focused training.[81] Americans believe that insiders are part of the problem.

If we remove those (four) incumbents running for reelection, there is only one insider George H.W. Bush who has won the presidency in the past forty years.

Table 5. Presidential Insiders and Outsiders.

Year	President	Insider	Outsider
1976	Carter		✓
1980	Reagan		✓
1984	Reagan	(✓)	✓
1988	HW Bush	✓	
1992	Clinton		✓
1996	Clinton	(✓)	✓
2000	W Bush		✓
2004	W Bush	(✓)	✓
2008	Obama		✓
2012	Obama	(✓)	✓
2016	Trump		✓

Source. Compiled by author.

THE CHARACTER QUESTION

This was an election decided more on personality and character than policies and ideas. As such, the voters were presented with the choice of two "character-challenged" candidates. Hillary Clinton generated very low scores on the trust meter; and Trump's comments on women, Mexicans, immigrants, war heroes, the handicapped, and other groups left many voters disgusted.

In judging a presidential candidate, there are three elements of "character" to consider: public, private, and constitutional character. Public character is one's moral and ethical compass in pursuit of the public good. It is about trying to do the right thing. Private character involves what one does, how one behaves in his or her private (i.e., family) life. Constitutional character involves "the disposition to act, and motivate others to act, according to principles that constitute the democratic process..." and "includes such questions as sensitivity to basic rights, respect for due process... willingness to agree to accept responsibility, tolerance of opposition, and most importantly a commitment to candor."[82]

How do the two candidates rate on these measures of character? Sadly, on all three categories of character Clinton and Trump are found wanting. Hillary Clinton's public character has been repeatedly called into question on matters from her e-mails to Benghazi. Where private character is concerned, the uses (and abuses?) of the Clinton Foundation also raised serious questions. On constitutional questions, Clinton fares considerably better, ranking high on most measures.

Donald Trump has a long history of shady business dealings[83] and could be seen as ranking low in public character. His record on private character is abysmal as the thrice-married Trump objectifies and insults women regularly,[84] and brags about his indiscretions.[85] Perhaps most frightening are Trump's low marks on constitutional character, as his unwillingness to accept the results of the election, unless he won,[86] his constant trashing of political opponents,[87] and his belittling of due process ("we're gonna have a deportation force")[88] indicate.

Trump's open contempt for the norms of our constitutional republic—evident in his threat to imprison his opponent;[89] stated goals of narrowing press freedoms by changing liberal laws; call for the resumption of torture; goal to ban all Muslim immigrants;[90] questioning the independence of the judiciary and the fairness of a federal judge who, while born in Indiana, but whose parents are from Mexico is said to be biased against Trump;[91] his plan to round up and deport millions of undocumented immigrants;[92] as well as his refusal to say that he would accept the outcome of the election[93]—all speak to Trump's failure to fulfill even the most minimal of constitutional ethics.

With two candidates who were seriously "character challenged," they seemed to cancel each other out on this issue.

THE ELECTORAL COLLEGE VOTES

Although Hillary Clinton won the popular (democratic) vote by roughly 2.9 million, she was not elected president; that's because the people don't actually elect the president, the Electoral College does. Winning *states*, not *votes*, is what matters.

When the presidency was created almost 230 years ago, the Framers were perplexed regarding just who should select the new president. Should it be the Congress? No, that would undermine the separation-of-powers model that was designed to prevent executive tyranny. The people? No, a skilled president could inflame the passions of the people and turn them into a mob at his disposal, or conversely, the people might demand that the president bend to their will, and that could mean the president would be a slave to the whim of the moment. After much deliberation and frustration, they ended up inventing an Electoral College, wherein each state would select a slate of electors from among the finest in local society, and they would choose the president. This mechanism protected the interests of the slave states of the South, and as such, paved the way for the creation of this unique process.[94] No other country in the world has such a bizarre system, and for good reason.

This Electoral College opens the door to two potential problems: 1) the winner of the popular vote might not win the electoral vote (2000 and 2016), or 2) between the time of the election and the actual voting and counting of the Electoral College votes, some form of mischief might occur.

There are 538 Electors comprising the Electoral College. On December 19, in their respective state capitols, they met to cast their electoral votes, presumably for the candidate to whom they were pledged, and who won in the state. These votes were then transmitted to the Congress where on the opening of the new Congress, the results are read out and the election is official. That five-week period between the November 8 vote and the December 19 electoral vote was a time of intense if hidden lobbying by the losers designed to sway votes away from the Electoral College vote winner.

Ordinarily the Electors are loyal to the candidate to whom they are pledged, but over our history there have been several "faithless electors" who ended up voting for someone else. Is that permitted? Several states prescribe a legal penalty to electors who are faithless, and more than twenty states require a party loyalty pledge of their electors, but apply no real punishment if they defect. So, most electors are in effect free agents whose vote might be bought or otherwise gained.

In 2004, 30 percent of the Electors said they had been contacted about switching their votes, and in 2012, 80 percent, according to Robert Alexander of Ohio Northern University, an expert on the Electoral College and presidential electors,[95] said they were lobbied to switch candidates. If past is prelude, we should not be surprised if similar and even more intense lobbying took place in 2016.

On several occasions in our history, the candidate who lost the popular vote has won the presidency, but never has an Electoral College vote actually overturned the College winner of a presidential election.

In the end, an Electoral College rebellion against Trump did not materialize. And while there were faithless electors, more of them turned against Hillary Clinton (5) than against Trump. He won the Electoral College 304-227 (Colin Powell got 3 votes).

How to Measure and Judge a New President

Taking the measure of any new president is a difficult and delicate task. But two things may illuminate our task: determining the new president's "level of political opportunity" (context), and employing a five-factor template (early test cases) of candidate/presidential achievement. We turn now to these two categories of analysis.

President Trump's "Level of Political Opportunity"

A president's *level of political opportunity*,[96] sometimes referred to as *political capital*, is the context in which a president governs and the political fuel he has to ignite the engine of governing. In calculating a president's political opportunity, we should consider:

> **1) The President's Party in Congress:** Is the party of the president the majority party in Congress? If so, by how much? A large majority opens a door to power, a slim majority gives the president some limited leverage, and when the opposition controls Congress, the president has very limited political clout.

> **2) The Results of the Last Election:** Did the president win in a landslide? Was it a squeaker? The bigger the electoral victory, the more the president can claim a *mandate to govern*.

> **3) What Type of Election was it?** Elections based on policy match more to a president's success than do elections based on personality, (see Reagan's 1980 victory which gave him high opportunity vs. 1984 where he had little).

> **4) Did the President have Coattails?** Did the president run ahead of members of Congress in their districts? If so, the president may argue that he or she helped Congressperson X electorally; If not, (e.g., Clinton in 1992) members feel less dependent on and indebted to the president.

> **5) Nature of the Opposition:** Is the opposition cohesive and unified against the president (e.g., Republicans during the Obama years), or are they willing to work *with* the president?

> **6) The Public's Mood:** Does the public demand action? Is public trust in government high?

7) The President's Skill and Experience: While not enough, skill and experience do matter.

8) The President's "Power Sense": Does the president know how to pull on the levels of power? When to? When not to? Does the president have a good "strategic sense?"

MEASURING TRUMP'S OPPORTUNITY

The President's Party in Congress: Donald Trump comes to office with majorities in both the House and the Senate. Having unified government should help him achieve some of his legislative goals.

Results of the Last Election: It was a hard fought election, and Trump won by a significant margin. While no landslide, Trump did convincingly beat Hillary Clinton. But while Trump won in the Electoral College, Clinton won the popular vote, thus neutralizing some of the glow on Trump's victory. Two days before the election, Donald Trump tweeted, "The Electoral College is a disaster for a democracy."[97] With Clinton beating Trump for the popular vote, that is probably something Trump and Clinton might agree on.

Type of Election: The 2016 race was dominated by the oversized personality of Donald Trump. Issues, while of some importance, paled in comparison to the personal. Hillary was unpopular and untrustworthy, Donald was unpopular and belligerent. It was a contest of character (or lack thereof), not issues. This added nothing to the victory.

Coattails: Republicans lost seats in the House and Senate in 2016, but not many. Trump seemed to have coattails, but fairly short ones. Trump ran behind most Republican legislators in their states or districts, thus his coattails, such as they were, will not help him govern. However, those Republican Senate candidates who stood squarely with Trump (Ron Johnson in Wisconsin, Richard Burr in North Carolina, and Roy

Blunt in Missouri)[98] did better than those who distanced themselves from Trump (Mark Kirk of Illinois and Kelly Ayotte in New Hampshire).[99]

The Opposition: The Democrats will be a thorn in Trump's side, but it remains to be seen just how obstructionist they will try to be, and how unified they are in the opposition to Trump. They will not—thankfully—be the mirror image of the Republicans, but they will not give Trump a free pass either.

The Public's Mood: Trump won the votes of angry voters. Can he keep them at bay, or will they eventually turn on him? Trust in government is low, and how long will it be before Trump takes full ownership of the government, and will he then be seen as part of the problem? What if he can't get his promises enacted, or the wall built, or … Trust in Government was at an all-time low; Trust in Trump was low; public cynicism was high; and political partisanship was high. The public was in an angry mood, unhappy with the direction in which the nation was moving, yet unwilling to lend much support to the new president to achieve policy goals.

Skills and Experience: Donald Trump has never held political office, and while experience in politics is not a requirement for the job, it is certainly of use. Only four of his predecessors never held elective office (Taylor, Grant, and Eisenhower who were generals, and Hoover who served as a Cabinet official). The world of politics is vastly different from the world of business—can Trump successfully make that transition?

Trump's "Power Sense": With his skill at self-promotion, Trump knows how to attract attention. He seems to have a good power sense, and that was part of the reason he did so well in the primaries and general election. But government is more than just posing and attacking. Does Trump have a good political or governing power sense?

Governing is hard in the best of circumstances, but in our age of hyperpartisanship, and with limited opportunities, the new president may have but a short time to prove his effectiveness. Given that trust in government has been steadily dropping since the 1970s, (there was a bump up in trust following 9/11; however, it did not last long), the ability of a president to lead amid low levels of trust is markedly limited. In the early 1960s, roughly 75% Americans said they had a fairly high level of trust in government. By 2016, that number hovered in the 20% mark.[100] How can anyone govern when trust in government is so low?

A Template for Measuring Presidential Success

In trying to assess Donald Trump as a president, we have to put Trump's presidency into context (his level of political opportunity) and measure how he governs by looking at a series of key early tests:

- Campaign Management
- The Selection and Organization of his Governing Team
- The Transition
- His Inaugural Address
- The First 100 Days

From these measures, we can make a preliminary assessment of Trump as he assumes power (did he hit the ground running or stumbling?), determine Trump's opportunity to lead, as well as make a long-range prediction of the type of president Trump will be. It is to these five tests of Trump's leadership that we now turn.

Notes

1. Portions of the following are adapted from: Michael A. Genovese, *The Trumping of American Politics: The Strange Case of the 2016 Presidential Election* (Amherst, NY: Cambria Press, 2017).
2. Liam Donovan, "The Blue Wall Crumbles," *National Review*, November 16, 2016.
3. Bernard L. Fraga, Sean McElwee, Jesse Rhodes, and Brian Schaffner, "Why Did Trump Win? More Whites – and Fewer Blacks – Actually Voted," *The Monkey Cage, The Washington Post*, May 8, 2017.
4. "2016 Election Expert Polls," *The Washington Post*, November 29, 2016.
5. Alexander Agadanian, "How the 2016 Vote Broke Down by Race, Gender, and Age," *Decision Desk HQ*, March 8, 2017.
6. Katie Rogers, "White Women Helped Elect Donald Trump," *The New York Times*, November 9, 2016, https://nyti.ms/2jKFJ35.
7. Agadanian, "How the 2016 Vote Broke Down."
8. Ibid.
9. Ibid.
10. Ibid.
11. Ibid.
12. Ibid.
13. Ibid.
14. Ibid.
15. Ibid.
16. *The Los Angeles Times*, "Why Trump Won," November 13, 2016, A1; See Edison Research national exit poll. Regarding African American voters, see also https://www.washingtonpost.com/news/monkey-cage/wp/201 6/11/11/trump-got-more-votes-from-people-of-color-than-romney-did-heres-the-data/?utm_term=.c32bb40bd497
17. Ibid.
18. Sarah Wheaton, "Van Jones: Trump Vote is a White-Lash," *POLITICO*, November 9, 2016.
19. Roper Center, "How Groups Voted in 2016," *The Roper Center*, April 24, 2017.
20. Ibid.
21. Ibid.
22. Ibid.

23. Ibid.

24. Ibid.

25. Ibid.

26. Amanda Taub, "Partisanship as a Tribal Identity," *The New York Times*, April 13, 2017, A10.

27. George Packer, "The Unconnected," *The New Yorker*, October 31, 2016, 51.

28. J.D. Vance, *Hillbilly Elegy: A Memoir of a Family and Culture in Crisis* (New York: HarperCollins, 2016).

29. Matthew Yglesias, "Why did the South Turn Republican?" *The Atlantic*, August 24, 2007.

30. James E. Campbell, "Forecasting the 2016 American National Election," *PS*, October 2016

31. Peter W. Stevenson, "Trump is headed for a win, says professor who has predicted 30 years of presidential outcomes correctly," *The Washington Post*, September 23, 2016 https://www.washingtonpost.com/news/the-fix/wp/2016/09/23/trump-is-headed-for-a-win-says-professor-whos-predicted-30-years-of-presidential-outcomes-correctly/?utm_term=.9d920973e393.

32. See Theda Skocpol and Vanessa Williamson, *The Tea Party and the Remaking of Republican Conservatism* (New York: Oxford University Press, 2013).

33. Ibid.

34. Ibid.

35. Ibid.

36. Fareed Zakaria, "Where were Republicans Moderates 20 Years Ago?" *The Washington Post*, March 3, 2016, https://www.washingtonpost.com/opinions/where-were-republican-moderates-20-years-ago/2016/03/03/4c1c49c2-e18b-11e5-846c-10191d1fc4ec_story.html

37. David Frum, "The Seven Broken Guardrails of Democracy," *The Atlantic*, May 31, 2016. ,

38. Dan Merica and Sophie Tatum, "Clinton expresses regret for saying 'half' of Trump supporters are 'deplorables'," CNN, September 12, 2016, http://www.cnn.com/2016/09/09/politics/hillary-clinton-donald-trump-basket-of-deplorables/.

39. Steve Phillips, "What About White Voters?" *Center for American Progress*, February 5, 2016.

40. Ibid.

41. Henry Enten, "Demographics Aren't Destiny," *Five Thirty Eight*, November 14, 2016.
42. "Compare U.S. Presidents," *Inside Gov*, http://us-presidents.insidegov.com
43. Ibid.
44. Eric Lipton, David E. Sanger and Scott Shane, "The Perfect Weapon: How Russian Cyberpower Invaded the U.S.," *The New York Times*, December 13, 2016.
45. Adam Entous and Ellen Nakashima, "FBI in Agreement with CIA that Russia Aimed to Help Trump Win White House," *The Washington Post*, December 16, 2016.
46. Michael V. Hayden, "Former CIA Director: Trump Proves He's Russia's 'Useful Fool'," *The Washington Post*, May 16, 2017.
47. Ibid.
48. Kurt Eichenwald, "Why Vladimir Putin's Russia is Backing Donald Trump," *Newsweek Magazine*, November 4, 2016.
49. See Nate Silver, "The Comey Letter Probably Cost Clinton the Election," *Five Thirty Eight*, May 3, 2017.
50. Liam Donovan, "The Blue Wall Crumbles," *National Review*, November 16, 2016.
51. Ibid.
52. Raymond Hogler, "What's Behind the Decline of Unions?" *New Republic*, November 30, 2016.
53. Hogler, "What's Behind the Decline of Unions?"
54. The American Presidency Project, "Presidential Elections Data," *University of California, Santa Barbara*, 2017.
55. Ibid.
56. Ibid.
57. Ibid.
58. See Matt Streb, Michael A. Genovese, et al, "Social Desirability and Support for a Female American President," *President Opinion Quarterly*, Spring 2008.
59. Michael A. Genovese and Janice Steckenrider, *Women as Political Leaders* (New York: Routledge, 2013).
60. Editorial Board, "Republicans Attempt to Rig the Vote by Suppressing It," *The Washington Post*, November 7, 2016.
61. Elizabeth Kolbert, "Drawing the Line: How Redistricting Turned America from Blue to Red," *The New Yorker*, June 27, 2016.
62. Jasmine C. Lee, "How States Moved Toward Stricter Voter ID Laws," *The New York Times*, November 7, 2016, A12.

63. Ari Berman, "Blocking the Ballot Box," *The Los Angeles Times*, February 5, 2016, A15.
64. David Daley, *RATF**KED: The True Story Behind the Secret Pan to Steal America's Democracy*, Liveright, 2016.
65. Anna North, "Five Ways Republicans are Threatening Voting Rights," *The New York Times*, November 7, 2016.
66. Theo Keith, "Former Republican staffer says GOP lawmakers were 'giddy; while crafting voter ID law," Fox6News, April 7, 2016, http://fox6now.com/2016/04/07/former-republican-staffer-says-gop-lawmakers-were-giddy-about-wisconsins-voter-id-law/.
67. Matt Gravatt, "Yelton was fired for saying what the NC GOP won't," *The Hill*, October 25, 2013.
68. Quotes from: Michael Wines, "Some Republicans Acknowledge Leveraging State Voter ID Laws for Political Gain," *The New York Times*, September 20, 2016, A15.
69. Jonathan Burr, "Election 2016's Price Tag: 6.8 Billion," *CBS Money Watch*, November 8, 2016.
70. Ibid.
71. Niv Sultan, "Trump's Free Media," *Open Secrets*, April 13, 2017.
72. Gallup, "America's Trust in Mass Media Sinks to New Low," *Gallup Poll*, September 14, 2016.
73. Ibid.
74. David Frum, "No One is Doing More for Democratic Turnout than Donald Trump, *The Atlantic*, August 17, 2016.
75. Jessica Chasmar, "Donald Trump changed political parties at least five times: report," *The Washington Times*, June 16, 2015, http://www.washingtontimes.com/news/2015/jun/16/donald-trump-changed-political-parties-at-least-fi/.
76. Cathy Burke, "Clinton Won Richest Counties-64 percent of U.S. G.O.P," *Newsweek*, November 22, 2016.
77. Ibid.
78. Matthew Rozsa, "Omarosa Hints at a Donald Trump Enemies List," *SALON*, November 9, 2016; and Mary Bowerman, "Omarosa: Trump Already has an Enemies List," *USA Today*, November 8, 2016.
79. Jonathan V. Last, "Dividers, Not Uniters," *Standard*, March 28, 2016.
80. Ibid.
81. Plato, *The Republic* (New York: Dover Thrift Editions, 2000).
82. See Dennis F. Thompson, "Constitutional Character: Virtues and Vices in Presidential Leadership," *Presidential Studies Quarterly*, March 2012, 23.

83. Celina Durgin, "The Definitive Roundup of Trump's Scandals and Business Failures," *National Review*, March 15, 2016, http://www.nationalreview.com/article/432826/donald-trumps-scandals-and-business-failures-roundup.

84. Editorial, "Donald Trump's List of Presidential Shortcomings Seems Bottomless. What Do We Do Now?" *The Los Angeles Times*, January 20, 2017.

85. Ibid.

86. Ibid.

87. Ibid.

88. Ibid.

89. Ibid.

90. Ibid.

91. Ibid.

92. Ibid.

93. Ibid.

94. Myra Adams, "How Slavery Birthed the Electoral College," *Washington Examiner*, July 31, 2017.

95. Robert M. Alexander, *Presidential Electors and the Electoral College: An Examination of Lobbying, Wavering Electors, and Campaigns for Faithless Votes* (Amherst, NY: Cambria Press, 2012).

96. Michael A. Genovese, Todd L. Belt, and William Lammers, *The Presidency and Domestic Policy* (New York: Paradigm Publishers, 2014).

97. Amy B. Wang, "Trump in 2012: 'The Electoral College is a Disaster for a Democracy," *The Washington Post*, November 9, 2016.

98. Brooke Singman, "Who's With Trump? Senate Republicans Deeply Split in Wake of Tape Controversy," *Fox News*, December 12, 2016.

99. Ibid.

100. Pew Research Center for the People and the press, "Public Trust in Government: 1958-2014" (www.people-press.org/2014/11/13/public-trust-in-government/).

Chapter 3

Campaign Management

The First Test

The first visible manifestation of a potential president's skill is how well—or poorly—they manage the primary campaign. Is the team that a candidate puts together cohesive or chaotic? Does the campaign show discipline and strategic thinking? Is the team on the same page or speaking with multiple, conflicting voices? Are resources expended with skill and intelligence? How involved is the candidate in campaign control?

The typical campaign team—such as was developed by Hillary Clinton —is large, specialized, expensive, with clear lines of authority and a bureaucratic hierarchy. Donald Trump's team was different. Donald J. Trump was an unconventional candidate who ran an unconventional campaign in an unconventional way.

Donald Trump *was* the Trump campaign. He did what he wanted, went with his instincts, defied tradition, upended logic, rejected custom, and eschewed civility. He simply could not be "managed."

Trump's slash-and-burn, take-no-prisoners style worked well for him in the primaries. He savaged opponent after opponent, caring little for the established rules of debate, going straight for the jugular. But when it came to the general election, Trump was pressured to act more presidential, to tone it down a bit, to be less "Trumpish." To be or not to be Trump, that was the campaign battle for Team Trump.

There are plenty of sage veterans of campaign craft who will, for the right price or the right candidate, sell their considerable expertise to a person or a cause. They generally follow the "rules" of campaigning, and their advice is valued by candidates. A true campaign pro can be a valuable asset in an election.[1]

But Donald Trump was Donald Trump. He didn't want to be "managed"; he wanted to be free to do what he did best: being Donald Trump.

The Trump campaign team was small—very small. Where Hillary Clinton had over 700 staffers, Trump had barely 100. He relied heavily on a few close associates and very heavily upon his children—especially son-in-law Jared Kushner. Plus, the Trump campaign team went through several major overhauls, with frequent changes at the top of the team. It should have spelled chaos, and in some ways it did—and yet, somehow it worked.

The Announcement

Down the Trump Tower escalator, he descended, like a god coming down from the heavens. Every detail had been micromanaged and it had to be perfect. Actors were allegedly paid $50 each to wear Trump shirts and enthusiastically wave Trump placards.[2]

On June 16, 2015, during his presidential announcement speech, Trump launched into his attack on Mexicans coming over the border, claiming "they're rapists, they're criminals."[3] And that was how Donald J. Trump announced his candidacy for president of the United States. This longest of longshots had been planning this moment for years.

Donald Trump caught the presidential bug in the 1980s and had flirted several times with making the plunge. This time he was all in. To run his campaign, Trump chose Corey Lewandowski, who was hired in January of 2015 and designated campaign manager. Lewandowski didn't seem to have the experience to run a national campaign.

It was by presidential standards, a bare-bones operation, more a family affair than a presidential race.

Corey Lewandowski was not one of the stars of the consultant class, but he was someone with whom Trump felt comfortable. Lewandowski had never run a presidential campaign, and by conventional standards (but remember, this would not be conventional) seemed ill-suited to such a large task.

Lewandowski's job was to help pick off rival after rival and win enough Republican delegates to capture the nomination *before* the July convention. The initial team consisted of Lewandowski, Roger Stone, Sam Nunberg, and Trump's lawyer Michael Cohen. Early in-fighting in the Trump campaign led to Stone (a long-time friend of Trump's) leaving the campaign, and then Nunberg's removal.

Meanwhile Trump began cultivating Republican National Committee Chairman Reince Priebus. From his meetings with Priebus in 2014 and 2015, Trump realized that the primary field would be crowded and that is where Trump decided on a campaign strategy: "to break out of the pack, he made what appears to be a deliberate decision to be provocative, even outrageous. 'If I were totally presidential, I'd be one of the many.'"[4] Thus began the Trump slash-and-burn primary style.

And so, Donald Trump went down the list of rivals, one by one, attacking, humiliating, and destroying each of his many establishment rivals. The Trump campaign knew they would have to cross the delegate threshold *before* the July convention, lest the Republican establishment steal the nomination from Trump in a deal at the convention.[5]

Being small, the Trump campaign team could be lean and mean, quick and responsive. If Lewandowski was the manager, and in the early days was firmly in control, Trump was—in his own words—the brains behind everything. "I'm the writer," and "I'm the strategist" he said. Lewandowski's job was to "let Trump be Trump." Lewandowski however, began to run afoul of the Trump children—a clear sign of his pending political death. In March, the campaign hired veteran Republican strategist Paul Manafort, and Lewandowski should have seen the writing on the wall.

As Trump advanced, rivals began to direct fire at Lewandowski.[6] But as the primary season drew to a close—and as Trump appeared to have the required number of committed delegates—Trump began to distance himself from Lewandowski. Although Lewandowski was a useful employee, he never seemed to be close to the candidate. If it is closeness you wanted to see, one had to look to the family.

By late April, the Trump campaign staff reorganization hit a major snag. Lewandowski was down; Manafort was up and by May was officially in charge of the campaign. But the veteran Manafort was caught on tape telling Republicans that Trump, up to this point, was merely playing a role, a part that would become more presidential later in the campaign.[7]

Trump blistered at the thought and demoted Manafort while elevating Lewandowski for a short time. Manafort was just too valuable to Trump as a convention manager and delegate hoarder. As Manafort negotiated the delegate victory to the convention, his star seemed on the rise. But in early August, Manafort was confronted with a scandal based on his consulting work in Ukraine. Reports circulated that he had received millions of dollars in cash from an associate of Vladimir Putin's and it was then an open secret that Manafort was on his way out.

THE MAGIC NUMBER

Lewandowski was getting results. Primary, by primary, Trump would win two, lose one; attack the nearest rival and bury him, only to go on to the next in line. By late June 2016, it was clear that Trump would have a lock on the convention delegates. As unlikely as it seemed at the start, Donald J. Trump was but one small step away from becoming the Republican Party's nominee for president.

But he still had to contend with the Dump Trump forces in the Republican Party. Angry, vanquished primary rivals, most of the Republican establishment, even elements in the RNC, all hoped to find an alternative to Trump, even at the eleventh hour.

As the convention approached, the campaign (Trump and Kushner) felt it was time to shift gears and campaign leadership. Lewandowski was fired, and Paul Manafort, a veteran Republican political consultant, was brought in to secure the nomination at the convention. He soon became Trump's second campaign manager.[8]

The Trump Children

Clashes in the Trump campaign organization were damaging the election effort, and by mid-June, the family got involved. The Trump children—led by Ivanka—pressed their father to dump Lewandowski in favor of Manafort having a greater role.[9] The Trump brand was being badly damaged by the candidate's inability to self-censor, and the children's intervention led to Donald Trump firing Lewandowski. The internal power struggle was over, but were Trump's troubles? The campaign was put in order, but could Trump get himself in order?

In Phase I, the Trump campaign was led by Lewandowski, whose goal was to let Trump be Trump. And in the primaries, this worked. But in Phase II, new campaign head Paul Manafort's approach was that in this new broader constituency he had to make Trump behave like a grownup. But Trump couldn't do it. He kept reverting back to Phase I Trump, to the applause of his loyalists and the dismay of the establishment.

Table 6a. Management and Strategy.

Individual	Role	Previous Experience
Paul Manafort	Campaign chairman and chief strategist	• Gerald Ford 1972 presidential • Ronald Reagan 1980 presidential • George H.W. Bush 1988 presidential • Bob Dole 1996 presidential • Viktor Yanukovych advisor
Michael Glassner	Deputy campaign manager	• Bob Dole 1988 presidential • Bob Dole 1992 U.S. Senate • Bob Dole 1996 presidential • George W. Bush 2000 presidential • Sarah Palin 2008 vice presidential • Sarah PAC chief of staff
Jim Murphy	National political director	• Gordon Humphrey 1984 U.S. Senate • National Republican Senatorial Committee • Bob Dole 1988 presidential • Brad Gorham 1990 Rhode Island Attorney General • Bob Dole 1996 presidential • DCI Group • JLM Consulting

Source. "Donald Trump Presidential Campaign Key Staff and Advisors, 2016—Ballotpedia."

Table 6b. Management and Strategy (*Cont'd*).

Ken McKay	Senior advisor	• Donald Carcieri (R-R.I.) 2002 and 2006 gubernatorial • Republican National Committee • Rick Scott (R-Fla.) 2010- gubernatorial • Ron Johnson (R-Wis.) 2011 U.S. Senate • Republican Governors Association • Chris Christie 2016 presidential
John Mashburn	Policy director	• Office of Sen. Jesse Helms • Office of Sen. Trent Lott • Office of Sen. John Ashcroft • Office of Rep. Tom Delay • Womble Carlyle Sandridge and Rice • Carleson Center for Public Policy • Office of Sen. Thom Tillis
Alan Cobb	Director of coalition	• Bob Dole 1996 presidential campaign • Koch industries • Tim Shallenburger 2002 gubernatorial • Mike Pompeo 2014 U.S. House • Pat Roberts 2014 U.S. Senate • Americans for Prosperity

Source. "Donald Trump Presidential Campaign Key Staff and Advisors, 2016—Ballotpedia."

Manafort Takes Over—Sort Of

Purging, then repopulating campaigns does happen. But usually that occurs after a series of failures, not on the eve of victory. Lewandowski had been pushed down, then pushed out. Trump and son-in-law Jared Kushner believed that Lewandowski was not up to the expected convention fight, so they went for a more experienced hand—someone who could get the delegate count across the finish line.

By early July, a new Trump team was in place (see tables 6a–b). More experienced, better suited to a possible convention floor fight, Phase II of the campaign was geared to delegate capture and nomination victory.

One advantage the Trump team had was that they were not required to spend massive amounts on fundraising. The combination of Trump "self-funding" his campaign, plus the billion-plus dollars in free publicity Trump was able to get, all freed the campaign staff to focus on getting Trump elected, as opposed to chasing funds.

All in The Family

For Donald Trump, family matters—so much so that his children are his key advisors. This is especially true when it comes to his daughter Ivanka and her husband Jared Kushner. In fact, Kushner emerged as the most important player on the Trump team as well as the de facto campaign manager.

Trump's team was low on experience ("I would take capable over experienced all day long," Trump once said).[10] He would also take less rather than more, allowing only a very few loyalists close to the core of his campaign.

Trump's "family first" approach reflects both his inexperience in politics as well as his personal demand for loyalty. It also reflects his belief that he needs very few people to help him—he is already, he believes, smart enough to win the presidency. "I'm speaking with myself, number one, because I have a very good brain..." he said.

The true inner circle of the Trump campaign is the Trump family. His adult children are his political family.[11]

THE CONVENTION

There was a time when national party conventions actually selected the party nominee. Back-room deals in smoke-filled rooms sometimes thwarted the will of the people, but more often, fairly capable, and electable candidates emerged from this behind-the-scenes process. The last time a convention actually selected the candidate was in 1952 when the Republican contest between party favorite Robert Taft and the people's favorite Dwight D. Eisenhower ended with Eisenhower being nominated.

Today, because candidates arrive at the convention with a sufficient number of delegates (from primaries and caucuses) to guarantee their nomination, the convention resembles more a coronation than a contest. Today's conventions are part infomercial, part celebration, and if there is anything that occurs that is unscripted—that is a problem.

The convention delegate strategy went rather smoothly with the Dump Trump forces withering away even before the convention began. With the nomination secured, the next step was to put on a good show for the public at the Cleveland Convention.

But the convention was anything but a celebration. Dark and menacing, the message, especially coming from the candidate himself, was gloom and doom—and only Trump could save us.

So poorly managed was the convention that what is supposed to be a three-day feel-good celebration of candidate and party, turned out to be one big, huge Trump family commercial. One after the other, the Trump children (except ten-year-old Barron) marched before the convention to praise their father and further monetize the Trump brand. The children all accorded themselves handsomely, but a major embarrassment occurred when the normally quiet Melania, third wife of Donald, gave a convention speech that was well received but was later revealed to have been plagarized from Michelle Obama.

Melania, not to mention the entire Trump team, was humiliated. Just when they were supposed to be in full celebration mode, everything shifted to a defensive posture. Had no one vetted Melania's speech? Were the Trump higher-ups really that incompetent? Someone would be made to pay.

That someone was Paul Manafort. In August, shortly after the Convention, going into the general election, Trump cleaned house again. Manafort was out, and Kellyanne Conway was in as manager, while the controversial spokesman for the alt-right and former head of right wing Breitbart News, Steve Bannon became CEO of the campaign.[12] Conway was Trump's third campaign manager.

Conway and Bannon were an odd couple; she was the mature Republican pollster while he was the firebrand political killer. Conway's Republican credentials were spotless; Bannon's far-right-wing affiliations were worrisome.

Would Trump's third campaign manager produce a Trump 3.0? Not likely—Trump seemed unmanageable.

As the campaign moved to the final stretch run, Trump remained a few points behind Clinton. And while Russian-Wikileaked Clinton e-mails were released, and in spite of the FBI fumbling and bumbling its way around the e-mail investigation, Clinton seemed to have weathered the storm and appeared on her way to victory.

In the final two weeks of the campaign, Trump, seemingly willing to take the advice of Conway, acted "presidential," and avoided his usual blistering rhetoric. This more "mature" Trump seemed more palatable to mainstream Republicans as they began drifting back to the fold. Taking the sage advice of seasoned veterans actually worked. Not being Trump seemed presidential and perhaps electable.

In the end, Trump's brief effort to act presidential—to comply with the wishes of the campaign experts—proved good advice...even winning advice. But did Donald Trump win the presidency *because* of himself or *in spite of* himself? It *was* a year of change, and he *was* the outsider, and he *did* run against a vulnerable opponent, but what tipped the scales for Trump? Was he the right man at the right time, or the wrong man at the right time who profited from the times and the opponent?

TEAM OF RIVALS OR DEN OF VIPERS?

Three campaign managers in fifteen months. Three managers for three different phases of the campaign. Was Trump smart enough to have figured out exactly what he needed at every stage of the campaign, or did Trump just fumble along?

And did Trump put together a team of rivals, a den of vipers, or was it, from start to finish, all about family? Trump seemed to spend little time on the managerial details of running for president and most of his time being the entertainer candidate.

WHAT TRUMP'S CAMPAIGN MANAGEMENT REVEALS ABOUT DONALD TRUMP

Effective leaders hire good people, empower them, and usually follow their advice. Intelligent people, when confronted with a problem—say a health issue—see a trained specialist and usually follow their advice. Trump seems to trust no one but his adult children and is reluctant to follow the advice of experts He is his own manager, and no one can tell him what to do. This brand of personal imperial arrogance is as frightening as it is dangerous.

Yes, Trump was always his own campaign manager, and yes, he liked to follow his instincts, and yes, at times that worked out just fine. But Trump's offhand remark during the campaign that "I know more about ISIS than the generals do."[13] reflects a narrow-minded arrogance that *will* get Trump into trouble as president.

It is not that the campaign was badly managed; it is that Trump refused to be managed, and had a heightened sense of self that suggests deep inner problems. Intelligent people know that there is a lot they do not know, and they know that at times one has to go to others for advice. Split an atom? I haven't a clue on how that is done. But if I were required to do so, I would consult a range of experts, sift through their advice, and *then* decide.

But going into every situation certain that you know all the answers ("I consult myself," Trump has said[14]), is a recipe for disaster. And now, that person is at the helm of our ship.

Donald Trump's management style, if a style it is, seems largely improvisational and ad hoc. His "out box" is often Twitter, and his information gathering consists primarily of watching "the shows,"[15] and reviewing social media,[16] this style of management may have served him well when running a family business, but it is hard to imagine this approach working as he tries to manage the executive branch of government.

Notes

1. Michael John Burton and Daniel M. Shea, *Campaign Craft: The Strategies, Tactics, and Art of Public Campaign Management* (Santa Barbara: Praeger, 2010).
2. Rick Jervis, "Allegations of fake protests spread as anti-Trump fervor grows," *USA Today*, November 12, 2016.
3. "Here's Donald Trump's Presidential Announcement Speech," *Time*, June 16, 2015, http://time.com/3923128/donald-trump-announcement-speech/.
4. Gabriel Sherman, "Inside Operation Trump, the Most Unorthadox Campaign in Political History" *New York Magazine*, April 3, 2016.
5. William Arruda, "Being Hated is Donald Trump's Campaign Strategy – and it's Working." *Leadership*. Forbes, 2 July 2016. Web.
6. Kenneth P. Vogel and Ben Schreckinger, "Trump Campaign Rift gets Personal" *Politico*, May 25, 2016.
7. Ryan Lizza, "Taming Trump," *The New Yorker*, October 17, 2016.
8. Kenneth P. Vogel and Ben Schreckinger "How Lewandowski Finally Ran out of Lifelines," 2016 Election. *Politico*. 20 June 2016. Web.
9. Lizzie Widdicombe, "Ivanka and Jared's Power Play," *The New Yorker*, August 22, 2016.
10. Sherman, "Inside Operation Trump."
11. Lizzie Widdicombe, "First Family: The Influence of Ivanka Trump and Jared Kushner," *The New Yorker*, August 22, 2016.
12. Connie Bruck, "How Hollywood Remembers Steve Bannon," *The New Yorker*, May 1, 2017.
13. Aaron Blake, "19 things Donald Trump knows better than anyone else, according to Donald Trump," *The Washington Post*, October 4, 2016, https://www.washingtonpost.com/news/the-fix/wp/2016/10/04/1 7-issues-that-donald-trump-knows-better-than-anyone-else-according-to-donald-trump/?utm_term=.ed7d38d17973.
14. Eliza Collins, "Trump: I consult myself on foreign policy," *POLITICO*, March 16, 2016, http://www.politico.com/blogs/2016-gop-primary-live-updates-and-results/2016/03/trump-foreign-policy-adviser-220853.
15. James P. Pfiffner, "Organizing the Trump Presidency," paper presented at the *American Political Science Convention* in San Francisco, CA, August 31, 2017.

16. James P. Pfiffner, "The Unusual Presidency of Donald Trump," *Political Insight*, September 2017.

Chapter 4

The Transition

Test Number 2

On Tuesday, November 8, 2016, the nation chose a new president. Months before, however, candidate Trump (as well as candidate Clinton) began preparing for the 73-day transition period that begins on November 9 and goes up to the inauguration. During that time (the transition), the newly elected president prepares to put the pieces of his administration together in anticipation of governing.[1]

The president-elect is assisted in this (sometimes hostile) takeover by, among others, the nonprofit Partnership for Public Service. Its 2016 report "Ready to Govern" serves as a primer on the presidential transition. But most presidents prefer to rely on loyalists.[2]

A presidential transition (sometimes called an interregnum) is actually quite an unusual thing. Most of the world's democracies have most of the pieces of a new government already in place and waiting. It takes minutes, not months, to transfer power and position. This can be done because many governments have some form of a "shadow government" (a government in waiting) already in place and ready to go.

Each new president, between election day and the inauguration, needs to select a cabinet, top White House staff, (usually) a chief of staff, agency heads; set legislative goals; deal with global issues; prepare a new budget; and hire a host of other government officials. One veteran of the process Martin Anderson, Assistant for the President to Policy Development, referred to it as a "delicious chaos." [3]

This whole transition begins *during* the presidential campaign. The candidate appoints someone to head a transition team which begins to set the process in motion.[4]

Not all transitions go smoothly. Sometimes the president of one party is replaced by a new president of another party. Cooperation between the outgoing and incoming administration is not always evident. The transition from Lyndon B. Johnson to Richard Nixon in 1968–1969 went well, as did the transition from George W. Bush to Barack Obama. A good transition depends on the goodwill of the outgoing administration and the skill of the incoming administration. If one or both are absent, it spells trouble.

Presidential transitions are about the "3 Ps": People, Policy, and Process. Here, we will examine how well or poorly the transition process went, as well as key policy decisions made during the transition.

The goal is to hit the ground running, not stumbling. To do this, the candidate must *start early* and appoint a highly *respected* and experienced *transition head.* The transition team must move swiftly as time is short. The top White House *staff* should be appointed first, followed by the *cabinet.* Decisions on *legislative priorities* have to be made, and the president and his team need to be prepared to move on day one.

The transition is designed to best prepare or lay the groundwork to help a new president prepare for governing.[5] American elections determine *who holds office, not who has power.* There is no clean transfer of power, only a change in the occupant of an office. Once in office, a president has to work to get power, and then retain and use it.[6]

Although rarely true, at times, a president may legitimately claim a *mandate* (authorization to do something). Not all elections produce mandates. In fact, few do. For an election to qualify as a mandate, the incoming president must register very high on the *political opportunity* scale. That is, they must win the election by a significant margin, the election choice must revolve around clear policy positions, and the president's party must win a large majority in both Houses of Congress[7] (see table 7).

Given that mandates are rare, trust in government is low, and we are a deeply divided nation, even a president with a good transition team will have trouble governing. Nevertheless, a good transition is a key to starting off well and hitting the ground running.

TOUGH TRANSITIONS

November 15, 2016: the transition had hardly started when Trump's first transition head New Jersey Governor Chris Christie was fired and replaced by Mike Pence. At that point, chaos set in. There was fierce jockeying for positions and open infighting among the transition staff. The Christie purge, instigated by Jared Kushner (it was personal),[8] led to the abrupt dismissal of many Christie associates such as the highly regarded former Congressman Mike Rogers, a foreign policy expert expected to have a high post in the new administration.

The new transition team, headed by Pence, shifted from outsider to insider mode. A large number of the transition team were lobbyists, just the kind of insiders Trump had promised to eschew. Among the lobbyists who worked on the transition team were Marc Shaw, Michael McKenna, Michael Catanzaro, Myron Ebell, and Norman Eisen. Insider and/or lobbyists formed the core of Pence's upper echelon team.

What was emerging was that the number-one criterion for high positions was loyalty to Trump. The president must hire roughly 4,000 federal employees, and not everyone can pass the loyalty test, but clearly, loyalty to Trump was a high priority in staffing the new administration.

Table 7. First-Term Presidential Election Performance.

Year	President	Party	Vote (%)	Margin (%)	House	Senate
1952	Eisenhower	R	54.9	10.5	22	1
1960	Kennedy	D	49.7	0.2	-22	2
1964	Johnson	D	61.1	22.6	37	1
1968	Nixon	R	43.4	0.7	5	6
1976	Carter	D	50.1	2.1	1	0
1980	Reagan	R	50.7	9.7	34	12
1988	G. H. W. Bush	R	53.4	7.8	-2	0
1992	Clinton	D	43.0	5.6	-10	0
2000	G. W. Bush	R	47.9	-0.5	-3	-4
2008	Obama	D	52.9	7.2	23	8
2016	Trump	R	46.2	-2	-6	-2
Averages			50.3	5.8	7.2	2.2

Source. Adapted from John P. Burke's *Presidential Power: Theories and Dilemmas,* "The Myth of a Presidential Mandate," 173. Gerhard Peters "Seats in Congress Gained or Lost by the President's Party in Presidential Election Years" and "Presidential Elections Data," *The American Presidency Project,* ed. John T. Woolley and Gerhard Peters (Santa Barbara: University of California, Santa Barbara, 1999–2017) http://www.presidency.ucsb.edu/index.php.

Transitions are rarely smooth. There are usually glitches and mistakes. But the Trump transition seemed especially erratic and mistake prone. They did not get in contact with the departments of State and Defense at the outset, setting off all sorts of alarm bells in D.C. and across the globe.

Among the first Trump appointments was to name the controversial alt-right champion Steve Bannon as his top political advisor, specifically Chief White House Strategist. Bannon's appointment met with an immediate chorus of condemnation from a wide range of sources. A sampling of some of Bannon's quotes reveal much about his political views. Referring to Ann Coulter, Michele Bachmann, and Sarah Palin in a 2011 interview on Political Vindication Radio, he said:

> These women cut to the heart of the progressive narrative. That's why there are some unintended consequences of the women's liberation movement. That, in fact, the women that would lead this country would be pro-family, they would have husbands, they would love their children. They wouldn't be a bunch of dykes that came from the Seven Sisters schools up in New England. That drives the left insane, and that's why they hate these women.

Bannon has also noted:

> I'm a Leninist, Lenin wanted to destroy the state, and that's my goal, too. I want to bring everything crashing down, and destroy all of today's establishment.

> What we need to do is bitch-slap the Republican Party.

> Let the grassroots turn on the hate because that's the ONLY thing that will make them do their duty.[9]

TWEETY BIRD

Donald Trump had a hard time shifting from campaign attack-shark mode to presidential mode. His voluminous late-night Tweet eruptions did not stop, as Trump railed against restaurant critics, television shows, union leaders who corrected his faulty math, major U.S. corporations whose CEOs had the nerve to disagree with Trump, actresses, and just about anyone who criticized the president-elect.

Using Tweets to go after average Americans is both unpresidential and dangerous. It is unpresidential because it suggests a smallness, a pettiness, and the insecurities of a fragile ego. It is dangerous for what Trump unleashed.

For example, Trump intervened with the Carrier Corporation, persuading them not to move some jobs to Mexico. Trump exaggerated the number of jobs saved, and when union leader Chuck Jones publicly corrected Trump, the president-elect blew this small incident into a national story when he blasted Jones on Twitter, writing that he was doing "a terrible job representing workers." It did not end there. Some unhinged Trump supporters went after Jones, harassing him at his home, and directly threatening Jones and his family ("We're coming for you" warned one, while another told him he'd better keep an eye on his kids).[10]

From his bully pulpit, Trump was inciting bullies. His verbal attacks on average citizens paint a target on their backs and open a dangerous door.

While Trump's use of Twitter gave him a direct and immediate connection to millions of citizens, allowing him to go around the mainstream media, it also revealed a thin-skinned and undisciplined nature, not to mention how unseemly it was for a president-elect to use Twitter as his personal attack mechanism.

Incoming First Lady Melania Trump said she intends to be a "long distance first lady,"[11] living in the Trump Tower in Manhattan, announced that the "issue" she wanted to promote was the prevention of bullying. Critics suggested she start by taking away her husband's Twitter account. Throughout the first seven months of the Trump presidency, the president continued to get off message by his repeated early morning tweets, many of which ran counter to stated policy or to the intended message of the day [12]

From Promises to Proposals

During the transition, an incoming administration must find a way to turn campaign promises into real-world policy proposals. The incoming president should set clear priorities, decide which proposals to push for first, and articulate a clear roadmap for the future.

During the campaign, candidate Trump made a number of bold statements and promises: I'll build a wall—and have Mexico pay for it; I'll ban all Muslims; I'll "lock her [Hillary Clinton] up,"; I'll repeal Obamacare on Day 1; I'll "take care of our Vets"; I'll "resume waterboarding, and worse"; "NATO is obsolete;" climate change was a "Chinese hoax."

As the transition progressed, Trump began retreating from many of his promises. Contrary to popular opinion, the modern presidents had *all* worked very hard to keep their campaign promises. Trump seemed to be running away from his. Prosecute Hillary Clinton? Off the table. Obamacare? There are actually a few parts he wanted to keep. Torture? Maybe that wasn't such a good idea. And the wall? Who knew? I "never settle" lawsuits? He settled on the Trump University lawsuit. File legal charges against the eleven woman who came forward charging Trump with sexual harassment? Nope. Drain the swamp? Not happening. Trump was abandoning many of his own promises that drew so many voters into his camp. Was he a hypocrite? A traitor to the cause?[13]

So just what did Donald Trump want to do coming out of the gate? Candidate Trump issued a bold series of promises from major "day one promises" to "one hundred day promises." This massive agenda was whittled down significantly in the first six months of Trump's presidency, as ambition far exceed ability. Beyond achieving the confirmation of Neil Gorsuch to the Supreme Court, Trump could point to very few legislative successes in his first six months.

ETHICS? NOT TODAY, THANK YOU

Given his vast business interests, there was no way for Donald Trump to avoid dilemmas regarding ethics and conflicts of interest. It should be pointed out that presidents are not bound by all of the governmental legal codes of ethics. Nonetheless, it is customary and expected that presidents release their tax returns and put their holdings into a blind trust while they are in office to avoid any conflict of interest.

Trump announced that he would neither release his tax returns nor would he put his assets into a blind trust, but that he intended to have nothing to do with running his business. He would let his adult sons run the business; at the same time, he also named children to his transition team. But with holdings spread across the globe, owing millions of dollars to banks controlled by China for example, having business ties to Uruguay, Azerbaijan, and elsewhere, and with more than 500 limited liability companies, Trump clearly faces conflict of interest issues.

Trump will also oversee the National Labor Relations Board, which would decide if Trump has violated labor laws in his dealing with employees. Such obvious conflicts of interest should raise red flags for even the most ardent Trump supporters.

It would be easier to get to the bottom of this mess if Trump released his tax returns—something every president for the past forty years has done —but Trump refused to do so. In addition, the U.S. Constitution contains the Emoluments Clause, which prohibits any government official from accepting gifts or payment from a foreign government or from sharing profits in a company with financial ties to a foreign government. Trump has numerous business deals with foreign individuals and governments.

The Emoluments Clause of the U.S. Constitution can be found in Article I, Section 9, Clause 8. It reads:

> No Title of Nobility shall be granted by the United States: And no Person holding any office of profit or trust under them, shall, without the consent of the Congress, accept of any present,

emolument, office, or Title, of any kind whatever, from any King, Prince, or foreign state.

An "emolument" is any fee, compensation, salary, financial benefit, or payment. It comes from the Latin *emolumentum* meaning profit or gain.

So what should Trump do? As the *New York Times* noted in an editorial:

> Even if he no longer manages his businesses directly, Mr. Trump will continue to own them and his family will be involved in deals, both foreign and domestic, to develop real estate projects or license his brand. He will still be aware of the existence of his business interests and how his actions as president will affect them. The conflicts between his private interests and his public role will be impossible to untangle.[14]

For example, the profitability of his investments in the Middle East, India, Turkey, the former Soviet republics and elsewhere could put his financial interests directly at odds with American foreign policy, whether it takes the form of sanctions against those governments or American investment and aid deals. In such situations, will he act to protect or grow his family's assets or advance the interests of the country? His businesses currently owe hundreds of millions of dollars to Deutsche Bank, which is negotiating a multibillion-dollar mortgage settlement with the Department of Justice. How would the public know if he or his Justice Department softened its stance because it involved a bank to which he owes money, or whether that bank cut him a sweetheart deal in hopes of currying favor?[15]

Having a family member in one's administration is not new. After all, President John F. Kennedy appointed his brother Bobby to be Attorney General. This led to the passage of a 1967 anti-nepotism law designed to prevent office-holders from hiring relatives. But Trump's tangled government/business/family caldron makes for a strange and strained brew.

The U.S. criminal conflict of interest statute does not apply to the president, but a series of other laws do. The most relevant, as mentioned, is the Emoluments Clause of the U.S. Constitution. Conflicts—perceived or real—are inevitable.

Trump has a history of playing fast and loose in his business dealings. He allegedly used funds illegally from the Trump Foundation for personal expenses (including a large painting of himself),[16] faced multiple lawsuits alleging housing discrimination,[17] was charged with fraud in his Trump University (he settled),[18] and other questionable activities.

As president, Trump's sprawling global business interests—the full extent of which is still held secret due to Trump's refusal to release his taxes—involve financial interests with nations Trump will be dealing with as president. Trump's deep association with South Korea's Daewoo Engineering and Construction Corporation raises questions regarding Trump's policy proposals.[19] Candidate Trump suggested that South Korea should develop nuclear weapons. As policy, this would undermine decades of U.S. nonproliferation policy, but if this happens, Trump would make millions of dollars. Does business drive policy? The specter of government for sale will loom large over the Trump presidency.[20]

Trump seemed unable to let go of his business interests. He even went so far as to sign on as executive producer of NBC's "The New Celebrity Apprentice" television program.[21] Trump will be working for a network—NBC News—that will also be commenting on and evaluating his performance as president.

Trump's many business interests scattered across the globe cannot help but muddy the ethical waters in which Trump as president must swim. He has said his children will run his business yet he also appointed them to formal roles in the transition, with daughter Ivanka given an office in the West Wing of the White House and son-in-law Jared Kushner serving as a key advisor to the president.[22] And Trump himself continued to involve himself in his business during the transition, mixing his roles and raising ethical concerns when—among other questionable business activities—after the election he spoke with British politician Nigel Farage, encouraging him to oppose offshore windmill farms off the Scottish coast near a Trump owned golf resort.[23]

When confronted with these ethically questionable activities, Trump responded that "the law's totally on my side. The president can't have a conflict of interest."[24] Additionally, Trump businesses owe hundreds of millions of dollars to banks in China and Germany, and perhaps elsewhere. How can President Trump distance himself from Businessman Trump? If he cannot, charges that he is running a kleptocracy are inevitable.

Trump's ownership of the new Washington Trump International Hotel (located in the Old Post Office Building, just a few blocks from the White House) also raised clear conflicts. Several nations scheduled events there *after* Trump was elected, some by choice possibly hoping to curry favor with the new president, others perhaps felt pressured to cancel events and rebook at Trump's hotel. Kuwait, for example, reserved space in the Four Seasons Hotel for the annual holiday party where they would be hosting 600 guests. After Trump's election victory, they cancelled the Four Seasons reservations (where they'd held their annual event for years) and rebooked at the Trump International Hotel.[25] Such activities led critics to wonder if Trump is the first occupant of the Oval Office to see the presidency as a money-making venture.

President Trump's global business interests—and his unwillingness to distance himself from those interests by placing his assets in a blind trust—means that there will clearly be the appearance of corruption— violation of the Emoluments Clause of the Constitution—if not the reality of corruption.[26] Many Trump companies do business with various entities controlled by foreign governments, making it almost certain that serious conflicts of interest will apply, and the Constitution will be violated.

And how did Republican leaders in Congress, so eager to "lock her up" react to the Trump conflict-of-interest issue? House Oversight Committee Chairman Jason Chaffetz of Utah, who announced before the election that his committee would hold "years" of investigation into possible

Clinton Foundation conflicts of interest, lost interest, claiming that he would not go on any "fishing trip" related to Trump's business interests and public policy.[27]

PAY FOR PLAY—OR—(WITH APOLOGIES TO BEN FRANKLIN) "A KLEPTOCRACY, IF YOU CAN KEEP IT"

The offer seemed too good to be true. It was an invitation from Donald Trump Jr. and his brother Eric. If only you will pony up half a million dollars, you too can be a part of a private, day-after-the-inauguration reception, get a photo opportunity with President Trump, and go on a hunting or fishing trip with one of the brothers. "Opening Day 45" as it was called was to be a "camouflage and cufflinks" themed fundraiser, and proceeds were to go to conservation groups.[28]

During the campaign, Donald Trump railed against the Clinton's for their "pay-for-play" ways. He promised to "drain the swamp." But during the transition, Trump sons Donald Jr. and Eric concocted a plan to trade access for money.[29]

In this access for money scheme, Trump's sons sent out invitations for a post-inaugural event called "Opening Day 45," where depending on how much money you bought in for, you were granted various levels of access to the new president and his family. Donald Jr. and Eric Trump sit on the board of directors of the nonprofit "Opening Day" foundation, and after this story broke, their status was changed to "honorary chairmen" of the event. Broken down by level of giving, this is what access could be bought (See figure 2).

Figure 2. The Trump Boys Go Hunting for Money.

WASHINGTON, DC
SATURDAY, JAN. 21, 2017

OPENING DAY
2017
45

BENEFITING
CONSERVATION CHARITIES

BALD EAGLE | $1,000,000

+ Private reception and photo opportunity for 16 guests with VIPs and celebrities associated with the event

+ Four guitars autographed by an Opening Day 45 performer

+ Elite Conservation Package with commemorative custom products
  - Multi-day outdoor excursion for 4 guests

+ Outfitter's Pro Package* with commemorative custom details

+ 85 VIP guest tickets
  - Early event entry
  - Access to VIP Lounge

+ 200 General Admission guest tickets

+ Priority company listing on all printed material
  - Logo on invitation, main stage branding, key branding throughout event and premier branded item in guests' swag bags

+ Name recognition on invitation materials, must respond immediately

GRIZZLY BEAR | $500,000

+ Private reception and photo opportunity for 8 guests with VIPs and celebrities associated with the event

+ Two guitars autographed by an Opening Day 45 performer

+ Elite Conservation Package with commemorative custom products
  - Multi-day outdoor excursion for 2 guests

+ Outfitter's Pro Package* with commemorative custom details

+ 45 VIP guest tickets
  - Early event entry
  - Access to VIP Lounge

+ 100 General Admission guest tickets

+ Company branding opportunities
  - Logo on invitation, branding throughout event and branded item in guests' swag bags

+ Name recognition on invitation materials, must respond immediately

ELK | $250,000

+ Private reception and photo opportunity for 4 guests with VIPs and celebrities associated with the event

+ One guitar autographed by an Opening Day 45 performer

+ Outfitter's Pro Package* with commemorative custom details

+ 20 VIP guest tickets
  - Early event entry
  - Access to VIP Lounge

+ 50 General Admission guest tickets

+ Company branding opportunities
  - Logo on invitation, branding throughout event and branded item in guests' swag bags

+ Name recognition on invitation materials, must respond immediately

MARLIN | $100,000

+ 8 VIP guest tickets
  - Early event entry
  - Access to VIP Lounge

+ Outfitter's Pro Package* with commemorative custom details

+ 30 General Admission guest tickets

+ Company branding opportunities
  - Logo on invitation, branding throughout event and branded item in guests' swag bags

+ Name recognition on invitation materials, must respond immediately

RAINBOW TROUT | $50,000

+ 4 VIP guest tickets
  - Early event entry
  - Access to VIP Lounge

+ Outfitter's Pro Package* with commemorative custom details

+ 16 General Admission guest tickets

WILD TURKEY | $25,000

+ 2 VIP guest tickets
  - Early event entry
  - Access to VIP Lounge

+ Outfitter's Pro Package* with commemorative custom details

+ 8 General Admission guest tickets

VIP PACKAGE | $5,000

+ 1 VIP guest ticket
  - Early event entry
  - Access to VIP Lounge

GENERAL ADMISSION TICKET | $1,500

+ 1 General Admission guest ticket

Source. https://www.nytimes.com/interactive/2016/12/20/us/politics/document-2016-12-20-OpeningDay-Sponsorship-12-20-16.html

Not that it stops there. Son Eric's foundation was auctioning off "coffee with Ivanka" to the highest bidders.[30] Such naked commercialization, selling access to the plutocrats, suggest that the U.S. was becoming a kleptocracy under the direction of the Trump family.

Shortly after Christmas, Trump announced that he would close his controversial Trump Foundation so as not to create any hints of a conflict of interest. But the foundation was already under investigation by New York's Attorney General for the improper use of funds (e.g., buying a large portrait of Trump himself, yet having his "foundation" pay for it). Legally, the foundation could not be shut down while under investigation.[31]

As inauguration day approached, numerous key positions in the Trump administration remained unfilled and in many cases, without even a nominee for the post. Things hardly got any better in the first fifty, then hundred days of the administration. At the State Department, Defense, the Pentagon, and elsewhere, senior posts remained vacant and it became clear that Trump's was one of the slowest in modern history to staff key positions. As a *New York Times* story noted:

> Mr. Trump's personnel problems are rooted in a dysfunctional transition effort that left him without a pool of nominees-in-waiting who had been screened for security and financial problems and were ready to be named on Day 1. In the weeks since, the problem has been compounded by roadblocks of his own making: a loyalty test that in some cases has eliminated qualified candidates, a five-year lobbying ban that has discouraged some of the most sought-after potential appointees, and a general sense of upheaval at the White House that has repelled many others.[32]

One of the oddest inaugural contribution sources came from Citgo Petroleum, which donated $500,000. The Citgo gift is odd because that company is the U.S.-based affiliate of PDVSA, Venezuela's state-controlled oil company, not to mention that Venezuela was going through devastating economic problems, as well as severe food and medicine shortages.

Foreign entities donating large sums of money to the incoming president raises serious ethical and political questions.

WHAT THE TRANSITION TELLS US ABOUT PRESIDENT TRUMP

Donald Trump had a hard time transitioning from campaign attack dog to president. Old habits die hard, as reflected in two news stories that appeared on December 2, 2016. The first reported on a phone call between president-elect Trump and Nawaz Sharif, Prime Minister of Pakistan. According to reports, Trump was effusive in his praise of Sharif: "You are doing amazing work which is visible in every way," said Trump, "You are a terrific guy." This proclamation seemed at odds with the view of the U.S. State Department, which scrambled to mend the Trump-broken fences with India, Pakistan's rival, as well as with the Pakistan people where Sharif is beset by accusations of widespread corruption. Moreover, Trump calling Pakistan a "fantastic place of fantastic people" seemed at odds with Trump's own proposed ban on all Muslims entering the U.S.[33] What does this inconsistency tell us about how Trump will govern as president?

The second piece of evidence occurred at a Trump victory rally in Ohio where against his staff plans and ahead of schedule, Trump announced that he would be appointing James "Mad Dog" Mattis as Secretary of Defense. This premature announcement reflected the lack of discipline on Trump's part, as well as his penchant for going over the top at rallies where crowds seem to bring out the worst rather than the best in him. As president, Trump would have to learn to control himself and not let the emotions of the crowd influence him so.

Winning the presidency is one thing, governing quite another. To win, Trump tore down the system. To govern, he must build up the system and run it. It is something like the dog that finally catches up with the bus: I've achieved my goal, now what do I do with it?

What, for example, does Trump do with the white supremacist supporters who so passionately backed him?[34] Trump created an atmosphere and said many things in his campaign that signaled to some of the more unsavory elements in our society that they had Trump's stamp of approval. He made it possible for sexists and misogynists to come out into the open. They were energized by Trump's attacks on Mexicans and Muslims. Many cheered at Trump's insulting comments about women.

Emblematic of this is Carl Paladino, former Republican candidate for Governor of New York, as well as the New York cochair of Trump's presidential campaign. In response to a series of questions posed by *Artvoice*, Paladino sent out an e-mail in which, in response to the question, what would you like to see "go away in 2017," he wrote: Michelle Obama, "I'd like her to return to being a male and let loose in the outback of Zimbabwe where she lives comfortably in a cave with Maxie, the gorilla." He also wrote that he wished "Barack Obama catches mad cow disease after being caught having relations with a Herford," adding "He dies before his trial and is buried in a cow pasture next to Valerie Garret (an Obama senior staffer) who died weeks prior, after being convicted of sedition and treason, when a Jihadi cell mate mistook her for being a nice person and decapitated her."[35]

Who writes such things? This is not from some sadly deranged fourteen-year-old isolated in his room afraid to face the real world; this was written by the cochair of Trump's New York campaign. Such crude behavior seen during the transition period has also been witnessed during the presidency—Anthony Scaramucci was appointed as White House communications director when he unloaded a profanity-laced verbal tirade against Reince Priebus and Steve Bannon in a conversation with a reporter. However, this time instead of remaining quiet as he did with Paladino, Trump had Scaramucci fired. During her announcement that Scaramucci was fired (not even two weeks into his job), White House press secretary Sarah Huckabee Sanders said that "The president certainly felt that Anthony's comments were inappropriate for a person in that position." So perhaps Trump, "who delights in pushing the boundaries of political and social decorum,"[36] now understands that as president he cannot let slide such unacceptable behavior.

During the transition, Trump—in refusing to sit through intelligence briefings, failing to deal adequately with business conflicts of interests, intruding inappropriately in dealings with foreign leaders, continuing to go on Tweet rants—exhibited an undisciplined, shoot-from-the-hip, dismissive brand of leadership that may serve him poorly as president. As an outsider, Trump's learning curve may take more time than a more seasoned politician, but as president there is little time for on-the-job learning—a president must be ready from Day 1.

During the transition, Trump took the unprecedented step of meddling in policymaking *before* he even became president. The U.S. has only one president at a time, yet that did not stop Trump from openly advocating certain actions (e.g., veto a UN resolution dealing with Israeli settlements) contrary to stated U.S. policy and the intent of the Obama administration. Then, after the U.S. refrained from vetoing the UN resolution, Trump took to tweeting not only how wrong the Obama administration was, but that soon things would be very different.

Transitions normally focus on the future. But events surrounding allegations regarding Russian interference and the 2016 presidential election forced Trump and others to be concerned about the recent past. As inauguration day approached, the case of Russian interference in the presidential election heated up. Numerous U.S. Intelligence agencies confirmed what they had long suspected and warned about, that the Russian government, under orders from Vladimir Putin, hacked into the computer systems of key Democrats—including Clinton's campaign Chief John Podesta—and gave the stolen information to Julian Assange's WikiLeaks, which released the materials. This proved damaging to the Clinton campaign and may have impacted the outcome of the election.[37]

Donald Trump simply refused to accept this, arguing that he was not convinced that the Russians were involved, going so far as to dismiss the allegations as a "witch hunt." Trump, siding with Vladimir Putin and Julian Assange, against what would soon become his own intelligence services, put Trump at odds not only with the Democrats in Congress (which might be expected) but also against most leading Republican legislators such as Senators John McCain and Lindsey Graham (not to mention the U.S. Intelligence agencies). Trump, sensitive to the possibility that this might tarnish his electoral victory, simply refused to believe the voluminous evidence and chose to believe what he wanted—perhaps "needed" to believe.

Late in the afternoon of Friday, January 6, the partially declassified Intelligence Report on the Russian hacking was released.[38] It was a devastating indictment of Vladimir Putin and Russia. The report confirmed that Russia carried out a comprehensive cyber campaign designed to hurt Hillary Clinton and help elect Donald Trump president. This cyber campaign was ordered by Vladimir Putin who "aspired to help" elect Trump.

That Friday afternoon, president-elect Trump also sat for one of his infrequent security briefings where the evidence of the Russian cyberattack was presented to Trump. After the meeting, Trump insisted that the cyber campaign had no impact on his victory, but he did seem to entertain the possibility that there might have been some sort of cyberattack.[39]

On January 11, president-elect Trump held his first press conference since the November election. The press conference was held amid a media frenzy over Russia's hacking scandal in which, on the order of Vladimir Putin, Russia hacked into e-mails of Democrats, gave the stolen e-mails to WikiLeaks who released it, interfering with the presidential election. As if Russia trying to help Donald Trump get elected were not enough, an unconfirmed addendum to the U.S. intelligence agency report included reports of bizarre sexual activities by Trump, supposedly filmed while Trump was visiting Russia several years earlier. These allegations, while unconfirmed, created an online sensation.

Trump tried to deflate accusations of conflict of interest at a news conference, with the main item being Trump's announcement on the measures he would take to avoid conflicts of interest as president. He announced that he would turn over operation of his business to his sons, but he would not divest his holdings and would not set up a blind trust.

In this, Trump took several steps in the right direction, but virtually all ethics experts said it did not go nearly far enough. Trump would still own the business, profit from them, and it would still be the family openly engaging in business. When Walter M. Shaub, Jr., Director of the U.S. Office of Government Ethics, announced that Trump's actions were insufficient, House Republican Chair of the Oversight Committee Jason Chaffetz of Utah threatened to hold hearings directed against Shaub and his agency. Of this, former White House ethics advisor under the George. W. Bush presidency Richard Painter said it was a "clear threat to pull the funding of the Office of Government Ethics."[40]

By all appearances, conflict of interest issues might well be the Achilles heel that takes Trump down. His failure to even do minimal due diligence surely would come back to haunt him.

On the issue of emoluments, an attorney representing Trump said that to offset any constitutional concerns, any profits made from Trump hotels would be donated to the U.S. Treasury. But this is only the tip of the emoluments iceberg. China's government rents space in Trump Towers, and there are many other Trump venues profiting from foreign governments.[41]

No president is above the law, and the law couldn't be clearer. From the moment Donald Trump took the oath of office, he was in violation of the emoluments clause of the constitution.[42]

Donald Trump, the anti-hero as president uses his poke-you-in-the-eye style—getting into Twitter fights with members of Congress (John Lewis), television shows (Saturday Night Live), the heads of U.S. intelligence agencies (John Brennan), movie stars (Meryl Streep)—as an operating or governing style. He is and will likely remain divisive and controversial, and he has tried to convert that into a method of governing. He faces a *divided nation* with a *unified party*, and he believes he can govern by being openly hostile to critics, while controlling his Republican majorities in the House and Senate.

Trump entered office as the most unpopular elected president in modern times. On the eve of his inauguration, Gallup Poll ratings showed Trump at 44% approval to be far behind past incoming presidents. Six weeks into his presidency, his rating was in the mid-thirty percent range. Can a president so unpopular govern effectively? And if so, for how long?

Table 8. Popularity of Incoming Presidents.

Year	Incoming President	Popularity
1993	Bill Clinton	68%
2001	George W. Bush	61%
2009	Barack Obama	83%
2017	Donald Trump	44%

Source. Compiled by author.

If Trump enters office with low popularity, it should be remembered that he also begins his presidency with Republican control of both Houses of Congress. This alone gives Trump a strong hand at getting his program passed. With the transition over, governing begins. His first test will be how he performs in his first hundred days.

There seemed to be two Trump transition teams: the transition team and Team Trump. During the campaign, Trump distanced himself from the transition team. After the election, Trump decided to get involved, and that is when things went off the rails. The transition team—located in Washington—immediately came into conflict with Team Trump, based in Trump Tower. The two rarely came together, often operating at odds with each other.

On election day, the transition team presented Trump with thirty binders. They were filled with detailed plans for the transition and the early months of the new administration. They took advantage of the two recent laws and Executive Orders funding and facilitating the transition process, plus they benefitted from the information made available by the White House Transition Project and the Partnership for Public Service. Pre-election day, the transition team was off to an excellent start. But days after the election, the transition team got displaced by the Trump children[43]—transition team chairman Chris Christie was fired and was replaced by Mike Pence. At this point the president-elect all but turned things over to his children who met regularly with transition officials. And at that point, the detailed policy plans, the appointment process, the transition itself all imploded; and all the long, hard work of the transition team was gutted by Team Trump.[44] Is this a sign of things to come?

Notes

1. See John P. Burke, *Presidential Transitions* (Boulder, CO: Lynne Rienner, 2000) and Ida E. Burkhalter, ed. *Presidential Transitions: Backgrounds and Issues* (New York: Nova Science, 2013).
2. www.whitehousetransitionproject.org; https://www.brookings.edu/blog/fixgov/2016/12/12/transition-in-three-easy-charts/; http://presidentialtransition.org/#band-1; https://www.washingtonpost.com/graphics/politics/trump-administration-appointee-tracker/database/?tid=ssmail
3. Martin Anderson Oral History, Assistant for the President to Policy Development, University of Virginia, Miller Center, Presidential Oral Histories.
4. See Martha Joynt Kumar, *Before the Oath: How George W. Bush and Barack Obama Managed a Transfer of Power,* John Hopkins University Press, 2015.
5. See Michael A. Genovese, *Memo to a New President,* Oxford University Press.
6. See Charles W. Dunn, Chapter 7 "The Laws of Management" in *The Seven Laws of Presidential Leadership,* (Harlow, Pearson, 2007). See also http://whitehousetransitionproject.org.
7. Robert A. Dahl, "Myth of the Presidential Mandate," *Political Science Quarterly* 105, no.3 (Autumn 1990): 335–372.
8. As a federal prosecutor, Christie sent Kushner's father to jail. See Byron York "The sordid case behind Jared Kushner's grudge against Chris Christie," *Washington Examiner,* April 16, 2017, http://www.washingtonexaminer.com/byron-york-the-sordid-case-behind-jared-kushners-grudge-against-chris-christie/article/2620427.
9. Daniel Victor and Liam Stack, "Bannon and Breitbart News, Quoted," *Los Angeles Times,* November 15, 2016, A16.
10. Michael D. Shear, "Trump as Cyberbully in Chief? New Twitter Attack on Union Boss Draws Fire," *The New York Times,* December 9, 2016, A1.
11. Catherine Lucey, "For now, Melania Trump plans to be long-distance first lady," Associated Press, November 25, 2016, http://www.pbs.org/newshour/rundown/now-melania-trump-plans-long-distance-first-lady.
12. Z. Byron Wolf, "Try to square Trump's tweets with his wife's plan to combat cyberbullying," CNN, June 29, 2017, http://www.cnn.com/2017/0

6/29/politics/melania-trump-cyberbullying-trump-counterpunch/index.
html.

13. Evan Halper, "Flip-flopping en route to White House," *The Los Angeles Times*, November 23, 2016, A1.

14. Editorial, "Donald Trump's Tangled Web," *The New York Times*, November 16, 2016.

15. Editorial, "Mr. Trump's Tangled Web," *The New York Times*, November 17, 2016, A28.

16. David A. Fahrenthold, "This is the Portrait of Donald Trump that his Charity Bought for $20,000," *The Washington Post*, November 1, 2016.

17. Jonathan Mahler and Steve Eder, "'No Vacancies' for Blacks: How Donald Trump Got His Start, and was First Accused of Bias," *The New York Times*, August 27, 2016.

18. Robert W. Wood, "Trump University Settlement Nets $25M Write-Off For Trump, Taxes For Students," Forbes, April 3, 2017, https://www.forbes.com/sites/robertwood/2017/04/03/trump-university-settlement-nets-25m-write-off-for-trump-taxes-for-students/#45d369997298.

19. Kurt Eichenwald, "How the Trump Organizations Foreign Business Ties Could Upend U.S. Security, " *Newsweek,* September 14, 2016.

20. Carolyn Kenney and John Norris, "Trump's Conflicts of Interest in South Korea," Center for American Progress, June 14, 2017, https://www.americanprogress.org/issues/security/news/2017/06/14/433958/trumps-conflicts-interest-south-korea.

21. Maggie McGrath, "How Can Trump Produce The Apprentice While Serving As President?", *Forbes*, May 4, 2017, https://www.forbes.com/sites/maggiemcgrath/2017/05/04/how-can-trump-produce-the-apprentice-while-serving-as-president/#6bdcc9d11d0c.]

22. Kevin Liptak, "Trump's Secretary of Everything: Jared Kushner" *CNN Politics*, April 3, 2017.

23. Editorial, "Fight the 'Blight' of Wind Farms Near my Golf Courses, Trump Urges Ukip Leader" *The Guardian*, November 22, 2016.

24. Rosalind S. Helderman and Tom Hamburger "Trump's Presidency, Overseas Business Deals and Relations with Foreign Governments Could All Become Intertwined," *The Washington Post*, November 25, 2016.

25. Jackie Northam, "Kuwait Celebration at Trump Hotel Raises Conflict of Interests Questions," *National Public Radio*, February 25, 2016.

26. Adam Liptak, "Business Could Test Presidential Limits," *The New York Times International Edition*, November 23, 2016, 7.

27. Alex Seitz-Wald and Benjy Sarlin, "Hillary Clinton's Victory Prize: Congressional Investigations," *NBC News*, October 26, 2016.
28. Matea Gold and David A. Fahrenthold, "Offer of Access to Trump and Family at Fundraiser is Pulled Back, but Ties Remain," *The Washington Post*, December 20, 2016.
29. Ibid.
30. Camila Domonosque, "Trump Family Tried to Auction Coffee with Ivanka, Raising Ethical Concerns," *National Public Radio*, December 16, 2016.
31. Tracy Wilkinson, "Trump to Close Charity to Avoid 'Possible Conflict of Interest,'" *The Los Angeles Times* December 25, 2016, A12.
32. Julie Hirschfeld Davis and Sharon LaFraniere, "Slowest Transition in Decades Has Dust Piling Up in Key Offices," *The New York Times*, March 13, 2017, A1.
33. Shashank Bengali and Aoun Sahi, "In phone call with leader, Trump lavishes praise on Pakistan, 'fantastic place of fantastic people,'" *The Los Angeles Times*, December 1, 2016, Web. http://www.latimes.com/world/la-fg-pakistan-trump-20161201-story.html.
34. Jaweed Kalseem, "'White Pride' Awakened," *The Los Angeles Times*, November 18, 2016, A1.
35. Jamie Moses, "WHAT DO WE WANT FOR 2017? We have a Lot of Different Opinions," December 23, 2016, *Artvoice*, http://artvoice.com/2016/12/23/want-2017-lot-different-opinions/#.WWtfkogrKUk. See also Maya Rhodan, "Donald Trump Backer Carl Paladin Defends His Call for President Obama's Death and Michelle Obama's 'Return to Africa,'" *TIME*, December 24, 2016.
36. Michael D. Shear, Glenn Thrush, and Maggie Haberman, "John Kelly, Asserting Authority, Fires Anthony Scaramucci," *The New York Times*, July 31, 2017, https://www.nytimes.com/2017/07/31/us/politics/trump-white-house-obamacare-health.html.
37. Brian Bennett and Noah Bierman, "Trump Renews Attack on Case for Russian Hacking," *The Los Angeles Times*, January 5, 2017, A1.
38. Office of the Director of National Intelligence, "Background to 'Assessing Russian Activities and Intentions in Recent US Elections': The Analytic Process and Cyber Incident Attribution," January 6, 2017, https://www.dni.gov/files/documents/ICA_2017_01.pdf. See also http://www.pbs.org/newshour/rundown/russian-president-vladimir-putin-ordered-campaign-influence-u-s-election-report-finds.

39. Greg Miller, "Declassified Report Says Putting 'Ordered' Effort to Undermine Faith in U.S. Election and Help Trump," and "U.S. Intelligence Agencies: Putin Ordered Intervention in Presidential Elections" *The Washington Post,* January 6, 2017.

40. Nicholas Fandos, "Government Ethics Chief Resigns, Casting Uncertainty Over Agency," *The New York Times,* July 6, 2017.

41. Linette Lopez, "And Here's Trump's Conflict of Interest with the Chinese Government..." *Business Insider,* November 28, 2016.

42. See Robert Spitzer, "Why Congress Won't Impeach Trump Now, Even Though it Should," *Syracuse.com,* January 13, 2017; Norman L. Eisen, Richard Painter, and Lawrence H. Tribe, "The Emoluments Clause: Its Text, Meaning, and Application to Donald J. Trump." Brookings Institution, December 16, 2016; and David Cole, "Trump is Violating the Constitution," *The New York Review of Books,* February 23, 2017.

43. Jonathan Lemire, "Trump Children's Roles Blur Line Between Transition, Company" *PBS News Hour the Rundown,* November 20, 2016.

44. Dan Balz, "'It Went Off the Rails Almost Immediately': How Trump's Messy Transition Led to a Chaotic Presidency," *The Washington Post,* April 4, 2017.

CHAPTER 5

PUTTING TOGETHER TEAM TRUMP

THE THIRD TEST

The president is one individual, but the presidency is a collection of people, departments, and agencies spread out over a vast network that comprises the "institutional presidency." How a president manages this institution speaks volumes to just how effective that president will be.

In the early days of the republic, presidents did not have to worry much about managing the executive branch. It was, after all, very small. But with the Great Depression of 1929 and the growth of the positive role of the federal government in being held responsible for solving many of society's problems, a large and unwieldy network has enveloped the president, making the role of chief executive more demanding.

Of the hazards of personnel selection during the transition, John F. Kennedy wrote that "I must make appointments now; a year hence I will know who I really want to appoint."[1] This may prove especially pertinent to a Trump presidency as the president-elect's unfamiliarity with D.C. and the major players means he must rely heavily on the input of others and is always uncertain about the people he appoints.

All the nominees must be screened and vetted before their appointments are announced. While vetting is an inexact science, and some nominees with disqualifying skeletons in their closets do get through, causing both embarrassment and conveying the impression that the new team is not competent, it is important to try to avoid nominees about whom damaging revelations and negative impressions are made.

So intrusive are the vetting and confirmation processes that some good potential appointees simply refuse to put themselves and their families through the indignity. Evan Bayh, at one time a potential Democratic vice-presidential pick, said that the vetting process was "totally invasive. It's like having a colonoscopy, except they use the Hubble telescope on you."[2]

Today, a new president appoints around 4,000 people to the Cabinet, Sub-Cabinet, staff, and agency posts. It is a daunting task but if poorly handled, will almost certainly lead to failure on the part of the new president. The first person a new nominee selects is the vice president.

SELECTING A RUNNING MATE

"I am nothing, but may be everything" said John Adams, the nation's first vice president of the office he occupied.[3] One of Franklin D. Roosevelt's vice presidents John Nance Garner said the office had the value of a "bucket of warm piss."[4] And for a good deal of history, our vice presidents were held in relatively low esteem.

The selection of a vice presidential running mate is the first true measure of a presidential candidate's gravitas and approach to politics and governing.

At the beginning of the nation, the person who finished second in the race for president became vice president, but an 1800 kerfuffle compelled the passage of the 12th Amendment which led to clear lines of distinction in the presidential and vice-presidential positions.

There was a time when the office had little but ceremonial significance. That changed when a vice president was unexpectedly thrust into the presidency.

The vice president's job depends on the president's wishes. It can be as big (e.g., Cheney) or as small (e.g., Quayle) as each president decides.

Article 2 of the Constitution states that the vice president must be a natural-born U.S. citizen, at least 35 years old, and an inhabitant of the United States for at least fourteen years at the time of his or her swearing in.

There are a few "unwritten" rules VP candidates are to follow: 1) do not overshadow the presidential nominee; 2) don't cause trouble for the nominee; 3) pass the "smell test" of being acceptable to a large portion of the public; 4) don't have any skeletons in their closets; and 5) if they can, help the nominee get elected.

The presidential nominee picks the vice-presidential running mate. Yes, the choice must be confirmed at the Party Convention, but that is a foregone conclusion. If the candidate is selected before the convention, the candidate may spend weeks narrowing down the list, vetting the potential nominee, polling or using focus group research on the person, and see how compatible the choice might be with the candidate.[5]

Prior to the 1980s, vice presidents were usually chosen to balance the ticket either regionally or ideologically. But ever since the presidency of Jimmy Carter, who gave his vice president Walter Mondale considerable substantive responsibilities, vice presidents have been drawn closer into the presidential orbit.

One of the first things a contemporary presidential candidate thinks about when selecting a vice president is "who can help me get elected?" Can Senator X deliver his or her state? An imported voting bloc? A wavering wing of the party? In truth, vice-presidential candidates make very little electoral difference. But some vice-presidential picks may heal party wounds from the primaries or be seen as a master of some particular issue.

Some vice presidents were called upon to materially assist the president. Walter Mondale, George H.W. Bush, and Joe Biden ably served the nation. Dick Cheney, the most powerful vice president in United States history, exerted a great deal of influence over the president, not always to positive effect.[6]

There have been a few obvious blunders in the modern era of vice-presidential selection. In 1968 Richard Nixon selected little-known Maryland Governor Spiro Agnew who resigned from office and pled *nolo contendere* (I do not contest) to bribery charges.[7] In 1972, Democratic nominee George McGovern selected Missouri Senator Tom Eagleton, but a few days later he withdrew from the ticket when it was revealed that he had undergone electroshock therapy.[8] In 1988 George H.W. Bush selected J. Danforth Quayle, Senator from Indiana. Quayle, it turned out, was a bit "slow" and became something of a national joke.[9] In 2000 John McCain chose Alaska Governor Sarah Palin. What at first appeared to be a stroke of genius very soon morphed into a major embarrassment when Palin turned out to be more than a bit goofy.[10] And in 2004, John Kerry picked John Edwards who was later revealed to have been involved in a strange affair with one of his "campaign workers."[11]

So, what *should* the candidate seek in a vice president? First, are they ready to be president should the need arise? Second, are they people the president-elect can work with? After that, think about what the VP would add to the ticket. It matters who is vice president. After all, nine vice presidents have succeeded to the presidency, and fourteen presidents first served as vice presidents.

Normally, the line of vice-presidential hopefuls is quite long. But due to the unusual qualities of the 2016 Republican nominee, and due to a mild revolt of the establishment Republicans, the usual waiting list was pared down quite a bit.

Clearly Trump needed a D.C. insider to balance his outsider status, but beyond that it was unclear just what Trump was looking for: a partner to help run the government? Someone who might help win a key state? An establishment figure to offset Trump's outsider image?

Ohio Governor John Kasich was—many insiders confess—offered the job, as well as a guarantee that the VP would be deeply involved in running the executive branch. But Kasich remained true to his "never Trump" stance and said no. Trump has denied offering Kasich the position.[12]

Former House Speaker Newt Gingrich rose to the top of Trump's list despite his notable liabilities (a Trump-Gingrich ticket would have totaled six marriages and might have proved a deal-breaker with certain religious voters)[13] as did Alabama Senator Jeff Sessions. Others on the list included New Jersey Governor Chris Christie (an early Trump supporter but had ethics-related baggage weighing him down), Oklahoma Governor Mary Fallin, Florida Governor Rich Scott, Tennessee Senator Bob Corker, and South Dakota Senator John Thune.

Trump was leaning towards Gingrich, but his children favored Mike Pence, Governor of Indiana and former member of the House of Representatives. Pence was the safer choice, but Gingrich caught the fancy of Trump. After some very public auditions before Trump and his children, Trump was finally persuaded that Pence was the one.

In his July 16, public announcement that Mike Pence would be his vice-presidential nominee, Trump repeatedly got off message. Trump's script was a promotion of Pence, yet he kept drifting off script to talk about himself.[14]

Almost as soon as he let word of the Pence choice leak out, Trump had second thoughts. He still wanted Gingrich. But Pence was already on his way to New York in preparation of a public announcement. Trump wanted to know if he could rescind his offer to Pence, going so far as to go on Fox News saying that he had *not* yet made up his mind.[15] Pence, getting word of Trump's cold feet, went public, announcing that yes, he was asked—and had accepted—the offer to be Trump's vice president.[16] Trump ended up keeping Pence on the ticket. But this very public fumble by Trump raised questions about his veracity and his judgment.

The choice of vice president sends an important signal and is seen as a crucial moment—a test if you will—of the nominee. How he (or she) handles this first key decision speaks volumes to the skill and soundness of the nominee. Trump's stumble was worrisome. It sent a bad message. Who was calling the shots, Trump or his children? And how could they so stumble on such an important a choice?[17]

In the early days of the Trump presidency, Pence served as a loyal, even sycophantic, vice president. And as Trump got into early trouble over the Russia investigations and conflict-of-interest charges, Pence seemed poised to move up, should the need arise.

CHIEF OF STAFF

Once elected, the president-elect must begin putting together the team. It is wise to select a Chief of Staff first because that person becomes the central hub of the new administration.

Trump moved quickly, selecting Republican National Committee Chair Reince Priebus. The choice of Priebus was widely applauded because he was an insider and a part of the Republican establishment with a deep knowledge of Washington D.C. and all the key players.

But what role would Preibus play? Would he direct the Trump presidency or be Trump's errand boy? Trump said he wanted to "encourage a lot of input, with multiple, competing voices at the table." He said he did not want a "top-down White House." But James Pfiffner warns against such a model, favoring instead greater reliance on the chief of staff:

> The White House now has more than 15 sub-units filled with more than 400 very ambitious people who will compete for the president's time to promote their priorities. Cabinet secretaries will do the same. Someone must organize demands on the president's time, moderate staff battles, and ensure that the right advice gets to the president.

Empowering a chief of staff does not mean that the president will or should have only one source of information or advice. In fact, it's just the opposite.

The chief of staff should ensure that the president is exposed to opposing voices on all important policy issues, and particularly to those at odds with the apparent consensus. If important people in the administration feel shut out, they will create back doors to the president. The result will be policy incoherence.

Furthermore, empowering a chief of staff does not mean that the president will or should ignore outside advice. Presidents should be able to consult with whomever they choose, including an outside 'kitchen cabinet.'

But advice must be mediated by the White House staff so that any serious proposal can be 'staffed out' to examine its full implications. If not, the president may accept what seems like a good idea without being aware of its full ramifications. It's not that staffers know better than the president. It's that the president needs to be aware of opposing views and potential pitfalls before making a decision.[18]

Priebus did not last long. Unable to bring discipline to the president or the administration, he was soon replaced by Homeland Security Secretary General John Kelly.

Along with the announcement of Priebus came the (much) more controversial announcement that Steve Bannon, a prominent alt-right spokesman, who worked on the Trump campaign, would serve as Trump's chief strategist and senior counselor. An alt-right leader and former head of Breitbart News who is seen by many as a white supremacist, Bannon's hard-right ideology even alarmed many Republicans who see him as too extreme and too willing to traffic in alt-right causes. Bannon, long associated with white supremacist views, "doesn't belong within 10 miles of the White House," editorialized *The Boston Globe*.[19]

Building the President's Cabinet

During the campaign, candidate Trump eschewed conservative orthodoxy and was all over the ideological landscape. Absent a clear ideology, voters were free to see in Trump a pragmatic businessman who got results, someone free from ideological rigidity.

Trump wanted to save Medicare and social security, initiate a massive infrastructure rebuilding program—liberal, big-government programs. At the same time, he was going to cut taxes, dismiss warnings about global climate change, increase defense spending—classic conservative Republicanism. Left and right, Trump was hard to pin down.

But when he put together his Cabinet, Trump revealed what was hidden during the campaign: a hard-right/alt-right conservatism.[20] One would expect a Republican president to choose a conservative, Republican Cabinet, but Trump went to extremes (see table 9).

Trump's Cabinet is short on political experience. Only ten Trump nominees are experienced politicians; this compares unfavorably with Obama (15) and George W. Bush (17). Trump's Cabinet is also less educated than past Cabinets. Only ten Trump nominees have graduate-level degrees, compared to Obama with thirteen and Bush with ten. On business experience, nine Trump nominees, two Obama Cabinet members, and nine Bush officials had significant business experience. And none of the Trump Cabinet members were Democrats, whereas Obama had two Republicans and Bush had one Democrat. Trump has two women in his Cabinet, while Obama, as did Bush, had four. Two of Trump's Cabinet nominees were nonwhite, compared to seven under Obama and six under Bush.

Table 9. The Trump Cabinet.

Name	Cabinet Post	Background	Party	Gender	Race	Political Orientation
Rex Tillerson	State	CEO Exxon Oil	R	M	W	Right
James Mattis	Defense	Marine General (Ret.)	R	M	W	Hard Right
Jeff Sessions	Attorney General	U.S. Senator, Alabama	R	M	W	Hard Right
Wilbur Ross	Commerce	Billionaire Investor	R	M	W	Wall Street
Andrew Puzder	Labor	Businessman	R	M	W	Hard Right
John Kelly	Homeland Security	Marine General (Ret.)	R	M	W	Right
Scott Pruitt	EPA	House of Representatives	R	M	W	Hard Right
Tom Price	HHS	House of Representatives (A)	R	M	W	Hard Right
Steven Mnuchin	Treasury	Finances	R	M	W	Wall Street Cons.
Betsy DeVos	Education	Major Rep. Donor	R	F	W	Hard Right
Elaine Chao	Transportation	Former Labor Secretary	R	F	Asian	Right/Wife of McConnell
Ben Carson	HUD	Medical Doctor	R	M	Af-Am	Hard Right
George Perdue III	Agriculture	Business/Governor of Georgia	R	M	W	Right
Ryan Zinke	Interior	House of Representatives, MT	R	M	W	Hard Right
Rick Perry	Energy	Former Texas Governor	R	M	W	Hard Right
David Shulkin	Veterans Affairs	Physician/ Under Secretary	I	M	W	Moderate

Source. Compiled by author.

Many of Trump's picks for Cabinet posts were on record as being hostile to the very departments they were to lead. As the *Los Angeles Times* editorialized: "Almost every one of Trump's picks will head a department that he or she has sued, fought, or sought to undermine."[21] Jennifer Rubin, writing in NYMag.com noted that instead of a "team of rivals," Trump looked as if he was putting together "a team of saboteurs."[22]

Trump also chose an unusually high number of generals to surround him, the most in fact of any president since World War II. With Lt. General Michael Flynn short lived as National Security Advisor, General James N. "Mad Dog" Mattis as Defense Secretary, and Marine General John Kelly heading Homeland Security, the Trump administration is top heavy with brass. Early in his presidency when Mike Flynn was let go, Trump chose another general, H. R. McMasters as his replacement. Ironically, Trump's military advisors were more prudent and less confrontational than their boss. While the Framers intentionally established civilian control over the military, Trump seems to be blurring the lines.

Donald Trump ran as an outsider, an insurgent who would "drain the swamp." But running the government may require experienced hands who can administer a vast bureaucracy. Trump seems little concerned that many of his appointees have little relevant experience. As Neil Irwin wrote of Trump's nomination of Steven Mnuchin as Treasury Secretary:

> But his appointment is part of a recurring theme as Mr. Trump has assembled his cabinet. Most of his appointees have little in the way of directly relevant policy experience. Mr. Trump, who has never worked in government at any level, has also named a chief of staff (Reince Priebus) and chief White House strategist (Stephen K. Bannon) of whom the same can be said.

Irwin further notes,

> Mr. Trump seems to be betting that nuts-and-bolts experience running government agencies and wrestling with the hard right technical details of public policy just don't matter...The swamp that is being drained is the one inhabited by wonkish technocrats

who have devoted their careers to the details of policy-making. If nothing else, the years ahead will be a fascinating experiment in how much policy expertise actually matters to effective governing.[23]

If Washington-based or policy-area experience matters little to Trump, Wall Street and Goldman Sachs experience seems highly valued.[24] Steven Mnuchin, Wilbur Ross, and deputy Commerce Secretary Todd Ricketts are the tip of the billionaire boys club iceberg in the new Trump administration. Wall Street insiders, not populist outsiders, have been called upon to drain the swamp (or, as critics argue, Trump is filling the swamp —with alligators).[25]

Trump is the first president since Ronald Reagan not to have a Latino in his initial cabinet. And Trump's was a predominantly white male cabinet. It was a Cabinet that decidedly did not look like today's America.

As Donald Trump took the oath of office, his Cabinet appointees confirmations lagged. Some of the delay was caused by Democrats whose goal was merely to delay. Some of the delay occurred because several Trump nominees failed to submit the required paperwork. And some of the delay occurred because of ethical questions about a few nominees.

Trump's Cabinet is also one of the oldest in history. Trump himself is 70, Wilbur Ross (Secretary of Commerce) is 79, Jeff Sessions (Attorney General) is 70, James Mattis (Secretary of Defense), John Kelly (Secretary of Homeland Security), Rick Perry (Secretary of Energy) and Andrew Puzder (Secretary of Labor) are all 66, Ben Carson (Secretary of Housing and Urban Development) is 65, and Rex Tillerson (Secretary of State) is 64.

TRUMP'S STAFF SELECTION

Over the past fifty years, the president's Cabinet has declined in importance and the president's staff has increased in power and importance. Most presidents grow to believe that Cabinet Secretaries—over time— become captured by their departments and become advocates for the needs of the department over the will of the president. In addition, many presidents question the loyalty of Cabinet secretaries because they also have strong connections to the congressional committee on whom they are dependent for funding and direction and/or to the client group (e.g., the Agricultural Secretary becomes the advocate for Agribusiness). This "iron triangle" that surrounds the Cabinet secretary—congressional committee, client group, department—draws the secretary's attention, and perhaps loyalty. Over time, presidents rely less on their Cabinet for advice and input, and more on their top staff and the Executive Office of the President (EOP).

The staff, in contrast, is loyal only to the president, serves the president's every need, and answers only to the president (see tables 10a–c).

From early indications, son-in-law Jared Kushner is a key advisor to Trump. Ivanka's husband enjoys a very close relationship to Trump, and the president trusts him.[26] Reports from inside the Trump campaign all verify Kushner's influence over Trump, and the word spread quickly within the campaign not to cross him.

As expected, son-in-law Jared Kushner was named a senior advisor to Trump. Kushner will not draw a salary, and he has said that he will set up firewalls between himself and his various business interests.

Kushner's appointment violates the 1967 anti-nepotism law barring government officials from hiring relatives. The law is clear:

> No federal official, including the president, may hire or appoint a relative, including a son-in-law, to "a civilian position in the agency in which he is serving or over which he exercises jurisdiction or control.

Table 10a. Top Trump White House Appointees (Non-Cabinet).

Name	Post	Background	Party	Gender	Race	Political Orientation
Reince Priebus	Chief of Staff	Head of RNC	R	M	W	Right
Steve Bannon	Senior Counselor	Head of Breitbart News	R	M	W	Alt Right
Kellyanne Conway	Counselor	Political Pollster/ consultant	R	F	W	Right
Omarosa Manigault	Communications	Reality TV Personality	R	F	Af-Am	-
Katie Walsh	Scheduling	RNC Official	R	F	W	Right
Rick Dearborn	Deputy Chief of Staff for Legislative and Intergovernmental Affairs	Senate Staff	R	M	W	Right
Joseph Hagin	Deputy Chief of Staff of Operations	Security Consultant	R	M	W	Right
Bill Stepien	WH Political Director	Aide to Governor Christie	R	M	W	Right
Marc Short	Legislative Affairs	Pence Advisor	R	M	W	Hard Right
John DeStefano	Director of Presidential Personnel	Mayor, New Haven, Connecticut	D	M	W	Right/Moderate
Sean Spicer	Press	RNC	R	M	W	Right

Source. Compiled by author.

Table 10b. Top Trump White House Appointees (Non-Cabinet; *Cont'd*).

Name	Position	Detail				
Dan Coats	Director of National Intelligence	House of Representatives	R	M	W	Hard Right
Ken Blackwell	Domestic Policy Advisor	Ohio Politician	R	M	Af-Am	Hard Right
Michael Flynn (withdrew in first month)	National Security Advisor	General	R	M	W	Hard Right
Peter Navarro	White House National Trade Council	Economist	D	M	W	Right
Gary Cohn	Director of National Economic Council	President of Goldman Sachs	R	M	W	Right
Jared Kushner	Advisor	Real-Estate/Son-in-Law	R	M	W	Right
Donald F. McGahn	White House Council	Attorney	R	M	W	Hard Right
Carl Icahn	Special Advisor	Businessman, Wall Street	R	M	W	Hard Right
Mick Mulvaney	Budget Director	Right Wing Interest Group	R	M	W	Hard Right
Nikki Haley	UN	South Carolina Governor	R	F	Indian	Right

Source. Compiled by author.

Table 10c. Top Trump White House Appointees (Non-Cabinet; *Cont'd*).

					Tea Party/Hard Right
Mike Pompeo	CIA	House of Representatives, KS	R	M	W	
Robert Lighthizer	Trade Representative	Former Trade Official, Lobbyist	R	M	W	Hard Right
Jay Clayton	SEC	Wall Street Lawyer	-	M	W	-
Stephen Miller	Senior Advisor for Policy	Senate Staffer	R	M	W	Hard Right

Source. Compiled by author.

Although she does not hold any official position in the administration, Trump's daughter Ivanka—who has moved into the First Lady's Office in the West Wing of the White House[27]—also holds considerable influence over her father. Between Ivanka and husband Jared, they are likely to be seen as *the* power couple in Washington D.C. in the age of Trump.[28]

Kellyanne Conway, who was called in at the eleventh hour of the Trump campaign to right the ship, was also selected to serve in the new administration. Conway was the first woman to serve as a major party campaign manager, and she has long been active in Republican campaigns. She was named as White House counselor and is tasked with messaging and political strategy.[29]

Trump also appointed Carl Icahn (investor, Wall Street guru, and opponent of government regulations) to serve as a special advisor on regulatory reform. This suggests that a Trump presidency will be serious about reducing regulations. Icahn, another billionaire appointee, is the fox put in charge of the henhouse. He will *not* be paid and will thus not be subject to conflict-of-interest laws.

Trump further signaled his move to the right in his selection of deficit hawk Mick Mulvaney, a member of Congress from South Carolina, as his budget director. Mulvaney, a cofounder of the hard-right House Freedom Caucus, is part of a group of members of Congress who propose draconian cuts in social spending in order to balance the federal government.

For White House Counsel, Trump selected hard-right Libertarian Donald F. McGahn. As an attorney, McGahn "fought for years to strip away limits on big money in politics long before the Supreme Court blessed the idea, and he has relied on a bare-knuckle style to defend politicians in trouble."[30] McGahn will be giving Trump advice on a wide range of legal issues, including Trump's potential conflicts of interest in his business dealings. But Trump does not need a legal enabler, he needs someone who will give prudent advice. However, it seems that McGahn's approach will be more of a "let Trump be Trump" one, when there may be times he needs to keep Trump's activities under tighter control.

Signaling that President Trump will indeed be tough on trade with China, Trump appointed China critic Peter Navarro to head the newly created White House National Trade Council. This appointment, along with Trump's stirring the pot by suggesting a new, more positive relationship with Taiwan, are designed to either put China on the defensive so as to extract a better trade deal with China, or signal an aggressive, even hostile, relationship of the U.S. vis-à-vis China.

PERSONNEL AND PROCESS

Apart from personnel, how a president organizes his staff is an important ingredient in governing. The "how" depends on a variety of questions: How does the new president like to receive information, make decisions, resolve conflicts, and handle pressure? Where does he turn when the U.S. is threatened? Whom does he most trust? What is at the core of the new president's cognitive thought process, and how does the new president process information? What are the president's cognitive strengths and weaknesses? Who gets to report directly to the president?

The organizational structure of the White House is almost entirely up to the president, but there are clear roles and expectations to which presidents must conform. Some presidents prefer a hierarchical structure while others like a more open process. Dwight D. Eisenhower, perhaps given his experience in the military, preferred a hierarchical system. Richard Nixon favored an even more rigid hierarchical system than did Eisenhower. John Kennedy and Bill Clinton liked a more open, accessible staff structure.

There are benefits and pitfalls built into each style. A hierarchical system can exclude information or isolate a president, but it also tends to produce an orderly process. More open systems can give a president access to a wide range of information, but such systems can also be undisciplined and chaotic.

Donald Trump prefers an unstructured, open system—in the extreme. Trump has experience operating a family business but no executive experience in corporate America or in government. His preferred style is to be open, accessible, unstructured, and unencumbered. In a December 14 meeting with heads of tech companies, Trump signaled his style telling them to "call me...we have no chain of command here."[31]

Trump's decision-making process is highly personal—and even backwards. As Kellyanne Conway noted, "He started with a conclusion, and the evidence brought him to the same conclusion." He often says that in making decisions, "I rely on my gut."[32] Evidence and facts are used to support decisions already made.

D.C. Veteran Elizabeth Drew, writing about Donald Trump's working style in the White House, noted that "People who have been to the Oval Office have come away stunned by Trump's minimal attention span, his appalling lack of information, and his tendency to say more than he knows (Intelligence officials have been instructed to put as much of his daily briefings as possible in the form of pictures)."[33]

Is this a sustainable model for a modern president whose inbox overflows with demands on his time every day? Most presidents rely on a Chief of Staff and eventually (it took Carter and Clinton some time, and or few mistakes before the came around to recognizing this) impose at least a bit of discipline and hierarchy into their management models. On this, letting Trump be Trump will almost certainly not work, as the president realized with his short-lived chief of staff Reince Priebus, replaced after barely five weeks by General John Kelly, who was brought in to bring some order up (to the president) and down (to the staff) to the Trump White House.

Donald Trump is a watcher, not a reader. He gets information, as he admitted, by "watching the shows" (cable news). By all accounts, Trump watches more television than any president in history.[34] This "information-lite" approach to gathering information means that on many issues the president will be ill- or underinformed. As president, he insisted that his briefing materials should be no more than a single page, have bullet points, and have no more than nine per page.[35]

Most leaders rely on advice, information, and evidence when making decisions. Not so with Trump. "I know more about ISIS than the generals do," said candidate Trump, and in his 2004 book *Trump: Think Like a Billionaire*, Trump described his decision process when he wrote that others "are surprised by how quickly I make big decisions, but I've learned to trust my instincts and not overthink things."

Additionally, like Richard Nixon before him, Trump is a collector of slights so as to be better able to get revenge: "If you do not get even, you are just a schmuck." He also suggested that it was good to "be paranoid."[36]

During the Senate confirmation hearings, a number of Trump nominees contradicted the president-elect's views and policy positions. General Mattis (Defense) openly disagreed with Trump on Russia, NATO, and the Iranian nuclear arms agreement. Mike Pompeo (CIA), who testified that he wanted to investigate Russian efforts to influence the U.S. election, said he would "absolutely not" use torture on prisoners and also agreed that Russia tried to aid Trump in the campaign. Jeff Sessions (Attorney General) opposed Trump's call for a ban on Muslims entering the United States, opposed waterboarding, and said that yes, Russia interfered with the election. Sessions was also asked whether "grabbing a woman by her genitals without consent" constitutes sexual assault. "Clearly it would be," he said. And on whether millions of undocumented immigrants had voted for Hillary Clinton as Donald Trump had tweeted, Sessions answered "I don't know what the president-elect meant or was thinking when he made that comment or what facts he may have to justify his statement."[37]

Rex Tillerson (State) disagreed with Trump on climate change, the Paris climate accord, NATO, the Muslim ban, Trans-Pacific Partnership (TPP), and on the spread of nuclear weapons. John Kelly (Homeland Security) also disagreed with Trump on issues such as the benefit of a border wall, a Muslim registry, torture, and domestic surveillance. Was such open disagreement a sign of the Trump administration's openness to a variety of views?

The president-elect, and later when he was president, was exceptionally slow in filling key posts in his administration. One reason for this is that as a political outsider, Trump simply did not know very many insiders who might be qualified to run departments and programs. But if, as the old Washington political saying goes "personnel *is* policy," then Trump was missing a golden opportunity to initiate the changes he promised.

By June 2, almost six months into his presidency, Trump had nominated only 110 people to fill positions that required Senate approval. At the same time in their first terms, George H. W. Bush was at 155, Bill Clinton at 207, George W. Bush at 202, and Barack Obama at 238, were all ahead of Trump. [38]

A team of rivals or a team of clones? As mentioned, this is a distinctly right-wing Cabinet, very conservative, very male, and very white. Will this team bring Trump competing choices, different options, a wide range of ideas and information from which to choose, or will Trump be given limited and ideologically slanted options and information?

WHAT TEAM TRUMP TELLS US ABOUT PRESIDENT TRUMP

Contrary to campaign indications where Trump sold himself as a pragmatic outsider, who spoke for forgotten Americans, president-elect Trump put together a team of highly right-wing ideologues, several billionaire businessmen, a number of Wall Street investors and Goldman Sachs employees. Trump also put together a largely white and male team.

Of course, a president is generally free to choose those he wishes to work with (subject to Senate confirmation), and in this, President Trump was the person selected to be president. But Trump's team is whiter, richer, and more conservative than several administrations that preceded him, and one less representative of the American people. Does the team he has put together help him pass the test of being an effective president? And reflecting on the first six months of the Trump presidency, staff chaos has reigned, making it more difficult for the president to govern successfully; however, the problem is not just staff chaos but also a lack of discipline at the top. John Kelly was brought in as chief of staff to create order below (staff) and discipline above (the president).

Trump won as a populist insurgent, gave an inaugural address with a populist insurgency message, but he appointed a government that was anything but populist. Once again, the elite few would rule; once again, the people would be left out. Could Trump enlist the elite to work on behalf of the people? That was his publicly stated goal—did he intend to keep that promise?

NOTES

1. Quoted in James P. Pfiffner, *The Strategic Presidency*, 2nd edition, (Lawrence: University of Kansas Press, 1996), 56.
2. "Inside the VP Vetting Process: A Guide to the Invasive Questions," *The Week*, 20 July 2012, http://theweek.com/article/index/230860/inside-the-vp-vetting-process-a-guide-to-the-invasive-questions.
3. Jaime Fuller, "Here are a bunch of awful things Vice Presidents have said about being No.2," *The Washington Post*, October 3, 2014.
4. Ibid.
5. Paul Light, *Vice-Presidential Power; Advice and Influence in the White House*, (Baltimore: John Hopkins, 1984); Christopher Devine and Kyle Kopko, *The VP Advantage: How Running Mates Influence Home State Voting in Presidential Election* (Manchester: Manchester University Press, 2016); Jody C. Baumgartner and Thomas F. Crumblin, *The American Vice Presidency: From the Shadow to the Spotlight* (Lanham: Rowman and Littlefield, 2015); Barton Gellman, *Angler: The Cheney Vice Presidency* ((New York: Penguin, 2009); Joel Goldstein, *The White House Vice Presidency: The Path to Significance, Mondale to Biden* (Lawrence: University Press of Kansas, 2016); Jules Witcover, *The American Vice Presidency: From Irrelevance to Power* (Washington, DC: Smithsonian Books, 2014).
6. Gellman, *Angler*.
7. Michael A. Genovese, *The Nixon Presidency* (Westport: Greenwood Press, 1990).
8. Lawrence K. Altman, "Hasty and Ruinous 1972 Pick Colors Today's Hunt for No.2," *The New York Times*, July 23. 2012.
9. See "Mr. Quayle's 'e' for Effort," The New York Times, June 17, 1992, http://www.nytimes.com/1992/06/17/opinion/mr-quayle-s-e-for-effort.html.
10. See Philip Bump, "Sarah Palin cost John McCain 2 million votes in 2008, according to a study," *The Washington Post*, January 19, 2016, https://www.washingtonpost.com/news/the-fix/wp/2016/01/19/sarah-palin-cost-john-mccain-2-million-votes-in-2008/?utm_term=.6badf49c2ad1.
11. See Marc Dorian and Lauren Effron, "John Edwards and the Mistress: A Breakdown of One of America's Most Sensational Scandals," ABC

News, November 12, 2013, http://abcnews.go.com/Politics/john-edwards-mistress-breakdown-americas-sensational-scandals/story?id=20854336.

12. Benjamin Oreskes, "Trump denies offering Kasich VP job," *POLITICO*, July 20, 2016, http://www.politico.com/story/2016/07/trump-john-kasich-vice-president-225840.

13. Shannon McCaffrey, "Why Donald Trump didn't pick Newt Gingrich for VP," *The Atlanta Journal-Constitution*, July 18, 2016, http://www.myajc.com/news/national-govt--politics/why-donald-trump-didn-pick-newt-gingrich-for/P0cYTivYOuHDqOQzEhxlNL.

14. Eric Bradner, Dana Bash, and MJ Lee, "Donald Trump Selects Mike Pence as VP," *CNN*, July 16, 2016.

15. Dave Jamison, "Donald Trump Wanted to Back Out of Choosing Mike Pence for Veep," *Huffington Post*, July 15, 2016.

16. Ibid.

17. Michael Finnegan and Michael A. Memoli, "Trump Settles on a Running Mate," *The Los Angeles Times*, June 20, 2016, A10.

18. James Pfiffner, "Trump Wants a White House That's Not Top Down," *Washington Post: Monkey Cage,* November 28, 2016.

19. See "Trump's Tumultuous Transition to Power," *The Week,* November 25, 2016, 4; and Connie Bruck, "A Hollywood Story: Did the Movies Really Make Steve Bannon?" *The New Yorker*, May 1, 2017, 34–45.

20. Evan Hunter and David S. Cloud, "Trump Goes Hard Right in First Choices for Top Posts," *Los Angeles Times* November 19, 2016, A1.

21. Editorial, *The Los Angeles Times*, December 14, 2016, A14. See also John Wagner, "Do Trump's Cabinet Picks Want to Ruin the Government – or Dismantle it?" *The Washington Post*, December 8, 2016.

22. See "Trump Rounds out Conservative, Pro-Business Cabinet," *The Week*, December 23 and 30, 2016, 5.

23. Neil Irwin, "Trump Betting Policy Expertise Will Not Matter," *The New York Times*, December 2, 2016, A16.

24. Landon Thomas Jr., and Alexandra Stevenson, "Cabinet Choices Signal Embrace of Wall Street Elite," *The New York Times*, December 1, 2016, A1.

25. Noah Bierman and Evan Halper, "Trump Picks at Odds with His Message," *The Los Angeles Times*, November 15, 2016, A1.

26. Jonathon Mahler and Maggie Haberman, "In-law With Outsize Power: Kushner is a Steadying Hand," *The New York Times*, November 20, 2016, A1; and Briefing, The Week, December 9, 2016, 11.

27. Kate Anderson Brower, "Ivanka Trump Could be the Most Powerful First Lady Ever: Non-Spouses Have Played Roles like Hers in Past Administrations, None Quite Like Her," *The Washington Post* December 16, 2016.
28. Lizzie Widdicombe, "First Family: How Donald Trump Came to Rely on Ivanka Trump and Jared Kushner," *The New Yorker*, August 22, 2016.
29. Ibid.
30. Eric Lichtblau, "In Donald McGahn, Donald Trump Gets a Combative White House Counsel," *The New York Times*, December 12, 2016.
31. James P. Pfiffner, "The Unusual Presidency of Donald Trump," *Political Insight*, September 2017.
32. Conway quoted in Daniel W. Drezner, "I Can't Stop Laughing at the Trump Administration. That's not a Good Thing," *The Washington Post*, June 2, 2017.
33. Elizabeth Drew, "Trump: The Presidency in Peril," *The New York Review of Books*, June 22, 2017.
34. Chris Sillizza, "Donald Trump Watches More Cable TV than You Do," *The Washington Post*, July 26, 2016.
35. Christina Wilkie, "Leaks Suggest Trump's Own Team is Alarmed by His Conduct," The Huffington Post, February 7, 2017.
36. All quotes from Even Osnos, "President Trump: what Would He Do?" *The New Yorker*, September 26, 2016.
37. Jenna Johnson and Matt Zapotosky, " Trump Seeks 'Major Investigation' into Unsupported Claims of Voter Fraud," *The Washington Post*, January 25, 2017.
38. Partnership for Public Service, cited in *The Los Angeles Times*, June 5, 2017.

CHAPTER 6

THE INAUGURAL ADDRESS

TEST NUMBER 4

Inaugural addresses are what rhetoricians call "epideictic"[1] or ceremonial speeches.[2] The word is derived from the Greek *diexis,* meaning "to display." For a president, the inaugural address, delivered at the swearing-in ceremony, acknowledges, displays, explains, and, hopefully, inspires. Often long on generalities and short on specifics, newly elected presidents use this address to signal a sense of vision and direction,[3] and to call for national unity. A president's first address sets a tone, points in a direction, and indicates a style and temperament.

Overall, most inaugural addresses have been fairly forgettable. After reading all previous inaugural addresses as preparation for writing John F. Kennedy's Address, Ted Sorenson noted that they were "a largely undistinguished lot, with some of the best eloquence emanating from some of the worst presidents."[4] If most inaugural address do not stand the test of time, they nonetheless reveal what a president hopes to achieve, how he hopes to be viewed, and how he approaches governing the nation, as well as dealing with the world. For this reason, inaugural addresses provide a vital insight into both the mind and hopes of the incoming president.

Certainly, the worst inaugural address was delivered by William Henry Harrison in 1841. The speech was long, (lasting one hour and forty-five minutes), and the day was cold (there was a snowstorm in Washington D.C. that day). Harrison caught pneumonia and died a month later. Hard for an inaugural address to turn out worse than that.

George Washington's second address was the shortest ever (134 words). It said next to nothing and was anything but epideictic. It did, however, reflect the stoic and distant personality of our first president.

Most of the memorable inaugural addresses occurred in times of national crises or upheaval. Great times call for great speeches. Among the best were Abraham Lincoln's two addresses (1861 and 1865). In 1861, as the nation faced a pending Civil War, Lincoln said that "though passion may have strained it must not break over bonds of affection. The mystic chords of memory, stretching from every battlefield and patriot grave to every living heart and hearthstone all over this broad land, will yet swell the chorus of the Union, when again touched, as surely they will be, by the better angels of our nature."

It hardly seems possible, but Lincoln's 1865 address topped his 1861 speech. It was perhaps the greatest inaugural address in history. While short, it faced squarely the cost of the war:

> Both parties deprecated war, but one of them would make war rather than let the nation survive, and the other would accept war rather than let it perish, and the war came." He concluded: "With malice toward none, with charity for al, with firmness in the right as God gives us to see the right, let us strive on to finish the work we are in, to bind up the nation's wounds, to care for him who shall have borne the battle and for his widow and his orphan, to do all which may achieve and cherish a just and lasting peace among ourselves and with all nations.

Thomas Jefferson's 1801 speech came after the first truly contested presidential election in which two political parties vied for power. As the winner in a bitter contest, Jefferson tried to heal the wounds and unify the nation. Power shifted from one party to another. Could this be done peacefully, or would the losers seek to delegitimize Jefferson? The new president tried to bridge the gap between the two rival parties: "every difference of opinion is not a difference of principle. We have been called by different names brethren of the same principle. We are all Republicans, we are all Federalists." Sage advice then, sage advice now.

Franklin D. Roosevelt's first inaugural address (1933) took place during the depths of the depression, with one-fourth of the nation's workers still jobless, the stock market having lost three-fourths of its value, and nearly half the nation's banks already folded. In the address, Roosevelt sought to reassure a frightened and anxious nation. "The only thing we have to fear is fear itself," he intoned. But the biggest applause line came when Roosevelt demanded "action, and action now."

John F. Kennedy's 1961 inaugural address was inspiring both in its delivery and content. Short by contemporary standards (fewer than 1,400 words), the speech was nonetheless packed with punch: "ask not what your country can do for you—ask what you can do for your country." The speech was delivered not in the midst of a national crisis but at the beginning of a national transformation where power and responsibility were being transferred to a new generation of leaders. "The torch," Kennedy said, had been "passed to a new generation of Americans—born in this century, tempered by war, disciplined by a hard and bitter peace..." It was a new generation for a new and threatening age; an age when American hegemony would be challenged by rivals and adversaries. In this age, Kennedy made a huge commitment: "Let every nation know, whether it wishes us well or ill, that we shall pay any price, bear any burden, meet any hardship, support any friend, oppose any foe, in order to assure the survival and the success of liberty." But ours would not be a belligerent Pax Americana: "Let us never negotiate out of fear. But let us never fear to negotiate."

DONALD TRUMP'S INAUGURAL ADDRESS

Donald Trump's inaugural address was delivered amid the backdrop of the Russian hacking scandal. Reports from the U.S. intelligence agencies unanimously concluded that Russia—on the orders of Vladimir Putin—hacked into computers of leading Democrats, gave the stolen materials to WikiLeaks (which released them), with the intention of hurting Hillary Clinton and aiding the Trump campaign.

The shocking revelations were met with scorn by Trump loyalists, but some leading Republican officials—for example, Arizona Senator John McCain, and South Carolina's Lindsey Graham—were incensed and insisted on congressional hearings to get the full story. Four questions were raised: 1) Did the Russians interfere with a U.S. election to hurt Clinton and help Trump? 2) Did this interference actually affect votes, thereby helping Trump and hurting Clinton? 3) Was the Trump campaign working with the Russians? and 4) Were the Russians able to hack into voting machines and change the votes? The answer to questions 1 and 2 is *yes*; the answer to question 3 is still to be determined; the answer to question four is *no*. Were enough voters influenced to vote for Trump to change the election outcome? It is very possible, but difficult to prove with certainty. With some critics questioning the very legitimacy of Trump, it was clear that Trump's inaugural address had added significance for the incoming president. Could he "bring us together," or would we continue to be a deeply divided nation?

THE SPEECH

January 20, 2017, an overcast day in the nation's capital, and the day of the 58th formal presidential swearing-in ceremony (six presidents were sworn-in outside Washington D.C.) and of the seventy-first time a president has taken the oath of office. A crowd estimated at about 600,000 people witnessed the inauguration, far fewer than the 1.8 million people who packed the Mall on the bone-chilling day of Barack Obama's first inauguration.[5]

Which Trump would we see, the in-your-face smash-mouth Trump, or a new "bring-us-together" Trump?

Donald Trump's first speech as president was relatively *short*—roughly 17 minutes—and *dark*—it soon became known as "the carnage speech"—and addressed almost solely to his white, angry, populist base. There was no olive branch held out to those who voted against him, no call for coming together or national unity, no binding of wounds, no pivot to a presidential style, no lofty summons appealing to "the better angels of our nature."

Trump did not rise, rather he sank, to the occasion. Rather than present himself as president of *all* the people, he drove the wedge even further among Americans. It may have been an honest expression of who Trump is and whom he intends to serve, but it drove many away, told them they were not in his plans, and it divided and did not unify the nation.

In a pugnacious tone, delivered to an aggrieved segment of the electorate, his inaugural address was little more than a repeat of the acrid tone of campaign 2016. In the address, he did not make reference to his opponent Hillary Clinton, nor did he appeal to her voters to join him. There was no extended hand of friendship, no statement that he would be president of *all* the people; it was all about and only aimed at *his* people. Ungenerous and unwelcoming, it sought not to heal the wounds, but to rub salt into the wounds. It struck an angry tone, not a conciliatory one. It was Trump as Polarizer-in-Chief.

Yes, he did throw breadcrumbs to unity, but there was no grace, no "we are all Americans," no outreach to those he insulted during the campaign. Words like *carnage, rusted out, bleed, unrealized, sprawl, ripped, tombstone, robbed, trapped,* and *despair* peppered his address. Trump blasted insiders and elected officials:

The establishment protected itself, but not the citizens of our country. Their victories have not been your victories. Their triumphs have not been your triumph. And while they celebrated in our nation's capital, there was little to celebrate for struggling families all across our land. That all changes starting right here and right now, because this moment is your moment. It belongs to you...the forgotten men and women of our country will be forgotten no longer.

Trump added that "for too long, a small group in our nation's capital has reaped the rewards of government while the people have borne the cost." Ironically, that small group was seated behind the new president. Trump painted an unusually glum portrait of the nation:

Mothers and children trapped in poverty in our inner cities; rusted-out factories scattered like tombstones across the landscape of our nation; an education system, flush with cash, but which leaves our young and beautiful students deprived of knowledge; and the crime and gangs and drugs that have stolen too many lives and robbed our country of so much unrealized potential. This American carnage stops right here and stops right now.

Full of disdain for the establishment he now headed, Trump's speech was backward looking (Make America Great Again) and confrontational (unusual for an inaugural address). It was also unusually negative. It was Donald Trump, bashing the club that wouldn't let him in as a member.

The new president also announced to the world that:

We assembled here today are issuing a new decree to be heard in every city, in every foreign capital, and in every hall of power... From this day forward, a new vision will govern our land. From this day forward, it's going to be only America first. America first.

That shining city on a hill would no longer cast its light on the world, but only on itself, "only."

The crowd at the Mall was almost all white. They saw Trump as a national savior. Trump's critics saw him as a national migraine.

The two-party system also seemed under assault. Attacking the "establishment" meant attacking Democrats and Republicans. Was the country splitting into three different parties: Democrats (the left), Republicans (on the right), and Trump's Tea Party Populists (nationalists)?

It was a speech addressed more to the 46% of Trump voters than to the nation as a whole. Trump's speech was somber, even dark. He spoke to and for the angry, left-behind, frightened Americans who looked at America and saw gloom and doom. Trump opened with an anti-government, anti-establishment, anti-D.C. note, separating "you, the people" from the government; the first was good, the latter, bad. With a Jacksonian flair, Trump trumpeted "This moment is your moment. It belongs to you." The "you" was a narrowly defined set of outsiders and insurgents whose anger lifted Donald Trump to these heights as a spokesman for their anger. "The forgotten men and women of our country will be forgotten no longer" he promised.

The state of America? A wreck. "This American carnage stops right here, it stops right now," he said. Trump's dystopian critique of an America at war with itself would be transformed: "America will start winning again, winning like never before," Trump would turn the loser nation into a winner nation. He would "make America great again." He even promised to "eradicate" radical Islamic terrorism.

Trump paid lip service to bring-us-together rhetoric, but did not long stray from his blunt, fiery message, a message that energized his supporters but alarmed many.

President Trump loudly proclaimed, "America first, America first!" signaling a retreat from the global leadership of the past, and signaling a new relationship with the rest of the world. No longer would the U.S. be animated by the high ideals of Wilson, FDR, Kennedy, and Reagan; no longer would we be the best hope of mankind and strong defender of freedom and democracy. It would be the end of American exceptionalism and a time to truly put America first.

Trump called on America to turn in on itself; to eschew the needs and troubles of others and think first of ourselves. That this would create a vacuum internationally was unmentioned, nor did Trump indicate who or what might replace the U.S. as global leader.

In the end, Donald Trump's inaugural address turned out to be the speech that got him elected. It was not a new, more presidential Trump, but the Trump of the campaign, a raw, slightly menacing populist insurgent issuing his populist manifesto. There was brand consistency, not transformational rhetoric reinforcement, not a new more presidential Trump. He spoke largely to his core constituency, caring little to appeal to those who did not vote for him or did not vote at all, and this was the way Donald Trump governed.[6]

The day after the inauguration, massive protest marches took place. The Women's March on Washington drew an estimated 500,000 protestors,[7] and marchers occurred in every state in the U.S. There were also large protests across the globe, in London, Paris, Berlin, Mexico City, Sydney, and elsewhere. Lines had been drawn, decisions hardened. A divided nation was turning into a fractured nation.

The First Versus the Forty-Fifth

In an effort to contextualize Donald Trump's inauguration, it might be useful to compare the first inauguration (George Washington's in 1789) with the 45th (Trump's 2017).

In 1789, in New York City, the temporary capitol of the United States, George Washington took the oath of office becoming the first president of the United States, adding "so help me God" at the end of the oath. Small by modern standards, the ceremony was one more befitting the leader of a republic than an empire. No grand balls, no huge parades.

After the ceremony ended, the new president very unceremoniously walked back to the Boarding House at which he was staying, ate dinner and then, for after-dinner entertainment in a pre-television age, the new president, along with some friends, read aloud Joseph Addison's play, *Cato*. The framers were enamored of republican Rome and in part modeled the new government as well as personal practice on republican heroes such as Cato and Brutus.

Washington read the part of Cato, one of the prominent defenders of the republic against the imperial pretensions of Caesar. Cato served as a role model for many of the framers, and Washington set his sights on following Cato's lead.

Washington was the man who could have been king, yet he chose a different path. He invested himself in the creation of a constitutional republic based on the rule of law with limited governmental powers.

At the end of the revolution, when it seemed clear that the colonial rebels would win, many in Washington's military circle called on the general to become king. It made perfectly good sense. After all, that was the way it was done in the 1770s. Nations were ruled by kings. Now, America would have its king.

But Washington would have none of it. He wanted something more, something different. His goal was to be part of the creation of a new order, a constitutional republic. He willingly gave up power, eschewed the opportunity to become king, in the service of an idea and an ideal. When Louis XVI of France got word that Washington had declined to become king, Louis recognized that this step distinguished Washington from the past and created a new point of comparison. "He has ruined it for all of us [kings]" Louis said. Indeed, he had.

This mightily contributed to the creation of what we today call *liberal democracy*, a rule of law system with limited and separated powers of government and with individual rights.

Today, 230 years later, liberal democracies across the globe are under assault from illiberal tendencies. These illiberal democracies hold elections, but the web of checks and balances, individual rights, and the rule of law that limit government are largely absent. The leader is elected and fully empowered to govern. In effect, they elect popular autocrats to govern. It amounts to an election to choose a "strongman." Thus, it has an element of democracy (elections) but beyond that, the two depart as one emphasizes limited government, the other empowered government (in the leader).

Modern examples of illiberal democracies are Russia (Vladimir Putin), Turkey (Recep Tayyip Erdogan), the Philippines (Rodrigo Duterte), and Hungary (Viktor Orbán). Several other traditionally liberal democracies are being pulled in the illiberal direction. Frustrated by liberal government's inability to solve the problems posed by globalization, "the people" demand strong government, strong leadership, and big changes.

Is the United States leaning in an illiberal direction? Many argue that in Donald Trump's repeated attacks on the media (threatening to change libel laws), the political establishment ("protected itself, but not the citizens"), his opponents (Lyin' Ted, Little Marco, Crooked Hillary), critics (threatening to sue women who claimed Trump sexually assaulted them), elections (rigged, until he won), and threatening to prosecute his political opponent ("lock her up") suggest a person with deeply illiberal tendencies.

Where Washington willingly gave up personal power, Trump relished it. Their two visions are in conflict. If the U.S. succumbs to illiberal tendencies, we lose a great deal, and what do we gain?

What Do We Learn of President Trump from His Inaugural Address?

Dark, dystopian, confrontational, angry, President Trump's inaugural address can be seen as a mirror of the man or an accurate assessment of the conditions facing America. Was the address about Trump or about the nation?

It clearly was not a bring-us-together speech. It was more a revenge speech with venom directed at the "establishment" along with a warning that the old order was about to be shattered.

In his speech, Trump viciously attacked the very politicians (of both parties) seated immediately behind him. Ungracious to the point of being mean-spirited, Trump was trying not only to distinguish himself from the political class but also to issue a warning that he would be a disruptive, perhaps even a transformational, president. He was here to take down the establishment, not fix things.

According to a report in *New York* magazine, former president George W. Bush, upon leaving the inauguration grandstand said, "That was some weird shit."[8]

Notes

1. Sometimes written in England as "Epidictic"
2. Aristotle's *Rhetoric* is still one of the best starting points on this.
3. John Gabriel Hart, *The Inaugural Addresses of the Presidents* (New York: Gramercy Books, 1997).
4. Sorenson reflects on JFK Inaugural, *Brandeis University*, International Center for Ethics, Justice and Public Life, speech delivered January 14, 2009.
5. Betsy Klein, "Comparing Donald Trump and Barack Obama's Inaugural Crowd Sizes, *CNN Politics*, January 21, 2017.
6. See "President Trump's Inaugural Address, Annotated," NPR, January 20, 2017, http://www.npr.org/2017/01/20/510629447/watch-live-president-trumps-inauguration-ceremony.
7. Tim Wallace and Alicia Parlapiano, "Crowd Scientists Say Women's March in Washington had 3 Times as Many People as Trump's Inauguration," *New York Times*, January 22, 2017.
8. Yashar Ali, "What George W. Bush Really Thought of Donald Trump's Inauguration," *New York Magazine*, March 29, 2017.

Chapter 7

The First Hundred Days

A Rocky Start: Test 5

Why We Look at the First Hundred Days

It all started with Franklin D. Roosevelt.[1] The 1929 economic depression devastated the nation. Roosevelt was elected in 1932 to get the country out of that mess. When he took office in March of 1933 he promised "action, and action now." And Roosevelt delivered on his promise...and then some.

In his first hundred days Roosevelt proposed, and the Congress passed, an unprecedented series of depression-busting bills. It was a whirlwind of activity with Congress passing bill after bill, all designed to get the country moving. And while these new laws did not end the depression, they gave the nation a sense of purpose, direction, and hope.

This unprecedented level of action came to be seen as the proper, and over time, expected role of any new administration. Success in the first hundred days was by no means a perfect measure, and it might not ever be a desirable outcome—critics have come to object to the liberal/activist bias that seemed inherent in the 100-day standard. But the first hundred days became the first way of gauging the skill of each new president.

Artificial and unfair though it may be—after all, Roosevelt had all the ingredients for success: great political skill and a crisis that created a structural opportunity to lead—this measure stuck and from the example of Roosevelt's first days in office, every subsequent president has been in his large shadow.[2]

Beyond Roosevelt, there is another logic by which this early measure makes some sense. Presidents are usually at a peak of power early because they have just come off an election victory and they have some political capital, they may claim a mandate to govern, they are new to the office and the media and Congress are still taking the measure of the new president, and the public is hopeful that their president will be successful. The paradox, however, is that presidents are often powerful at the very beginning of their presidencies, when they are least seasoned and least knowledgeable.

Presidents do not like the 100-day standard. After all, how could any president live up to the bar set by Roosevelt? Thus, the hundred days both define and imprison a new president: it defines a president because it establishes a high set of expectations; it imprisons the president because even a president who does not raise expectations must try to meet public and media demands lest they be seen as failures—a criticism that could shape long-term estimations of an entire term from which a president may never recover (as Jimmy Carter discovered).

As mentioned earlier, leaders are usually at the peak of their power in the early days of a new term,[3] which is ironically when the new administration is also least knowledgeable and least prepared to decide. Over time, power wanes as knowledge rises. So, presidents are generally more powerful when less capable, and less powerful when more capable.

Case in point: John F. Kennedy and the Bay of Pigs fiasco. Upon taking office, President Kennedy inherited from the Eisenhower administration a plan to invade Cuba to oust the Communist government of Fidel Castro, using Cuban exiles as the invading force. Project Zapata (as it was called) should have been halted so as to give the new president the opportunity to review the plan fully. But no such review took place, and the plan moved forward. Kennedy's policy team was new and unprepared to explore fully the merits of Project Zapata. No one put the brakes on. When the invasion failed, Kennedy was asked to directly send U.S. forces into the battle. He refused. It was one big disaster. This was an avoidable error, one a more seasoned, experienced president (and his team) would likely have avoided.

Presidents don't like the hundred days, but they can't ignore it. Like it or not, that is how the president will be judged.

HITTING THE GROUND RUNNING OR STUMBLING?

What did President Trump hope to accomplish in his first hundred days? He gave the *New York Times* a checklist of what was in store, including deciding whom to nominate to the Supreme Court, rescinding the Obama executive order on immigration, calling to threaten corporate executives of serious consequence if they shift jobs out of the U.S., build the wall across the Mexican border, banning Muslim immigration, auditing the Federal Reserve, and repealing the Affordable Care Act (Obamacare).

Lord Acton asserted that power *corrupts*. Abraham Lincoln believed that power *reveals*. On January 20, Donald Trump had the power of the presidency in his hands. What did he do with that power, and what does it reveal about Donald Trump?

PROMISES, PROMISES

During the campaign, candidate Trump made an unusually large number of promises. Among them:

- ban all Muslims from entering the U.S.
- build a wall (across U.S.–Mexican border)
- make Mexico pay for the wall

- repeal and replace Obamacare
- appoint a special prosecutor to indict and convict Hillary Clinton ("Lock her up!")
- resume waterboarding (and worse)
- "take out" the families of terrorists
- develop new trade agreements with China
- cancel the nuclear agreement with Iran
- develop better relations with Russia
- "get" ISIS ("big and fast")
- withdraw U.S. from Trans-Pacific Partnership (TPP)
- withdraw from NAFTA (or renegotiate)
- withdraw U.S. from Paris Climate Accord
- round up and deport 11-12 million illegal immigrants
- cut corporate and personal taxes
- "drain the swamp"
- prevent U.S. companies from moving jobs abroad
- revive the steel and coal mining industries
- increase economic growth by more than 4%
- invest in infrastructure jobs
- eliminate many regulations
- rebuild the military
- take care of our vets
- promote school choice (and Common Core)

On August 1, 2016 (during the campaign), the Trump transition team moved into office space at 1717 Pennsylvania Avenue. One of their first tasks was to put together a policy game plan for the incoming Trump presidency. Past transition teams, in an effort to convert campaign promises into tangible policy proposals, put together a "promise book" listing all the candidates campaign promises.

TRUMP REVEALS HIS 100-DAY PLAN

In October of 2016, candidate Donald Trump released his plans for the first 100 days of his administration. Entitled "Donald Trump's Contract with the American Voter," it is reproduced below in its entirety:

> What follows is my 100-day action plan to Make America Great Again. It is a contract between myself and the American voter — and begins with restoring honesty, accountability and change to Washington

> Therefore, on the first day of my term of office, my administration will immediately pursue the following six measures to clean up the corruption and special interest collusion in Washington, DC:

> * FIRST, propose a Constitutional Amendment to impose term limits on all members of Congress;

> * SECOND, a hiring freeze on all federal employees to reduce federal workforce through attrition (exempting military, public safety, and public health);

> * THIRD, a requirement that for every new federal regulation, two existing regulations must be eliminated;

> * FOURTH, a 5 year-ban on White House and Congressional officials becoming lobbyists after they leave government service;

> * FIFTH, a lifetime ban on White House officials lobbying on behalf of a foreign government;

> * SIXTH, a complete ban on foreign lobbyists raising money for American elections.

> On the same day, I will begin taking the following 7 actions to protect American workers:

> * FIRST, I will announce my intention to renegotiate NAFTA or withdraw from the deal under Article 2205

* SECOND, I will announce our withdrawal from the Trans-Pacific Partnership

* THIRD, I will direct my Secretary of the Treasury to label China a currency manipulator

* FOURTH, I will direct the Secretary of Commerce and U.S. Trade Representative to identify all foreign trading abuses that unfairly impact American workers and direct them to use every tool under American and international law to end those abuses immediately

* FIFTH, I will lift the restrictions on the production of $50 trillion dollars' worth of job-producing American energy reserves, including shale, oil, natural gas and clean coal.

* SIXTH, lift the Obama-Clinton roadblocks and allow vital energy infrastructure projects, like the Keystone Pipeline, to move forward

* SEVENTH, cancel billions in payments to UN climate change programs and use the money to fix America's water and environmental infrastructure

Additionally, on the first day, I will take the following five actions to restore security and the constitutional rule of law:

* FIRST, cancel every unconstitutional executive action, memorandum and order issued by President Obama

* SECOND, begin the process of selecting a replacement for Justice Scalia from one of the 20 judges on my list, who will uphold and defend the Constitution of the United States

* THIRD, cancel all federal funding to Sanctuary Cities

* FOURTH, begin removing the more than 2 million criminal illegal immigrants from the country and cancel visas to foreign countries that won't take them back

* FIFTH, suspend immigration from terror-prone regions where vetting cannot safely occur. All vetting of people coming into our country will be considered extreme vetting.

Next, I will work with Congress to introduce the following broader legislative measures and fight for their passage within the first 100 days of my Administration:

Middle Class Tax Relief and Simplification Act. An economic plan designed to grow the economy 4% per year and create at least 25 million new jobs through massive tax reduction and simplification, in combination with trade reform, regulatory relief, and lifting the restrictions on American energy. The largest tax reductions are for the middle class. A middle-class family with 2 children will get a 35% tax cut. The current number of brackets will be reduced from 7 to 3, and tax forms will likewise be greatly simplified. The business rate will be lowered from 35 to 15 percent, and the trillions of dollars of American corporate money overseas can now be brought back at a 10 percent rate.

End The Offshoring Act. Establishes tariffs to discourage companies from laying off their workers in order to relocate in other countries and ship their products back to the U.S. tax-free.

American Energy & Infrastructure Act. Leverages public-private partnerships, and private investments through tax incentives, to spur $1 trillion in infrastructure investment over 10 years. It is revenue neutral.

School Choice and Education Opportunity Act. Redirects education dollars to give parents the right to send their kid to the public, private, charter, magnet, religious or home school of their choice. Ends common core, brings education supervision to local communities. It expands vocational and technical education, and make 2 and 4-year college more affordable.

Repeal and Replace Obamacare Act. Fully repeals Obamacare and replaces it with Health Savings Accounts, the ability to purchase health insurance across state lines, and lets states manage Medicaid funds. Reforms will also include cutting the red tape at the FDA: there are over 4,000 drugs awaiting approval, and we especially want to speed the approval of life-saving medications.

Affordable Childcare and Eldercare Act. Allows Americans to deduct childcare and elder care from their taxes, incentivizes employers to provide on-side childcare services, and creates tax-free Dependent Care Savings Accounts for both young and elderly dependents, with matching contributions for low-income families.

End Illegal Immigration Act Fully-funds the construction of a wall on our southern border with the full understanding that the country Mexico will be reimbursing the United States for the full cost of such wall; establishes a 2-year mandatory minimum federal prison sentence for illegally re-entering the U.S. after a previous deportation, and a 5-year mandatory minimum for illegally re-entering for those with felony convictions, multiple misdemeanor convictions or two or more prior deportations; also reforms visa rules to enhance penalties for overstaying and to ensure open jobs are offered to American workers first.

Restoring Community Safety Act. Reduces surging crime, drugs and violence by creating a Task Force On Violent Crime and increasing funding for programs that train and assist local police; increases resources for federal law enforcement agencies and federal prosecutors to dismantle criminal gangs and put violent offenders behind bars.

Restoring National Security Act. Rebuilds our military by eliminating the defense sequester and expanding military investment; provides Veterans with the ability to receive public VA treatment or attend the private doctor of their choice; protects our vital infrastructure from cyber-attack; establishes new screening procedures for immigration to ensure those who are admitted to our country support our people and our values

Clean up Corruption in Washington Act. Enacts new ethics reforms to Drain the Swamp and reduce the corrupting influence of special interests on our politics.

On November 8th, Americans will be voting for this 100-day plan to restore prosperity to our economy, security to our communities, and honesty to our government.

This is my pledge to you.

And if we follow these steps, we will once more have a government of, by and for the people.[4]

THE FIRST HUNDRED DAYS

After a dark and confrontational inaugural address, one that invited division and opposition, President Trump got to work on his ambitious agenda. Given his brash oppositional style and sagging popularity, some doubted Trump would have a traditional "honeymoon" period (Obama was denied one by Republican rivals, and the Democrats seemed intent on returning the "favor").

Day 1 was nothing like promised. There were a few executive orders (one limiting implementation of Obamacare), but the long list of major day-one promises never materialized. In the first 100 days, a president tries to put his stamp on Washington's politics and policies. A good start matters because it is difficult to dig out of a first-hundred-days hole.

Trump had promised that on his first day in office he would take more than a dozen actions designed to keep his promises and advance his priorities. But, there was no constitutional amendment introduced that would impose term limits on Congress, no beginning of a renegotiation of the North America Free Trade Agreement (NAFTA), all promised for day one.

The Trump transition team put together a Day 1, Day 100, and Day 200 action plan, but the sluggish start contradicted the bold campaign pledges.

The conditions under which Trump took office were far better than when his predecessor, Barack Obama, took office. Then, our economy was in free fall, unemployment had spiked up, the U.S. auto industry was collapsing, a housing crisis swept the nation, and the U.S. was engaged in two wars. Trump took office with a strong economy, a profitable auto industry, a strong stock market, a stable housing industry, and low unemployment.[5] The two wars—Iraq and Afghanistan—have morphed into a Syrian crisis and Al Qaeda was largely replaced by ISIS, but overall U.S. international military involvements (and U.S. deaths) were greatly reduced. Under Obama, there were no large foreign terrorist attacks on the United States.

Coming into office under such conditions allowed Trump and his team to focus less on crisis management and more on advancing the agenda. The freedom to pursue his priorities absent major crises meant that Trump could be Trump and not have to clean up much of a mess left behind by his predecessor. Trump's plate is quite full, but compared to what the Obama administration inherited, Trump had a great deal of freedom to advance his campaign pledges. Trump disagrees with this viewpoint and asserted during a press conference on February 16, 2017, that "our administration inherited many problems across government and across the economy," noting:

> To be honest, I inherited a mess. It's a mess. At home and abroad, a mess. Jobs are pouring out of the country; you see what's going on with all of the companies leaving our country, going to Mexico and other places, low pay, low wages, mass instability overseas, no matter where you look. The Middle East is a disaster. North Korea – we'll take care of it folks. We're going to take care of it all. I just want to let you know, I inherited a mess.[6]

According to PolitiFact, "Obama took an economy with a big hole in it and was able to fill it in and give it stability," said Brookings Institution economist Gary Burtless. That stability was passed on to Trump." As far as foreign policy goes, the report notes that "Trump can make a stronger case that he inherited a foreign policy 'mess' than an economic one, though most foreign policy specialists said the situation is more nuanced than he makes it out to be."[7]

TRUMP'S UNFOLDING PRESIDENCY

On Saturday, January 21, 2017, the day after his inauguration, President Trump picked a fight with the media. Donald Trump said that his inauguration had the highest attendance in history and that more people watched his inauguration on television than any other. This was the biggest crowd and the most-watched inauguration, Trump asserted. Various news outlets reported that Trump was not correct. President Obama's 2009 inauguration drew far more than twice as many people as did Trump's. It was also reported that viewership was far below other inaugurations (see figure 3).

Not willing to give in, Trump sent press secretary Sean Spicer out to dispute media reports that contradicted Trump, and lash out at the media for bias, accusing reporters of engaging "in deliberately false reporting." Spicer's attack on the media met with a great deal of blowback, but it was not until the following morning, Sunday, that the truth hit the fan. Trump advisor Kellyanne Conway went on the Sunday morning talk show tour to defend Trump and Spicer. On CNN, she was pressed with the evidence that Trump was wrong and that Spicer had tried to mislead the public. Conway defended the administration by insisting that they were operating with "alternative facts." *Alternative facts*. Enough said.

Often in the first 100 days, a president will face a situation or crisis he did not anticipate. Such events take the new president by surprise and distract him from his own goals and agenda. But presidents do not get to choose the circumstances in which they govern; they must react to whatever is thrown at them.

Figure 3. How Many Attended?

President Trump and organizers of women's marches disputed reports of crowd sizes published over inaugural weekend. Here are the estimated ranges of attendance:

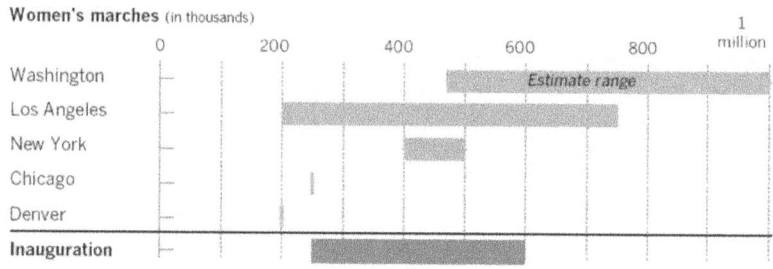

Sources: Jeremy Pressman, University of Connecticut; Erica Chenoweth, University of Denver, PolitiFact

Source. Kurtis Lee, "The Trouble with how crowd size is calculated," *Los Angeles Times*, January 24, 2017, A2. Copyright © 2017 Los Angeles Times. Reprinted with permission.

Figure 4. Inauguration Viewership Over the Years.

An estimated 30.6 million viewers tuned in to watch President Trump's inauguration on Friday.

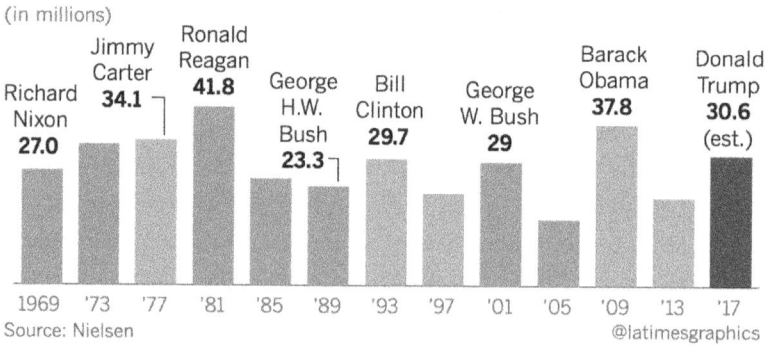

Source. Stephen Battaglio, "New Era of Turmoil: Fewer TV Viewers," *Los Angeles Times*, January 22, 2017, A18. Copyright © 2017 Los Angeles Times. Reprinted with permission.

Roughly a month into his presidency, President George W. Bush ordered the bombing of the military installations in Iraq in response to Saddam Hussein's interference with U.S. and British patrols supervising a no-fly zone in Iraq. Bush Press Secretary Ari Fleischer recalls:

> We're at [Mexican President Vicente] Fox's ranch. And Campbell Brown [NBC News White House correspondent] comes up to me and says, "Why are you bombing Iraq?" I said, "What do you mean?" And she said, "There's a bombing raid going on in Iraq, and you don't know about it?" So I go into the lunch and pull Condi [Condoleezza Rice, the national security adviser] out, and said, "Are we bombing Iraq?" She said no, Then Condi and I go into a secure room Condi calls Rumsfeld [Donald H. Rumsfeld, the defense secretary] and sure enough...[8]

And Karen P. Hughes, Counselor to the President noted:

> I just remember being totally surprised. I knew our pilots were enforcing the no-fly zone in Iraq. What I didn't know was that the military had recommended that we take a little more aggressive action.
>
> It was the first state visit designed to show that the Bush administration was making our relationship with Mexico and Latin America a priority. Here we are at an event designed to showcase one message, and all of a sudden the message is something else.[9]

President Obama was also distracted from his already-overflowing 100 Days inbox when on April 8, 2009, Somali pirates hijacked the Maersk Alabama, a U.S. cargo ship. Chief of Staff Rahm Emanuel noted "This is not in the handbook." And Senior Advisor David Axelrod recalled:

> The president was given 10 minutes to decide whether to authorize the Navy SEALS to take a shot at the pirates. The SEALS were on the water 100 yards away. They said, "We think we can get the pirates, but we might hit [Capt. Richard Phillips]. And you have 10 minutes." That's a day in the life of a president.[10]

Trump: Week One

Donald Trump's first week was a flurry of activity, sometimes chaotic, often policy driven, and very controversial. His tumultuous start matched the controversial and tumultuous personality of the president himself.

He often imposed his will (executive orders) and just as often shot himself in the foot (his ongoing obsession with Obama-versus-Trump inaugural crowd size estimates in dispute); and he claimed that he would have won the popular vote (which he lost by nearly 3 million votes) if only the 3–5 million illegal immigrants hadn't voted.[11]

The week was marked by a series of executive orders, many of which were designed to undo policies of the Obama presidency. These orders were controversial not only for their policy content but due to the fact that for the past five years, Republicans railed against President Obama for bypassing Congress and changing policies via unilateral executive action. Republicans called Obama a "dictator" who disregarded the constitution, going so far as to take Obama to court over some of his executive orders. As Carl Hulse noted,

> Now President Trump, at the start of his tenure, is relying heavily on executive actions not just to reverse Obama administration initiatives, but to enact new federal policies covering immigration, health care and other areas in ways that could be seen more as the province of the House and Senate. And he is doing that with clear Republican majorities in Congress.[12]

Trump used executive orders to allow for under-enforcement of Obamacare, to pull the U.S. out of the Trans Pacific Partnership (TPP), to allow the construction of Dakota Access and Keystone XL pipelines, and, among other things, to order "extreme vetting of immigrants" as well as ban immigrants from seven predominately Muslim countries President Trump believed were especially active in sending terrorists abroad (effectively banning 134 million Muslins from entering the United States). When asked by ABC reporter David Muir if these new immigration barriers might stoke anger in the Muslim world and might also motivate ISIS terrorists, Trump responded, "Anger? There's plenty of anger right now. How can you have more? The world is a mess. The world is as angry as it gets. What? You think this is gonna cause a little anger? The world is an angry place."[13]

Trump's executive order on building a wall on the border between the U.S. and Mexico led Mexican President Piña Nieto to cancel a scheduled goodwill trip to the U.S., and in response the Trump administration raised the possibility of a 20% tax on all Mexican imports coming into the United States, perhaps sparking a trade war. Trump's perceived "bad neighbor policy" caused an unnecessary rift between neighbors that would be hard to repair.

It seemed Trump just could not sublimate his ego needs to the demands of reality. He repeatedly peddled untruths as if the more he said it, the truer the falsehood would become. In an ABC interview with David Muir Trump returned to his obsessions that his inaugural crowd was "huge" and that his electoral victory was among the largest in history, "I had a tremendous victory, one of the great victories ever," adding "they say I had the biggest crowd in the history of inaugural speeches."[14] Did Trump believe this, or did he *need* to believe it? And which would be worse?

President Trump's propensity to exaggerate and tell outright falsehoods (e.g., millions of illegals voted for Clinton, or his inaugural crowds were bigger than Obama's) led several news organizations, including the *New York Times* and CNN, to cross a line and say directly that Trump lied.[15] Normally, a more genteel, less accurate word is used, but the sheer volume of Trump's falsehoods led to a blunter characterization of Trump's practice of being "distant from the truth."[16]

Trump sent out surrogates to push back on the media. As mentioned earlier, Kellyanne Conway humiliated herself when she dismissed criticism of her boss by saying that he operated with "alternative facts[17]," and press secretary Sean Spicer announced that the administration reserved the right to "disagree with the facts."

But policy wonks were most disturbed by what appeared to be Trump's retreat from U.S. global leadership and a ceding of influence to China and others. The abandonment of TPP opened the door for China to dominate trade and politics in the Pacific rim. China's President Xi Jinping, at the 2017 World Economic Summit in Davos, was openly gleeful, offering the services of China as the new dominant power that would be responsible for global trade.

Critics also believed that added to this was the ceding of the moral high ground internationally by President Trump in reopening the door to "enhanced interrogating" or torture, which Defense Secretary James Mattis has advised against.[18] These, along with distancing himself from NATO and warming up to Russia, caused alarm in the capitals of traditional U.S. allies as it caused optimism in Russia and China.

And it was no surprise that in week one of the Trump presidency, the president was sued in federal court in New York for violations of ethics laws. Citizens for Responsibility and Ethics in Washington (CREW) argued that from the moment he took the oath of office, President Trump was in violation of the Emoluments Clause of the Constitution, which bans government officials from taking gifts or payments from foreign governments. Some saw this as just the tip of the conflict-of-interest iceberg that might ultimately take the new president down.

This series of policy changes, unforced errors, and playing fast-and-loose with the truth demonstrated three things about the new administration: 1) they were very serious about enacting transformational change; 2) they were governing with a different behavioral style; and 3) if they didn't stop making rookie mistakes and stepping on toes, things would be very messy.

AND THEN, THE EXECUTIVE ORDER HIT THE FAN

"Rookie errors," said some. "Shooting themselves in the foot" said others. The Trump administration got off to a stumbling, and many believed bumbling, start. Confused messages, policy advances, then retreats.

The biggest blowback came in reaction to the travel ban placed on seven predominately Muslim countries. The rollout of the ban was badly handled. Confusion reigned. Local airports were not warned to be prepared and became overwhelmed. People with visas and proper paperwork were detained for hours.

On Saturday, Judge Ann Donnelly of the U.S. District Court in Brooklyn blocked deportations, and moments later U.S. District Court Judge Leonie Brinkema issued a temporary restraining order. Acting Attorney General Sally Yates, a career prosecutor, questioned the legality of the Trump ban and announced that the Justice Department would not defend the ban in court. Trump fired her. Protests erupted across the U.S. It looked like the 1960s.[19]

Inside the White House, Steve Bannon quickly emerged as the most influential Trump advisor. Trump's dark "carnage" speech at the inauguration was vintage Bannon; the ban looked to be the handiwork of Bannon; and the Trump persona of anger and self-absorption all demonstrated who had the president's ear. Bannon's influence was cemented when on Saturday, January 28, 2017, President Trump issued an order that demonstrated a politicizing of the national security process by elevating Bannon, his top political counselor, to a place on the National Security Council while downgrading Joseph F. Dunford, chairman of the Joint Chief of Staff, and James Clapper, director of National Intelligence by leaving them *off* the list. It was as unprecedented as it was alarming.

The avalanche of bad news and blunders had an impact. By February 3, Trump's popularity dropped. In a CNN/ORC poll, only 44% of Americans supported the president while 53% disapproved of the job Trump was doing. It was the lowest popularity rating of any president at this time in office since such polls were taken in the 1950s.

Table 11. Presidential Popularity: The First 100 Days.

President	Popularity Day 1	Popularity Day 100
Bill Clinton	58%	58%
George W. Bush	57%	62%
Barack Obama	68%	65%
Donald Trump	45%	40%

Source. Adapted from Jeremy W. Peters, "Grand Plans vs. Reality in the First 100 Days," *The New York Times,* January 25, 2017, A12.

Table 12. Days Until Each President Achieved Majority Disapproval in Gallup Polls.

President	Number of Days
Ronald Reagan	727
George H. W. Bush	1, 136
Bill Clinton	573
George W. Bush	1, 205
Barack Obama	936
Donald Trump	8

Sources: William Jordan, pollster; Gallup.

A STUNNING COURT REBUKE

The massive protests at airports across the nation in reaction to President Trump's refugee ban reflected the scope and depth of public disapproval of Trump's policies. But while the protests created a firestorm on the streets, it was in the courts that the president was being blocked.

Trump could fire his acting attorney general, but he could not fire federal judges. A judge in Washington state temporarily blocked enforcement of the ban and the government immediately challenged, but not before the president ungraciously tweeted:

> The opinion of this so-called judge, which essentially takes law-enforcement away from our country, is ridiculous and will be overturned![20]

The "so-called judge," James L. Robart, was appointed to the bench by Republican President George W. Bush.

The administration appealed the 9th Circuit Court of Appeals, but that court unanimously (3-0) and in a bipartisan (2 Democrats, 1 Republican) manner, rejected the administration's appeal and upheld Judge Robart's halting of the ban. In oral arguments before the Court the administration's lawyer was asked if the president was arguing that his actions were "non-reviewable"? "Yes," said the president's lawyer. But this question had been litigated several times during the George W. Bush presidency, and every time the courts—including the Supreme Court—said that in point of fact, the president's acts were reviewable by the courts, thereby striking a blow for both the rule of law and the system of checks and balances.

In all caps, the president tweeted:

> SEE YOU IN COURT, THE SECURITY OF OUR NATION IS AT STAKE![21]

THE LOOMING COURT BATTLE

Amid the chaos and confusion of the travel ban, Donald Trump paused to nominate Neil Gorsuch to replace the late Antonin Scalia to the Supreme Court. Gorsuch, a highly respected and very conservative judge of the 10th Circuit Court of Appeals, had strong support from establishment Republicans and seemed an ideal appointment.

But Democrats, still fuming from the Republican's failure to give Obama Court nominee Merrick Garland so much as a hearing, seemed poised for a fight. The Republicans held a 52-48 seat majority in the Senate, suggesting that eventually, Gorsuch might be confirmed, but not before "the nuclear option" (lowering the bar on the minimum vote required to bring Gorsuch to the full Senate from the customary 60 votes, to a simple majority). Gorsuch was eventually confirmed and quickly established himself as one of the most conservative Justices in a conservative court.

THE NATIONAL SECURITY ADVISOR AND THE RUSSIANS

On December 28, 2016, President Obama ejected thirty-five suspected Russian intelligence operatives from the U.S. in retaliation for Russia's hacking of the United States presidential election. Uncharacteristically, Russia (Putin) did not respond in kind. According to *The New York Times*:

> Mr. Putin, betting on improved relations with the next American president, said he would not eject 35 diplomats or close any diplomatic facilities, rejecting a tit-for-tat response to the actions taken on Thursday by the Obama administration.
>
> The switch was remarkable, given that Russia's foreign minister, Sergey V. Lavrov, had just recommended the retaliation in remarks broadcast live on national television. He called for punitive measures mirroring the ones imposed by the Obama administration, which accuses Russia of intimidating American diplomats and hacking institutions like the Democratic National Committee to influence the 2016 election.[22]

President-elect Trump (@realdonaldtrump) tweeted "Great move on delay (by V. Putin)—I always knew he was very smart!"[23]

At the same time, Michael T. Flynn, Trump's pick for National Security Advisor, spoke on the phone with Russia's ambassador to the United States, Sergey Kislyak. When it was later revealed that the two had spoken, Flynn insisted that the subject of sanctions did not come up. But rumors persisted. Flynn told Vice President Pence that he had not discussed sanctions with Kislyak, and the vice president went on a very public defense of Flynn.

A few days later, as rumors of the existence of a recording of the conversation might exist, Flynn changed his story—having "no recollection." Such discussions would have potentially been illegal (under the Logan Act).

As it turns out, almost a month earlier, Acting Attorney General Sally Yates (who was recently fired by President Trump because he said she had "betrayed" the country for refusing to implement the president's travel ban) informed White House Counsel Don McGahn that indeed tapes did exist and they might be used by the Russians to blackmail Flynn.

Late on Monday night, February 13, Flynn submitted his letter of resignation, which read in part: "I am tendering my resignation, honored to have served our nation and the American people in such a distinguished way."[24]

Less than one month into the Trump presidency and his National Security Advisor was forced out. It was unpresidential and signaled the ongoing confusion in the Trump White House.

On Tuesday afternoon, February 14, further confusion erupted when White House Press Secretary Sean Spicer confirmed that President Trump was informed that Flynn had misled White House officials, including the vice president, weeks before Flynn's resignation. The president was briefed by White House Counsel Dan McGahn that Flynn had discussed sanctions with Russian ambassador Sergey Kislyak—despite Trump's claims to the contrary—during a January 26 meeting.

This report contradicts statements made by Trump on February 10, 2017, aboard Air Force One when Trump said he was not familiar with reports that Flynn had lied about the calls. "I don't know about that," the president said, "I haven't seen it. What report is that? I'll look into that."

It's Miller Time

The president continued to fume over court rebuffs of his executive order instituting an immigration ban. The courts had no right, the president claimed, to challenge his authority. To defend his position, Trump sent out Stephen Miller, his Senior Advisor for Policy, to make the rounds of the weekend interview programs. It was Miller who wrote some of Trump's most strident campaign speeches, and it was Miller who wrote Trump's dark, almost apocalyptic Republican Convention Address.

On *Face the Nation*, host John Dickerson asked Miller:

> "When I talked to Republicans on the Hill, they wonder, what in the White House—what have you all learned from this experience with the executive order?"

To which Miller replied:

> "Well, I think that it's been an important reminder to all Americans that we have a judiciary that has taken far too much power and become, in many cases, a supreme branch of government. One unelected judge in Seattle cannot remake laws for the entire country. I mean this is just crazy, John, the idea that you have a judge in Seattle say that a foreign national living in Libya has an effective right to enter the United States is—is—is beyond anything we've ever seen before.

> The end result of this, though, is that our opponents, the media and the whole world will soon see as we begin to take further actions, that the powers of the president to protect our country are very substantial and will not be questioned."

"Will not be questioned." It was a statement so unmoored from American constitutional history that on Morning Joe (MSNBC) the following day, Jeff Greenfield quipped in reference to Miller's statement: "It sounded better in the original German."

PUZDER FALLS

As if things weren't bad enough, amid a controversial confirmation battle Trump's nominee for Labor Secretary Andrew Puzder, after losing the support of some key Republicans on the Senate Health, Education, Labor and Pensions Committee, withdrew his name from consideration on Thursday, February 16. Puzder faced opposition for hiring an undocumented immigrant as a housekeeper and was strongly opposed by labor unions and Democrats on the Committee, especially because of his position on overtime pay and the minimum wage. In addition, Puzder's ex-wife had leveled abuse charges against Puzder in 1990, making his confirmation doubtful. She later retracted the allegations.

The Hardee's and Carl's Jr. fast food executive withdrew his name a day before his Senate confirmation hearing was set to begin. It appeared that at least four to seven Senate Republicans were set to vote against Puzder's confirmation.[25]

RUSSIAN PROVOCATIONS

Amid the chaos of the Russian hacking, Trump surrogates talking with Russian agents during the campaign, Flynn's misleading statements about contact with Russia's ambassador leading to his forced resignation, and calls for congressional and independent investigations of Trump, his administration, and the Russian connections came a flurry of provocative steps by the Russians that seemed designed to challenge the U.S. and test Trump's resolve.

In the space of a few days, Russia test-fired a cruise missile in obvious violation of U.S.-Russian treaty obligations as Russian jets buzzed a U.S. destroyer in the Black Sea, Russian military activity in the Ukraine escalated, and a Russian spy ship sailed off the coast of New England—the farthest north any such ship has sailed in decades. All of this led the Head of U.S. Special Operations Command, General Raymond Thomas, to go public, warning that, "Our government continues to be in unbelievable turmoil. I hope they sort it out soon because we're a nation at war."[26]

Clearly the Russians were testing the new president. How did he respond? He did not. The U.S. leadership was in such disarray that a coordinated response seemed out of reach. Was this weakness or confusion?

Trump's Changing Positions on Leaks

Candidate Trump loved leaks. He even went so far as to call on an adversary—Russia—to leak stolen Clinton campaign documents to WikiLeaks so they could be made public. "I love WikiLeaks," Trump said in October of 2016.

As president, Trump started singing a different tune. With leaks coming out of the government revealing malfeasance by his campaign officials and White House strategists, the president began a full-throttled condemnation of leaks, leakers, and those who publish leaked materials.

He delivered his critique (how else?) via a twitter storm:

> "The fake news media is going crazy with their conspiracy theories and blind hatred. @MSNBC & @CNN are unwatchable. @foxandfriends is great!"[27]

> "This Russian connection non-sense is merely an attempt to cover-up many mistakes made in Hillary Clinton's losing campaign."[28]

> "Information is being illegally given to the failing @nytimes & @washingtonpost by the intelligence community (NSA and FBI?). Just like Russia"[29]

> "The real scandal here is that classified information is illegally given out by "intelligence" like candy. Very un-American!"[30]

"Leaking, and even illegal classified leaking, has been a big problem in Washington for years. Failing @nytimes (and others) must apologize!"[31]

Republicans in Congress wanted investigations into *who* leaked the material damaging to Trump. Democrats in Congress wanted investigation into *what* those leaked documents revealed about Trump and his team. Whom to pursue: the leader or the one whose malfeasance was leaked? This prompted late-night comedian Stephen Colbert to quip "Your honor, I did not kill that man—the real criminal is whoever filmed me strangling him."[32]

TRUMP AND HIS OPPONENTS

Opposition to Trump came from five key sources:

1. The Democrats. But as the minority party in Congress, there was just so much they could do. Generally, the Democratic response to Trump was tepid and little more than a minor irritation to the president.

2. The Media. Trump saw the media as his enemy and constantly attacked them. Of course, the media was more of an attack dog than a lap dog to Trump, but he often went out of his way to attack and antagonize the media, seemingly in the hopes of delegitimizing them in the eyes of the public.

3. The Bureaucracy. Trump's attacks on the intelligence community (which may have leaked material harmful to Trump) and the bureaucracy's reaction to Trump's ban on immigration (where they were caught off guard and made to look the fool sometimes) left them at odds with the president.

4. The Anti-Trump People: Angry mass protests such as the Women's March the day after the inauguration and protests over the ban served as rallying points in opposition to Trump.

5. The Republican Establishment. Trump was an outsider who was often at war with the establishment. At first there was a marriage of convenience between Trump and mainstream Republicans, but with Trump's very public attacks against Senator John McCain and others, the marriage of convenience could become a bit inconvenient and if that occurred, Trump would be in deep trouble.

More pushback could come from the states. During the Obama presidency, the state of Texas filed numerous suits against the administration hoping to block or delay Obama's action. California seems poised to serve a similar role to Trump.[33]

Donald Trump was elected to break up the old corrupt order. It should come as no surprise that the old order would oppose him. But while Trump proved very good at *breaking*, he was very bad at making. It is one thing to tear down the old building, but what if you don't know how to build a new one?

We Love Russia

Story after story, day after day. Trump's campaign contended with Russia reports that not only wouldn't go away but, with every passing day, Trump and his team seemed more and more deeply connected to Russian hacking and other activities.

According to sources in the U.S. intelligence community, several members of the Trump team had repeated contacts with Russian officials during the campaign, and questions were raised that Trump associates might be coordinating activities with Russian intelligence operatives. Clearly the Russians had hacked Clinton campaign staffers and released the stolen material to WikiLeaks who then released them to the public. And just as clearly, this was done on the order of Vladimir Putin for the express purpose of hurting Hilary Clinton and helping Donald Trump. But was there outright collusion? On January 11, an NBC reporter asked Trump whether members of his staff were in contact with Russian officials during the campaign. "No," he replied.[34] On January 15, Mike Pence was asked basically the same question on two Sunday shows. "Of course not," he replied on both Fox and CBS.[35] But a February 14, 2017 *New York Times* article said otherwise. "Phone records and intercepted calls show," the story said, "that members of Donald J. Trump's 2016 presidential campaign and other Trump associates had repeated contacts with senior Russian intelligence officials in the year before the election."[36]

TRUMP'S FIRST LATINO IN THE CABINET

With the withdrawal of the labor nominee Andrew Puzder, President Trump had an opportunity to broaden the makeup of his Cabinet, and he did so by nominating Alexander Acosta as his new Secretary of Labor. Acosta was the dean of the law school at Florida International University. He was a former U.S. attorney for the Southern District of Florida and had also served on the National Labor Relations Board. He was the first Latino appointment to the Trump Cabinet.

THANKS, BUT NO THANKS

With Flynn out, the president went on the hunt for a new national security advisor. The position was offered to Vice Admiral Robert Harward, a former Navy Seal who had strong support from both Democrats and Republicans.

Harward, aware of the obvious disarray of the Trump Administration, said that he would only take the job if allowed to pick his own team. The White House was wary and refused. Harward withdrew his name. Several reports revealed that Harward saw the White House as too chaotic and undisciplined, referring to it as a "sh**t sandwich."[37]

A WORLD OF ENEMIES

Donald J. Trump openly and often displays anger, pique, impatience, hostility, and rudeness. He sees enemies around him and lashes out at these enemies. He picks fights often and almost indiscriminately. He rails against the U.S. intelligence community, the judiciary, immigrants, the Democrats, members of the Republican Party who do not willingly follow his lead, and, of course, the media.

In his penchant to see adversaries as enemies, Trump resembles Richard Nixon. It was Nixon who put together an enemies list, and used the levers of government (e.g., the IRS) to harass and try to crush these enemies. Nixon, knowing that he had much to hide and that if anyone revealed his dark secrets, it would likely be the media, set out to undermine them before they could go after him. In conditioning the public to see the media as his enemy who would stop at nothing to bring him down, Nixon hoped that if and when the media did reveal his secrets, he would have immunized himself from criticism.

Nixon used his vice president, Spiro Agnew, to assault the press. "In the United States today," Agnew said, "we have more than our share of the nattering nabobs of negativism," adding, "They have formed their own 4-H Club—the hopeless, hysterical hypochondriacs of history."[38]

When the press did report on Nixon's sometimes criminal activities, Nixon shrouded himself in the cloak of victim, blaming the press for unfairly trying to take him down. In a 1972 phone call recorded by the White House, Nixon told National Security Advisor Henry Kissinger "the press is the enemy. The press is the enemy." Kissinger agreed with the president, and Nixon added, "It's the enemy."[39]

Trump has taken a page out of the Nixon playbook. On Friday, February 17, Trump tweeted that the media purveyors of fake news were the "enemy of the American people."[40] In a rally, the following day Trump went back to his attack mode calling the media "dishonest," "disgusting," and "fake." He called the media "fake" nearly twenty times in that rally.[41]

And during the campaign, Trump blacklisted nearly a half-dozen news organizations that he banned from receiving media credentials.[42] There is an old Washington D.C. saying: "Never pick a fight with anyone who buys ink by the barrel."

A free press is an essential ingredient in a thriving democracy. As imperfect and flawed as it may be, it is also one of our last best hopes for exposing corruption and thwarting tyranny.

MESSAGE FROM McCAIN

A variety of forces began to challenge the policies as well as the political disposition of the Trump administration. The *judiciary* entered into the fray surprisingly early. The *Democrats*, tepid and disheartened, posed but minor headaches for the president. The *bureaucracy*, stung and embarrassed by the rollout of the immigration ban, began to push back. The protesters took to the streets early in the Trump presidency. But it was the Republican establishment—especially the Republican majorities in the House and Senate—that held the fate of the president in their hands.

And the key to the Republican establishment was Senator John McCain of Arizona. From the start, Trump and McCain had a very troubled relationship. During the 2016 presidential campaign, Trump attacked McCain saying that although he had been in a North Vietnamese prison camp and refused to be released unless his men were also released, that he "was not a hero." "He got captured," Trump said, "I like people who weren't captured."[43]

In a February 17 speech at the Munich Security Conference in Germany, McCain unloaded on Trump.[44] Although not mentioning Trump by name, McCain nonetheless stuck a knife in the very heart of Trumpism, with its xenophobic hypernationalism and "America First" attitude. A brief sampling from the speech should suffice. McCain said that the founders of the Munich conference:

would be alarmed by an increasing turn away from universal values and toward old ties of blood and race and sectarianism. They would be alarmed by the hardening resentment we see towards immigrants and refugees and minority groups—especially Muslims. They would be alarmed that more and more of our fellow citizens seem to be flirting with authoritarianism and romanticizing it as our moral equivalent...But what would alarm them most, I think, is a sense that many of our peoples, including in my own country, are giving up on the West, that they see it as a bad deal that we may be better off without, and that while Western nations still have the power to maintain our world order, it's unclear whether we have the will.

He added:

I know there is profound concern across Europe and the world that America is laying down the mantle of global leadership. I can only speak for myself, but I do not believe that that is the message you will hear from all of the American leaders who cared enough to travel here to Munich this weekend. That's not the message you heard today from Secretary of Defense Jim Mattis. That is not the message you will hear from Vice President Mike Pence. That's not the message you will hear from Secretary of Homeland Security John Kelly. And that is certainly not the message you will hear tomorrow from our bipartisan congressional delegation.

McCain concluded with a more direct shot at Trump:

I refuse to accept that our values are morally equivalent to those of our adversaries...I am a proud, unapologetic believer in the West, and I believe we must always, always stand up for it. For if we do not, who will?

LITTLE TO SHOW AT 30 DAYS

One-third of the way to the 100-day mark and the president's list of achievements seemed quite underwhelming. There was a lot of noise, a flurry of executive orders, but little real change. CNN's Fareed Zakaria called it "a rocking horse presidency," with a lot of movement back and forth, but no progress.[45] And while Trump himself said in typical bombastic exaggeration that "there's never been a presidency that has done so much in such a short period of time,"[46] the reality is that most of the action was high on style and short on substance.

Most of his executive orders were calls for reports or statements of belief, and the one substantive executive order—the one banning entry to the U.S. from seven Muslim-majority countries—was so poorly written that it was thrown out in court after its chaotic unveiling.

Almost all of Trump's campaign promises that "on day 1, I will..." (e.g., label China a currency manipulator, demand a constitutional amendment instituting term limits on Congress, withdraw from the Iran Nuclear Arms Deal) remained undelivered. And most of the action within the administration was chaotic mistake making (e.g., the Flynn firing, the ban, explaining away "alternative facts").

TRUMP GUYS, RUSSIAN TIES

Accusations of electoral collusion with Russia just kept mounting. Things became so bad that Trump's chief of staff Reince Priebus went so far as to ask the FBI if they might go public and dismiss the charges of collusion. Of course, the FBI refused.

James Comey, director of the FBI, met with the Senate Intelligence Committee to discuss Russia's interference in the election. The FBI was investigating several different leads, and calls for the appointment of an independent prosecutor continued.

In late February, things became more bizarre—if that were possible—when the *New York Times* reported that Michael Cohen, the president's personal lawyer and a former Trump business associate Felix Sater, along with a pro-Moscow Ukranian legislator, delivered to the White House a plan for a resolution of the crisis in the Ukraine that would give Russia control of the Crimea while lifting U.S. sanctions.[47]

After the Flynn disaster, President Trump selected Lt. Gen. H. R. McMaster as his new national security advisor. The selection was met with near universal approval, and McMaster had strong bipartisan support. Known as a man who would speak his mind, some wondered how long it would be before he and Trump would clash. McMaster is not a "yes man," and along with the Secretaries of Defense and State, it seemed only a matter of time before friction with the president turned into fireworks.

Meanwhile, Trump tried to distance himself from Russia, but after a series of bankruptcies and the 2008 economic recession, Trump had trouble borrowing money from U.S. and European banks. Russian investors were heavily involved in several Trump-branded properties, especially in Florida. And Donald Jr. told a 2008 real estate conference that "Russians make up a pretty disproportionate cross-section of a lot of our assets;" adding, "We see a lot of money pouring in from Russia," Donald Sr.'s refusal to release his tax returns makes it difficult to see just how invested the Russians are in his businesses.[48]

ANOTHER ONE BITES THE DUST

The Flynn resignation/firing, coming so early in the president's administration was an embarrassment. Then the second Trump nominee, Vincent Viola, who was slated to be Secretary of the Army stepped down. And shortly after that, a third Trump nominee bailed. Businessman Philip Bilden was chosen as Secretary of the Navy, but he withdrew his name for consideration.

A Pentagon statement said that Mr. Bilden decided he could not comply with the Office of Government Ethics requirements without "undue disruption and materially adverse divestment of my family's private financial interests." Army secretary nominee Vincent Viola said substantially the same thing when he dropped out.[49]

An Enemy of The State

The president kept going after the media. It was a strategy to undermine the credibility of the media so that when the reported stories critical of Trump, he could (perhaps) dismiss such stories as yet another effort by the "dishonest media" to get the president.

Conflicts between presidents and the press are as old as the republic, but Trump's rhetoric escalated that conflict to new heights. In a long and combative press conference held in late February, the president repeatedly used words like "dishonest," "fake news," and "out of control," then going so far as to label the "fake" mainstream media "the enemy of the American people."[50]

"Enemy of the people." The phrase had a chilling history. It was used by the most brutal dictators of the past eighty years: Hitler, Lenin, Stalin, Mao, to discredit and paint as dangerous, anyone who threatened their power. Republican Senator John McCain reminded us that attacking the legitimacy of a free press was "how dictators got started."[51]

Trump's ire was further raised by a series of leaks coming out of his own administration that proved embarrassing to the president. There are two types of leaks: *controlled* (leaks intentionally revealed by the administration) and *uncontrolled* (leaks that work against the administration and are not released by the administration).

During the campaign, candidate Trump applauded Julian Assange and called on WikiLeaks to release more stolen and leaked information against Hillary Clinton, going so far as to call on Russia to find and publish more Clinton e-mails.[52] Now, Trump was singing a different tune. Complaining that leaks were "illegal" and "un-American," the president ordered his staff to identify who was doing the leaking. This led Press Secretary Sean Spicer to confiscate the cell phones of his staff to see if he could find anything.[53]

Trump's war against the media got even hotter when several mainstream media outlets were "banned" from a press gaggle with Spicer.

CNN, the *New York* and *Los Angeles Times*, *Politico*, and others were not allowed to attend the Spicer briefing.[54] Ironically, two months earlier Spicer said that open access to the media was "what makes a democracy a democracy versus a dictatorship."[55]

FOLLOW THE MONEY

Prior to his February 28 address to a joint session of Congress, the president released guidelines for a new budget. Trump called it an "America first" budget and it included a 10% ($54 billion) increase in defense spending, and a comparable cut in money to domestic agencies (especially the Environmental Protection Agency). No cuts were planned for Social Security and Medicare. Surprisingly, there was *no increase* in spending for infrastructure improvements, as the president had promised during the campaign.

The budget was largely the work of Mick Mulvaney, Office of Management and Budget (OMB) Director; Gary Cohen, National Economic Council Director; and Stephen Bannon, the White House chief strategist. Budget hawks were disappointed that entitlements went uncut, but populists applauded the budget proposals, setting up a clash later when the deficit grows and entitlements are put back on the table.

The new budget came at a time when virtually all the leading economic indicators were headed in the right direction. President Obama left Trump a strong and growing economy. In the campaign, Trump promised to more than double the United States' rate of economic growth, but his budget forecasters quickly backed away from that promise. Likewise, the promise of massive infrastructure spending was also dropped.

A BOTCHED RAID

Days after taking office, President Trump signed off on a military intelligence-gathering operation in Yemen that was initially discussed in the waning days of the Obama presidency. Trump gave the go-ahead for the operation. It was a disaster. During the raid, U.S. navy seal William "Ryan" Owens was killed. It was the first death of a military service member under the new Trump administration. The U.S. gathered little actionable intelligence from the raid.[56] Qasim al-Raym, an Al Qaeda leader, was believed to be the target of the raid, but he was not found and the U.S. was compelled to call in an air strike to destroy a V-22 Osprey helicopter damaged in the mission. More than twenty-five civilians, including nine children, were killed in the raid.

Initially, Trump praised the mission as a success and took credit for his own leadership in the matter.[57] "Absolutely a success," is how press Secretary Sean Spicer referred to the raid, and added that anyone who questioned the raid "owes an apology and [does a] disservice to the life of Chief Owens."[58] But soon after these remarks, a different version of the raid emerged. As it became clear that it was a botched raid, the president began to distance himself from responsibility. On February 27, he said that, "This was a mission that was started before I got here. This was something they wanted to do," the president told Fox News. He added, "They came to see me, they explained what they wanted to do—the generals—who are very respected, my generals are the most respected that we've had in many decades, I believe. And they lost Ryan."[59] *They* lost Ryan. The president did not appear to take responsibility for something on which he himself had signed off.

Administration officials "leaked" word that President Obama was responsible for the failure because the raid was first planned while he was president.[60] It was the generals; it was Obama. But in point of fact, it was Donald Trump who had signed off on the go-ahead order. Trump had failed to do due diligence or ask the right questions.

This was a far cry from the Bay of Pigs fiasco that occurred in the early days of the Kennedy administration. Kennedy inherited a plan drawn up by the Eisenhower administration to invade Cuba. Kennedy did not do his due diligence and approved the obviously flawed plan. When it failed, Kennedy took responsibility for the mistake.[61] That is what leaders do.

Early in his presidency, Trump has displayed a worrisome inability to admit or take responsibility for mistakes. As a candidate, Trump admitted that while he believed in God, he had never asked God for forgiveness. When directly asked the question Trump responded, "I am not sure I have. I just go on and try to do a better job from there, I don't think so. I think if I do something wrong, I think, I just try and make it right. I don't bring God into that picture. I don't."[62]

Trump added that while he hasn't asked God for forgiveness, he does participate in Holy Communion. "When I drink my little wine—which is about the only wine I drink—and have my little cracker, I guess that is a form of asking for forgiveness, and I do that as often as possible because I feel cleansed," he said. "I think in terms of 'let's go on and let's make it right.'"[63]

This attitude seems to be applied across the board as President Trump continued to deny responsibility for mistakes and refused to ask for forgiveness. He blamed President Obama for anti-Trump protests and also blamed him for the leaks that were coming out of his own administration. "I think he is behind it," said Trump of the leaks.[64] Just how would this refusal to take responsibility play out in Trump's presidency?

NOTES

1. Anthony J. Badger, *FDR: The First Hundred Days* (New York: Farrar Straus and Giroux, 2009); and Jonathan Alter, *The Defining Moment: FDR's Hundred Days and the Triumph of Hope* (New York: Simon and Schuster, 2007).
2. William E. Leuchtenburg, *In the Shadow of FDR: From Harry Truman to Barack Obama* (Ithaca: Cornell University Press, 2009).
3. Valerie Bunce, *Do New Leaders Make a Difference?* (Princeton: Princeton Legacy Library, 2014).
4. Amita Kelly and Barbara Sprunt, "Here is What Donald Trump Wants To Do in His First 100 Days," *NPR*, November 9, 2016.
5. Brooks Jackson, "What President Trump Inherits," *FactCheck.org*, Annenberg Public Policy Center, January 20, 2017.
6. Louis Jacobson, "Did Donald Trump inherit 'a mess' from Barack Obama?" PoltiFact, February 17, 2017, http://www.politifact.com/truth-o-meter/article/2017/feb/17/did-donald-trump-inherit-mess.
7. Jacobson, "Did Donald Trump inherit 'a mess'
8. Jeremy W. Peters, "Grand Plans vs. Reality: White House Veterans Recall Their First 100 Days," *New York Times*, January 24, 2017.
9. Ibid.
10. All quotes from Jeremy W. Peters, "Grand Plans vs. Reality in the First 100 Days," *The New York Times*, January 25, 2017.
11. Glenn Kessler, "Donald Trump's Bogus Claim that Millions of People Voted Illegally for Hillary Clinton," *The Washington Post*, November 27, 2016.
12. Carl Hulse, "For New President, Unlikely Role Model on Flexing Executive Muscles" *The New York Times* January 27, 2017, A10.
13. Transcript, ABC News Anchor David Muir Interviews President Trump, *ABC News*, January 25, 2017.
14. David Lauter, "A First Week Both Normal and Far From It," *The Los Angeles Times*, January 29, 2017, A12.
15. The front page of the *New York Times*, January 24, 2017 featured a story with the headline: "Meeting with Top Lawmakers, Trump Repeals an Election Lie."
16. Frida Ghitis, "Trump's Relationship with the Truth is Becoming a National Embarrassment, *CNN Opinion*, March 17, 2017.

17. Molly Ball, "Kellyanne's Alternative Universe," *The Atlantic,* April 2017, https://www.theatlantic.com/magazine/archive/2017/04/kellyannes-alternative-universe/517821/

18. Associated Press, "Trump: Mattis' view on torture will override his own beliefs," January 27, 2017, http://www.foxnews.com/politics/2017/01/27/trump-mattis-view-on-torture-will-override-his-own-beliefs.html.

19. Gabriel H. Sanchez, "This is What US Protests Looked Like in the '60s," *Buzzfeed,* January 23, 2017.

20. Donald Trump, Twitter post, February 4, 2017, 5:12 a.m., http://twitter.com/realDonaldTrump.

21. Donald Trump, Twitter post, February 9, 2017, 3:35PM, http://twitter.com/realDonaldTrump.

22. Neil MacFarquhar, "Vladimir Putin Won't Expel U.S. Diplomats as Russian Foreign Minister Urged," *The New York Times,* December 30, 2017, A1.

23. Donald Trump, Twitter post, December 30, 2016, 11:41 a.m., https://twitter.com/realdonaldtrump.

24. Read Michael T Flynn's Resignation Letter, *CNN Politics,* February 14, 2017.]

25. William Finnegan, "The Rejection of Andy Puzder," *The New Yorker,* February 15, 2017.

26. Ryan Browne and Barbara Starr, "US Special Ops Chief: US Government 'In Unbelievable Turmoil,'" *CNN Politics,* February 14, 2017.

27. Donald Trump, Twitter post, February 15, 2017, 3:40 a.m., https://twitter.com/realdonaldtrump.

28. Donald Trump, Twitter post, February 15, 2017, 4:08 a.m., https://twitter.com/realdonaldtrump.

29. Donald Trump, Twitter post, February 15, 2017, 4:19 a.m., https://twitter.com/realdonaldtrump.

30. Donald Trump, Twitter post, February 15, 2017, 5:13 a.m., https://twitter.com/realdonaldtrump.

31. Donald Trump, Twitter post, February 16, 2017, 3:58 a.m., https://twitter.com/realdonaldtrump, https://twitter.com/realdonaldtrump.

32. Stephen Colbert, "So Much Russian Influence, So Little Time," The Late Show with Stephen Colbert, February 16, 2017, https://youtu.be/f31otqid2wc.

33. See Cathleen Decker, "Trump versus California: The Feud Turns from Rhetorical to Real," *The Los Angeles Times,* January 26, 2017.

34. Editorial, "Timeline: Trump and Associates Denied Russia Involvement at Least 20 Times," *The Guardian*, July 11, 2017.

35. Jenna Amatulli, "Meghan McCain: Mike Pence's Denial About Russia Communication was 'a lie,'" *Huffington Post*, July 11, 2017.

36. Michael S. Schmidt, Mark Mazzetti, and Matt Apuzzo, "Trump Campaign Aides Had Repeated Contacts with Russian Intelligence," *The New York Times*. February 14, 2017

37. Julie Hirschfield Davis and Eric Schmitt, "Trump's Pick to Replace Flynn Turns Down the Job," *The New York Times*, February 16, 2017.

38. Michael A. Genovese, *The Nixon Presidency: Power and Politicians in Turbulent Times* (New York: Greenwood, 1990).

39. Ibid.

40. David Jackson, "Trump Again Calls Media 'enemy of the people'", *USA Today*, February 24, 2017.

41. Ibid.

42. Kurtis Lee, "Presidents vs. Press, Then and Now," *The Los Angeles Times*, February 19, 2012, A8.

43. Ben Schreckinger, "Trump Attacks McCain: 'I Like People Who Weren't Captured,'" *Politico*, July 19, 2015.

44. Phil Stewart and Robin Emmott, "Trump's Team in Disarray, U.S. Senator McCain Tell Europe," *Reuters*, February 17, 2017.

45. Eric Mack, "Zakaria: This 'rocking-horse presidency' has done 'hardly anything,'" *Newsmax*, Febrary 19, 2017.

46. Ibid.

47. Megan Twohey and Scott Shane, "A Back-Channel Plan for Ukraine and Russia, Courtesy of Trump Associates," *New York Times*, February 19, 2017.

48. Rosalind S. Helderman, "Here's What We Know about Donald Trump and His Ties to Russia," *The Washington Post*, July 29, 2016.

49. Adam Davidson, "Donald Trump's Worst Deal," *The New Yorker*, March 13, 2017.

50. Alexandra Wilts, "Donald Trump Renews Attack on Media," *Independent*, July 2, 2017.

51. Chuck Todd, Phil Helsel, and Matt Rivera, "McCain Warns Supressing Press 'is how dictators get started,'" *NBC News*, February 19, 2017.

52. Rem Rider, "The Bizarre Alliance of WikiLeaks and Trump," *USA Today*, October 12, 2016.

53. Chas Danner, "White House Staffers Leak News of Sean Spicer's 'Phone Check' Targeting Their Leaks," *New York magazine*, February 26, 2017.

54. Scott Bixby, "President Trump's White House Media Blackout has Reporters Talking Mutiny," *Daily Beast*, June 19, 2017.

55. Phillip Bump, "In December, Spicer said Barring Media Access is what a 'Dictatorship' Does. Today, He Barred Media Access," *Washington Post*, Feb 24, 2017.

56. Tina Nguyen, "Trump Blames Obama, Generals for Botched Raid He Authorized," *Vanity Fair*, February 28, 2017, http://www.vanityfair.com/news/2017/02/trump-blames-obama-generals-for-botched-raid-he-authorized.

57. Ibid.

58. Ibid.

59. Ibid.

60. Ibid.

61. Trumbell Higgins, *The Perfect Failure: Kennedy, Eisenhower, and the CIA at the Bay of Pigs*, Norton, 1989.

62. Michelle Boorstein, "Trump on God: 'Hopefully I won't have to be asking for much forgiveness'," *The Washington Post*, June 8, 2016, https://www.washingtonpost.com/news/acts-of-faith/wp/2016/06/08/trump-on-god-hopefully-i-wont-have-to-be-asking-for-much-forgiveness/?utm_term=.e3188f326fa6.

63. Eugene Scott, "Trump Believes in God, But Hasn't Sought Forgiveness," *CNN Politics*, July 18, 2015.

64. Jennifer Epstein, "Trump Blames Obama for Protests: 'I Think He's Behind It," *Bloomberg*, February 28, 2017. https://www.yahoo.com/finance/news/trump-blames-obama-protests-think-130715651.html.

Chapter 8

The First Hundred Days

A Reboot Or Limping To The Finish Line:
Test 5 Continued

It was a rough start for the new president, but he hoped to press the restart button. And the restart was to begin with his address to the Congress and the nation. It was an ideal opportunity to turn around the flagging fortunes of his presidency.

The President Addresses a Joint Session of Congress

On the evening of February 28, 2017, President Donald J. Trump took center stage at his first address to a joint session of Congress. Which Trump would show up, combative Trump or presidential Trump? After his dark "carnage" inaugural address, viewers did not know what to expect. Was it time to reinforce the disruptive impact of Trump, or time to pivot, to press the reset button?

Expectations were not high as most commentators, anticipating combative Trump, set the bar pretty low. But Trump came out displaying little of the petty snark for which he was rightfully famous. He was considered more "presidential" than usual; because Trump exercised a good deal of impulse control, he was given high marks for the address.

Long on symbols and short on specifics, the address to Congress sounded more like the inaugural address he should have delivered than an annual address to Congress wherein presidents would normally present a specific list of legislative priorities, followed in the next few weeks by actual legislative proposals. Trump's address was less confrontational, less accusatory, and almost upbeat and inspiring. True, there was no clear agenda proposed, but in tone, this speech was welcome and reassuring.

That some of Trump's coming agenda to Congress would rub many establishment Republicans the wrong way (i.e., infrastructure spending, Trump's praise of Russia) and may cause friction, for now, Republicans in Congress were backing their president. Some Republicans saw Trump as their chance to pass major changes to the tax code, cut regulations, repeal Obamacare, and achieve other conservative goals. But there was little love lost between Trump and the Republican establishment. For now, it was a marriage of convenience. At what point might it become inconvenient?

Another Domino Falls

President Obama first learned of Russia's hacking in the early summer of 2016. He was reluctant to act too boldly because a) Clinton appeared to hold a safe lead over Trump, and b) he did not want to appear overly partisan. But at the September G-20 meeting in China, Obama directly confronted Putin, telling him to "cut it out," and warned of "serious consequences" if he tried to meddle with the November election.[1]

Two weeks before inauguration day U.S. intelligence officials briefed both President Obama and President-elect Trump about an explosive report compiled by former British intelligence officer Christopher Steele that contained material on Trump that Russia might use to blackmail the incoming president. The report contained unconfirmed details of a personal nature that, if true, would place Trump in jeopardy.

By inauguration day, the evidence of Russia's complicity in interfering with the election was certain, and a joint task force of the CIA, FBI, and NSA, along with the Treasury Department was formed to further verify the Russian activities. Also, three Senate Committees began inquiries.[2]

Trump and Russia. It just wouldn't go away. The first Trump domino to fall in the Russia scandal was campaign chair Paul Manafort. Next came national security adviser Michael Flynn (who was paid $40,000 by RT, the Russian propaganda station, to speak at one of its dinners. At the dinner, Flynn was seated next to Vladimir Putin). On March 2, a third domino seemed ready to fall: Attorney General Jeff Sessions.

In his confirmation hearings Sessions testified (under oath) that during the campaign, he had no contacts with any Russian officials. That was not true. Sessions changed his story several times, but a firestorm had started.

Pressure mounted on Sessions to resign. Instead, he announced that he would recuse himself from the Department of Justice's investigation into charges of Russia meddling in the 2016 campaign on behalf of Donald Trump. This sent Trump into a tailspin; later Trump declared that had he known Sessions might recuse himself, he would never have appointed Sessions as Attorney General.

RUSSIAN TIES, ADMINISTRATION LIES

An unfolding web of connections directly linking Trump associates to Russia, Julian Assange, and WikiLeaks came into deeper focus. Paul Manafort was let go, Mike Flynn was let go, Jeff Sessions continued to hang on. But the Russia connection expanded.

Many believed that Trump's repeated defense of Putin and Russia involved more than Trump's "he said nice things about me" rationale. From complimenting Putin to calling sanctions against Russia over the invasion of Ukraine into question to scoffing at evidence that Russia intervened in the 2016 presidential to help get Trump elected, to Trump associates forcing Republican Party platform writers to softer language on Russian sanctions, to Trump's very public (July 27) call for Russia to release more information on Hillary Clinton's e-mails ("Russia," Trump said, "if you're listening, I hope you're able to find the 30,000 e-mails that are missing."[3]). Moreover, there was no expression of outrage that Russia interfered with a U.S. election.

Over the years Trump repeatedly praised Putin. In 2007 he said, "Putin is doing a great job,"[4] and in a 2013 MSNBC interview Trump bragged about his relationship with Putin.[5] At a National Press Club luncheon, he said "I spoke indirectly and directly with President Putin, who could not have been nicer." But during the 2016 campaign, Trump was singing a different tune: "I never met Putin, I don't know who Putin is."[6]

The circle of Trump associates linked to Russia began to expand: Carter Page (who in July gave a speech in Moscow, condemning sanctions against Russia), and J. D. Gordon, another Trump campaign official, also met with Russians during the campaign, as did Jared Kushner and Walid Phares. Additionally, three weeks before the election, Donald Jr. flew to Paris to give a speech to a pro-Russian group that had nominated Putin for a Nobel Peace Prize. On top of this, former Trump adviser Roger Stone —after denying meeting with Russians—admitted on March 4 that he did have "back channel" contacts with Julian Assange whose WikiLeaks was releasing stolen e-mails from Democrats.[7] In fact, Stone's contacts proved embarrassing when the following Twitter exchange came to light in the following exchange:

> Caroline O. (@RVAwonk): "Stone denies contact w/ Assange. 10/2016: Stone says "I do have backchannel communication w/ Assange." (miami.cbslocal.com/2016/10/12/tru...) twitter.com/RogerJStoneJR/..."[8]

> Roger Stone (@RogerJStoneJR): "@RVAwonk you stupid bitch—never denied perfectly legal back channel to Assange who indeed had the goods on #CrookedHillary"[9]

When Russian ambassador Sergey Kislyak visited Trump campaign officials at Trump Tower, he was secreted in by a back entrance, so as to avoid the media.

Where would all this end? When would all this end?

THE TRUMP CIRCUS COMES TO TOWN

On Saturday morning, March 4, the president went on one of his frequent Twitter rants. Starting at 6:35 a.m., Trump began tweeting a rapid-fire assault against his predecessor, Barack Obama.

> "Terrible! Just found out that Obama had my "wires tapped" in Trump Tower just before the victory. Nothing found. This is McCarthyism!"[10]

> "Is it legal for a sitting President to be "wire tapping" a race for president prior to an election? Turned down by court earlier. A NEW LOW!"[11]

> "I'd bet a good lawyer could make a great case out of the fact that President Obama was tapping my phones in October, just prior to Election!"[12]

> "How low has President Obama gone to tapp my phones during the very sacred election process. This is Nixon/Watergate. Bad (or sick) guy!"[13]

> "Arnold Schwarzenegger isn't voluntarily leaving the Apprentice, he was fired by his bad (pathetic) ratings, not by me. Sad end to great show"[14]

Mr. Trump had accused his predecessor, Barack Obama, of committing a felony. Offering no evidence to support this charge, Trump wrote that Obama was a "Bad (or sick) guy!"[15]

There were three possibilities of what might have happened: 1) while president, Barack Obama illegally tapped (or had tapped) Trump's phones.

That would be a felony; 2) a legal FISA or Title 3 wiretap was attained where a federal judge, agreeing that there was "probable cause" of someone on Trump's team committing a crime or impropriety, signed off on a wiretap. If this were so, it might raise questions of impeachment against Trump; or 3) the charge was false, in which case serious questions would be raised relating to the mental health or veracity of the president. If this were so, there likely would be calls to invoke the 25th Amendment, removing President Trump from office on grounds of incapacity.[16]

Five days earlier, Trump was blaming Obama for the leaks coming out regarding Trump associates' campaign contacts with Russians. Now, Trump upped the ante. The fact that a president cannot authorize a wiretap seemed lost on Trump. Only through a Title 3 warrant or authorization from a FISA (Foreign Intelligence Surveillance Act) court can a judge— not a president—authorize wiretaps.

FBI director James Comey contacted the Department of Justice (DOJ), asking them to publicly refute the claim that Obama had wiretapped Trump, but the DOJ rejected this request. Comey's denial of the Trump accusation was reinforced by James R. Clapper, Director of National Intelligence who, on NBC's *Meet the* Press, said that "there was no such wiretap activity mounted against the president-elect at the time, as a candidate or against his campaign."[17] Obama spokespersons also denied Trump's claim.

Now the British Too?

President Trump's claim that during the campaign, President Obama had ordered a wiretap on Trump Towers got even more bizarre—if that is even possible—when on Thursday, March 16, administration press spokesman Sean Spicer, citing a Fox News commentator Andrew Napolitano, accused the GCHQ (a division of British Intelligence) at the request of Obama, of spying on candidate Trump's Trump Towers offices.[18] Both the British government and GCHQ immediately denounced the Spicer announcement as false, with GCHQ issuing a statement reading in part that the accusations are "nonsense. They are utterly ridiculous and should be ignored."[19]

Both Spicer and U.S. National Security Adviser General H.R. McMaster were forced to apologize formally to our ally and assure then that such false accusations would not be repeated.

Was the administration so desperate to confirm Trump's false charge as to risk relations with our ally? What if the U.S. *needs* Great Britain's support in an important international conflict, or a future military campaign; why would the British believe an administration that so casually peddles in falsehoods?

British Liberal Democrat leader Tim Farron called Spicer's accusation "shameful," adding, "Trump is compromising the vital U.K.-U.S. security relationship to try to cover his own embarrassment...This harms our and U.S. security."[20]

The Twitterer-in-Chief kept crying wolf, but there was no wolf. At what point would people no longer believe him—even when he does tell the truth? Oh, and while all this was going on, North Korea test-fired four missiles into the Sea of Japan. This would not be the last time North Korea got the attention of the new president.

KITCHEN APPLIANCES ARE WATCHING YOU: FROM ALTERNATIVE FACTS TO AN ALTERNATIVE REALITY

To make matters worse, Trump's 3:35 a.m. tweet on March 4, 2017, accusing Barack Obama of wiretapping him (calling Obama a "Bad (or sick) guy")[21] wouldn't go away. The president had insisted that Congress investigate, and to his surprise, they did, The House asked Trump to supply evidence, but he did not. They gave him an extension, and still he did not comply. In the meantime, Trump underlings strained to explain away what Trump "really" meant, with Kellyanne Conway going so far as saying that your microwave might be spying on you. Social media had a field day.[22] This was followed by Conway saying—and yes, she actually said this—that she was "not in the job of having evidence."[23] Life in Trump World seemed to have officially sunk into a Saturday Night Live skit.

Rep. Devin Nunes (R–California), the Chair of the House Intelligence Committee, and Adam Schiff (D–California), minority leader of the committee, held an impromptu press conference in which both reaffirmed that there was no evidence to support President Trump's accusation against Barack Obama.[24]

Trump's "Obama wiretapped me" tweet, referred to as "one of the most consequential accusations made by one president against another in American history, remained an unsubstantiated as well as ruthless charge." If it damaged the president's credibility—as seemed to be the case—it would also be damaging to Trump and to the United States.[25]

IMMIGRATION BAN 2.0

On Monday March 6, the president signed a new executive order banning immigration from six (originally seven) Muslim majority countries. Iraq was removed from the original list, and a few other changes took place such as opening up the process a bit more and addressing some of the objections that led courts to stop execution of the first travel ban. Would ban 2.0 pass the judicial test?

As one of his signature issues and one of his more visible campaign promises, the administration needed to get the Muslim ban just right. Another failure and the Trump team could very well get a reputation for incompetence. One doesn't always get a second chance in politics, but the reworked ban gave Trump an opportunity to learn from his previous mistake and perhaps get it right this time. He didn't.

REPEAL AND REPLACE

One of the key "day one" promises of candidate Trump was to repeal and replace Obamacare. On March 7, Republicans in Congress released an outline—it was not scored (no price tag) by the Congressional Budget Office as was customary, and there was no estimation of changes in coverage—of their Obamacare replacement program.

Democrats did not like the proposed changes, and more importantly, several conservatives, such as Republican Senator Rand Paul, called it "Obama Lite," and vowed to block the proposal. Repeal and replace would be considerably more complicated and difficult than candidate Trump had imagined—governing, it turned out, was hard.

At 4:04 a.m., President Trump tweeted yet another in his stream of attacks against Barack Obama—and yet again, it was largely a false claim: "122 vicious prisoners, released by the Obama Administration from Gitmo, have returned to the battlefield. Just another terrible decision![26]

The problem? While it was true that 122 released Guantanamo Bay detention center prisoners were identified to have reengaged in terrorism, Trump's charge that they were "released by the Obama Administration" was simply not true. In point of fact, 113 of the 122 former detainees were released before January of 2009—during the administration of George W. Bush. Nine were released during President Obama's presidency.

Scores to settle—against Barack Obama or Arnold Schwarzenegger—seemed higher on the Trump to-do list than changing government policy.

STEAMING, RAGING MAD

Flub after flub, mistake after mistake, was not what Donald J. Trump had in mind when he took office. He did not hit the ground running or stumbling, but seemed to repeatedly trip over his own feet. On an early March weekend trip to his Florida resort Mar-a-Lago, Trump exploded. Reports were published that he was "feeling besieged," was "seething," and was "steaming, raging mad."[27] Russia, Sessions, Flynn, leaks, sinking popularity, and a host of other problems seemed too much for the president. Trump, the disruptive force, didn't like getting disrupted. He was used to being the hammer; he didn't like being the nail.

And quietly, with little fanfare, the administration lifted a Clean Water rule, rolling back an Obama executive order.[28] Deregulations were something he would do all on his own.

A Danger to The World

America's allies were not comforted with the new Trump presidency. His criticism of NATO and his embrace of Putin made him (and the U.S.) too much the disruptive force and too little the reliable ally.

European Council President Donald Tusk called Trump "an existential threat to Europe," calling him "dangerous."[29] Germany's Foreign Minister Frank-Walter Steinmeier warned Trump would be "dangerous to the world,"[30] and the German magazine *Der Spiegel* published a blistering editorial, comparing Trump to Nero, and arguing that "the United States president is becoming a danger to the world."[31]

Repeal and Replace, Again

Republicans had made opposition to Obamacare (the Affordable Care Act) a central rallying point since it first went into effect on March 3, 2010. They voted more than 50 times to repeal it, and failing that, vowed that if elected they would "repeal and replace."

Now, with Republicans in control of the White House as well as both Houses of Congress, the time for talk was over and the time for action had arrived. But replace it with what? On Tuesday, March 7, 2017, Republican leaders from the House revealed their plan. That same day, a member of conservative Republicans from the "Freedom Caucus" came out against the plan.

Repeal and replace was the signature Republican electoral mantra; and if they failed, it would be a huge dent in both the Republican brand and the reputation of President Trump as a master negotiator.

HALTING BAN 2.0, PLUS

On Wednesday, March 15, a district court judge in Hawaii issued another setback to President Trump by putting a hold on Trump's second ban on grounds of religious discrimination. Early on Thursday, District Judge Theodore D. Chuang in federal court in Maryland also put a halt to the revised travel ban. In both cases, the judges cited religious discrimination against one's religion as the reason for their decision. Judge Derrick K. Watson of Hawaii cited candidate Trump's repeated verbal assaults against Muslims as well as his call "to ban all Muslims" from entering the United States, as evidence of motive.

It was a crushing blow to the president himself and his goal to ban entry into the United States from six (down from the original seven) predominantly Muslim countries.

KEEP FOLLOWING THE MONEY

On Thursday, March 16, 2017, the president released his proposed budget numbers. His new budget marked—as he promised during the campaign —a radical departure from the past.

The winners in Trump world? Defense was up 10%, vets by 6%, Homeland Security and Border Control by 7%. The losers? The Environmental Protection Agency (EPA; more than fifty programs were to be eliminated) was down 31%, the State Department by 28%, Department of Health & Human Services (HHS) by 18%, Department of Housing and Urban Development (HUD) by 13%. Slated for elimination was Public Broadcasting Service (PBS) and the National Endowment for the Humanities (NEH).

Figure 5. The Trump Budget.

President Trump's spending plan envisions deep cuts to many Cabinet departments and agencies. It is sure to face opposition from both parties in Congress.

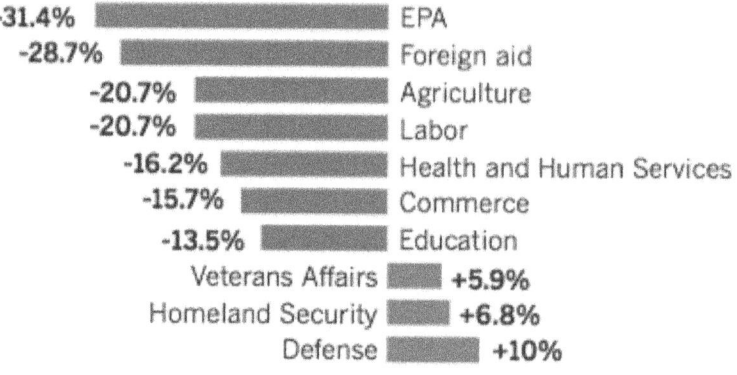

-31.4%	EPA
-28.7%	Foreign aid
-20.7%	Agriculture
-20.7%	Labor
-16.2%	Health and Human Services
-15.7%	Commerce
-13.5%	Education
Veterans Affairs	+5.9%
Homeland Security	+6.8%
Defense	+10%

Source: Office of Management and Budget

KYLE KIM Los Angeles Times

Source. "Trump's sweeping cuts would fund 'hard power'" *The Los Angeles Times*, March 17, 2017, A1. Copyright © 2017 Los Angeles Times. Reprinted with permission.

In addition, there were to be big cuts through the elimination of funding for United Nations Climate Control, United Nations Peacekeeping, the World Bank, Meals on Wheels, and Amtrak. Surprisingly absent was money for the large infrastructure program Trump repeatedly promised during the campaign.

Would Congress go along? Probably not. But the proposed Trump budget revealed much about the new president's goals and priorities.

THOSE PESKY RUSSIANS

Russia was proving to be yet another itch President Trump could not scratch. First Manafort, then Flynn, then Sessions got damaged, then his son-in-law Jared Kushner was reported to be involved, then Carter Page, and then, and then, and then...

And then there was Roger Stone, a long-time Trump friend and associate, who following denial after denial, finally—after proof surfaced —admitted that yes, he had some incidental contacts with people who might have been Russian. It was revealed that there were sixteen contacts between Stone and Guccifer 2.0, the Russian hacker who broke into and stole data from the computers of leading Democrats that proved so damaging to the Clinton campaign, leading Stone to insist that he had done nothing wrong.[32] However, Stone did announce during the campaign that Clinton campaign head John Podesta would soon have his "time in the barrel." Two weeks later, WikiLeaks released the Podesta e-mails that hurt Clinton's campaign.

While, at the 100-day mark, headlines about Trump campaign connections to Russia receded, House Senate and Special Prosecutor investigations continued, drawing Russia closer and closer to insiders in Team Trump.

TRUMP TRAIN DERAILED

Relations with Great Britain understandably hit a snag when Sean Spicer cited the report that British intelligence was used by President Obama to spy on the Trump campaign. Fevered denials followed, along with harsh words for Theresa May, the British prime minister.[33] To complicate matters, when soon afterward the president met in the White House with German Chancellor Angela Merkel, Trump, at a post meeting press conference, made the ill-suited joke that, referring to Merkel being wiretapped in the past, said, "at least we have something in common perhaps." The usually stoic Merkel shot the president what seemed like an incredulous look.

And then things got really bad. On March 20, FBI Director James Comey and National Security Agency Director Admiral Mike Rogers testified before Congress. It was all bad news for the president.

There were two key questions: 1) was there any evidence that President Obama had candidate Trump wiretapped? And 2) was the FBI investigating possible collusion between Trump associates and the Russians during the campaign? The answer was "no" to question one, and "yes" to question two. Additionally, Admiral Rogers verified that the charge that Obama had gotten the British to spy on Trump was false.

The president's credibility—both at home and abroad with our allies —took a big hit. Could President Trump be trusted? Could the word of the United States be trusted?

The case against President Trump was perhaps best made by Adam Schiff, ranking minority member of the House Intelligence Committee, who in his opening remarks made a strong circumstantial case that the administration was in hot water.[34]

Over time, key Trump advisers changed their stories about contacts with Russian officials. Denials turned into "maybes," and "maybes" into "yeses," but then "yes but" into "OK, I did." For example, after denying contact with "Guccifer 2.0," the online persona of the GRU Russia's military intelligence service, Roger J. Stone ended up having contact, but it was about some trivial matter.[35] However, in August, Stone sent out a tweet that John Podesta (Clinton's campaign chairman) would soon go through his "time in a barrel." Just weeks later, WikiLeaks published a pile of Podesta's hacked e-mails.

It is what the Republicans had been wanting and working for; it is what candidate Trump promised: repeal and replace Obamacare. It would be the first big test of the man who sold himself as the great deal maker.

But in this first test, negotiator Trump failed. His self-proclaimed deal-making power never materialized.

Even before the new "Trumpcare" plan came up for a vote in the Republican-controlled House of Representative, the bill was pulled on March 24, 2017. Some moderate Republicans worried that the new plan cut too many people off the insurance rolls; some conservative Republicans felt the bill did not cut enough. His own party failed him, maybe because it never really was *his* party. The president did not have the votes. He bailed—there was no Plan B. Those who believed Jared Kushner would top Steve Bannon in influence were surprised when, during the repeal-and-replace battle, Kushner, instead of being at the president's side, was off skiing in Aspen.

What next? The president said the defeat was really a blessing in disguise: "Here's the good news. Healthcare is now totally the property of the Democrats ... I've been saying for years that the best thing is to let Obamacare explode and then go make a deal."[36]

The president wanted the nation's healthcare system to "explode?" Explode? How many Americans would be hurt if that happened?

And President Trump actually set it up to explode by signing an executive order directing the IRS to back away from enforcing the Obamacare mandate.[37] Trump was contributing to the coming time bomb. But he is president of the entire nation, and took an oath to "faithfully execute" the laws of the land. Now he was pushing the law over a cliff. It was like showing up at a fire, pouring gasoline on the fire, then saying, "This fire started with my predecessor, so I'm not responsible for putting it out."[38] The problem? It is manifestly the job of the president to put out that fire, not fan its flames; dereliction of duty is not in the presidential job description.[39]

Russia, Russia, and More Russia

FBI director Comey's testimony confirming that there was an ongoing investigation focused on possible Trump associates colluding with Russia became a dark cloud hanging over the administration. One-time Trump campaign manager Paul Manafort faced new charges of questionable practices with the Russians,[40] and chair of the House Committee Devin Nunes who was investigating Trump and the Russians—rather than informing his House Committee—went to the White House to tell President Trump that there might be some evidence that indeed he might have been part of a wiretap. Nunes's committee exploded, with members openly wondering for whom Nunes was working, Trump or the committee?

As the *New York Times* editorialized:

> In a possible violation of the law, Mr. Nunes described intelligence reports that he said had suggested that American intelligence agencies incidentally intercepted communications of then President-elect Trump and people close to him, and then disseminated the information widely throughout the intelligence community. His disclosures, which have destroyed the credibility of his committee in investigating Russian interference in the election, make clear that he is unfit for the job and should be replaced.
>
> Mr. Nunes's remarks, which appeared to be deliberately vague, gave President Trump cover for his baseless claim that President Barack Obama had illegally wiretapped his phones. After making his disclosures during a news conference on Wednesday, Mr. Nunes went to the White House to brief the president. In a startling break with tradition, Mr. Nunes, a Republican, briefed reporters before sharing his findings with fellow members of the committee, who are from both parties. Mr. Trump portrayed the congressman's assertions as a vindication of his widely discredited accusation. "I very much appreciated the fact that they found what they found," Mr. Trump said.[41]

Could Nunes be trusted to investigate the president he was trying to assist? Was Nunes in Trump's back pocket? Pressure to appoint a special prosecutor mounted, but innocent or guilty, team Trump was *acting* like it was guilty.

WITH FRIENDS LIKE THIS...

During the campaign and even into his presidency, Donald Trump kept criticizing NATO and our European allies. He welcomed Brexit, believed NATO was obsolete, made several anti-EU comments, complained that European nations were not paying their fair share on defense, and suggested that he might not keep our defense treaty agreements with NATO.

Early in his presidency, he had already rankled the British by alleging that British intelligence, at the behest of President Obama, had bugged Trump Tower during the 2016 campaign. It was an odd accusation, made against our strongest ally, based on zero evidence. Trump tweeted this accusation, press spokesman Sean Spicer repeated it, and the British were outraged and insulted. Why pointlessly antagonize a US ally?

But that was not the end of it. Trumps' America First agenda began morphing into an America Alone agenda as shortly, the president had a rocky meeting with German Chancellor Angela Merkel. During her March visit to the U.S., the two leaders met but did not hit it off. Trump's behavior bordered on rude as he seemed unwilling to make eye contact with Merkel, and during a photo op Trump sat there staring at his lap sulking. When a reporter asked for a handshake between the two, Merkel turned to Trump and asked, "Do you want to have a handshake?" Trump, "who seemed to be grimacing as he sat alongside Merkel, did not respond."[42]

TRUMP'S HOT AIR

In keeping with his campaign promise, President Trump on Tuesday March 28, 2017, signed an executive order that rolled back Obama administration programs designed to address climate change, limit coal use, cut carbon emissions, and do a host of other things designed to protect the environment. The president also loosened car-mileage standards put in place by President Obama.

Scott Pruitt, Trump's EPA head, also questioned the role humans played in global climate change, arguing that there is just too much disagreement on the science of the issue. In tandem with this, Trump's OMB director Mick Mulvaney announced that "we're not spending money on that [climate change] anymore. We consider that to be a waste of your money."[43] Add to this the proposed 31% cut of the EPA budget, and the message is clear: the Trump administration does not consider climate change to be a threat to the U.S. The next shoe to fall? Would Trump pull the U.S. out of the Paris climate accord?

Even before he hit the campaign trail, Trump was a climate change denier. A sample of his pre-presidential tweets (below) reveal a man unwilling to follow the science and one for whom productivity and business competitiveness take precedence over environmental protection. This attitude was converted to government policy when Trump issued a March 28 executive order gutting a number of Obama-era pro-environmental regulations. Trump, claimed that this order "starts a new era of production and job creation" that would end "the theft of property."[44]

In his first 100 days, President Trump has systematically sought to reverse Obama-era environmental policies. From cancelling programs dealing with climate change, to eroding regulations on clean air and water, to opening up the coastline to oil drilling, to dismantling the Clean Power Plan, to halting a plan to increase fuel mileage standards, Trump, along with his EPA chief Scott Pruitt, has given the fossil fuel industries virtually everything they have asked for.[45]

> "In the 1920's people were worried about global cooling-it never happened. Now it's global warming. Give me a break!"[46]

"We can't destroy the competitiveness of our factories in order to prepare for nonexistent global warming. China is thrilled with us!"[47]

"Another freezing day in the Spring—what is going on with 'global warming'? Good move changing the name to 'climate change'—sad!"[48]

"Ice storm rolls from Texas to Tennessee—I'm in Los Angeles and it's freezing. Global warming is a total, and expensive, hoax!"[49]

"We should be focused on clean and beautiful air-not expensive and business closing GLOBAL WARMING-a total hoax!"[50]

"Any and all weather events are used by the GLOBAL WARMING HOAXSTERS to justify higher taxes to save our planet! They don't believe it $$$$!"[51]

The candidate who called climate change a "Chinese hoax" was now the president who promised to "end the war on coal." Reaction was swift and harsh.[52]

OFF TO THE SENATE

On March 30, 2017, the Senate Intelligence Committee opened its hearing into Russian interference in the 2016 U.S. presidential election. In stark contrast to the House, where chair Devin Nunes was engaged in an Opera Bouffe of cloak and dagger missteps, the Senate committee chair Richard Burr (R–North Carolina) and ranking minority member Mark Warner (D–Virginia) took great pains to emphasize their vow to be a bipartisan effort to get to the bottom of Russia's interference in our election.

Bipartisan, perhaps (hopefully), but make no mistake, the Democrats intended to ensure that any Trump associates implicated in the Russia plot were identified. As Senator Warner's opening remarks suggested, the Russians—and perhaps some Trump associates—were under the microscope.[53]

As the hearings were getting underway, new information about "Source D," the person identified as the source of salacious information linked to then private citizen Trump from one of his trips to Moscow, was revealed to be Sergei Millian, president of the Russian American Chamber of Commerce. Millian also told reporters that Mr. Trump had long standing connections to Russian officials and that Trump was given information that proved harmful to the Clinton campaign.[54]

And the noose kept tightening. It was revealed that Russia hired more than 1,000 people to "create fake anti-Hillary news stories targeting key swing states." Senator Warner said:

> We know about the hacking, and selective leaks, but what really concerns me as a former tech guy is at least some reports—and we've got to get to the bottom of this—that there were upwards of a thousand internet trolls working out of a facility in Russia, in effect taking over a series of computers which are then called botnets, that can generate news down to specific areas. It's been reported to me, and we've got to find this out, whether they were able to affect specific areas in Wisconsin, Michigan, Pennsylvania, where you would not have been receiving off of whoever your vendor might have been, Trump versus Clinton, during the waning days of the election, but instead 'Clinton is sick', or 'Clinton is taking money from whoever for some source' ... fake news.[55]

This Is Guatemala (With Apologies to Guatemala)

Events seemed to unfold at warp speed, leaving citizens dizzy from the whirlwind activity. Trump, a self-proclaimed disruptive force, was also a 24/7 action figure, always stirring the political pot. Might this lead to Trump-fatigue, or would this be seen as a mark of leadership?

The tale of Devin Nunes shifted from hire-wire intrigue to pity as the congressman was exposed as sadly over his head in a complex game of "who said what and when." As more information was made public it became clear that Nunes was called to the White House by Trump staffers to view materials that might be interpreted as supportive of the president. Nunes then took his story to the president to inform Trump that he had seen documents that might be useful to the president. He went to see the president before informing his committee. It seemed highly likely that Nunes was being used by the White House to provide the president with some cover. It was later revealed that two of the White House staffers who met with Nunes were Ezra Choen-Watnick, senior director for intelligence at the National Security Council, and Michael J. Ellis, a lawyer serving in the White House counsel's office.

The next day Trump said that he felt "partly vindicated" by the information Nunes had revealed to him—information that the White House already knew but needed a useful stooge to release it.

Calls for Nunes to step down as Intelligence Committee Chair mounted. Nunes was, it seemed, more interested in shielding President Trump than investigating him. In fact, in an interview Nunes admitted that he briefed Trump of his "findings" because the president was taking "heat in the news media."[56] John McCain argued that the Congress no longer had the "credibility to handle this [the investigation] alone."[57]

And in the middle of this, former national security advisor Mike Flynn, through his lawyer, said he would talk *if* he received immunity (it should be noted that during the campaign, Flynn said that people seeking immunity were probably guilty of a crime, a view candidate Trump supported a few days later).

And the Russia story just kept getting hotter and hotter. On March 31, 2017, during a press briefing Trump spokesman Sean Spicer gave what amounted to a three-pronged response to questions about Trump, wiretap claims, and the Russians: 1) Obama did it; 2) Obama did it; and 3) Obama did it.[58]

The old Watergate mantra, "follow the money," was, in 2017 revised to read "follow the *Russian* money." Despite the president's often repeated claims that he did not have any business relationships with Russians, a report by *USA Today* found that ten wealthy Russians and oligarchs from some ex-Soviet republics (some of whom were linked to organized crime) had invested in Trump-brand real estate projects.[59] Absent Trump releasing his tax returns, which Trump refused to do, questions of financial links to Russia persisted.[60]

And the Flynn story wouldn't go away. Flynn failed to disclose—as required by law—payment from Russia and Turkey when he reapplied for a security clearance. Flynn accepted $45,000 in speaking fees from the Russian news network *RT*, and he received over $500,000 for lobbying work on behalf of Turkey. When House Oversight Committee Chairman Jason Chaffetz (Rep–Utah) was asked if Flynn had committed a crime he responded, "I see no data to support the notion that General Flynn complied with the law."[61]

To further complicate the "follow the Russian money" effort, a bank in Cypress was investigating accounts linked to former Trump campaign manager Paul Manafort for possible money laundering. Manafort has been linked to over a dozen banks and 10 companies on Cypress, and one of his companies was paid $1 million by Russian oligarch Oleg Deripaska, an ally of Vladimir Putin. The Associated Press reported that Manafort had a $10 million-a-year consulting contract with Mr. Deripaska in 2006.[62]

Reaping What You Sow

During the campaign, candidate Trump was, on numerous occasions, accused of inciting violence at his rallies when he would say things like "I'd like to punch him [a peaceful protestor] in the face," or " I'll beat the crap out of you," adding, "part of the problem...is nobody wants to hurt each other anymore." He even said he would pay the legal feeds of any of his supporters who faced legal problems when assaulting protestors.[63]

And this list goes on and on. Trump has said he does not condone violence at his rallies, but his sometimes-thuggish rhetoric belies such a claim.

Judge David J. Hale, a federal judge in Kentucky, ruled against the president's attorneys who attempted to get a lawsuit filed against Trump for inciting violence against protestors at his March 2016 Louisville rally, thrown out of court. At the rally, candidate Trump repeatedly said, "get 'em out of here." According to the protestors, they were shoved and punched by Trump supporters. "It is plausible," said Judge Hale "that Trump's direction to 'get 'em out of here' advocated the use of force." Hale added, "It was an order, an instruction, a command."[64]

On April 2, the *Los Angeles Times* published an editorial, written by the newspaper's editorial board, entitled: "Our Dishonest President," the first of what was promised as "first in a series." The editorial opened with:

> it was no secret during the campaign that Donald Trump was a narcissist and a demagogue who used fear and dishonesty to appeal to the worst in American voters. The Times called him unprepared and unsuited for the job he was seeking, and said his election would be a "catastrophe."

> Still, nothing prepared us for the magnitude of this train wreck. Like millions of other Americans, we clung to a slim hope that the new president would turn out to be all noise and bluster, or that the people around him in the White House would act as a check on his worst instincts, or that he would be sobered and transformed by the awesome responsibilities of office.

> Instead, seventy-some days in — and with about 1,400 to go before his term is completed — it is increasingly clear that those hopes were misplaced.

> In a matter of weeks, President Trump has taken dozens of real-life steps that, if they are not reversed, will rip families apart, foul rivers and pollute the air, intensify the calamitous effects of

climate change and profoundly weaken the system of American public education for all.

His attempt to de-insure millions of people who had finally received healthcare coverage and, along the way, enact a massive transfer of wealth from the poor to the rich has been put on hold for the moment. But he is proceeding with his efforts to defang the government's regulatory agencies and bloat the Pentagon's budget even as he supposedly retreats from the global stage.

These are immensely dangerous developments which threaten to weaken this country's moral standing in the world, imperil the planet and reverse years of slow but steady gains by marginalized or impoverished Americans. But, chilling as they are, these radically wrongheaded policy choices are not, in fact, the most frightening aspect of the Trump presidency.

What is most worrisome about Trump is Trump himself. He is a man so unpredictable, so reckless, so petulant, so full of blind self-regard, so untethered to reality that it is impossible to know where his presidency will lead or how much damage he will do to our nation. His obsession with his own fame, wealth and success, his determination to vanquish enemies real and imagined, his craving for adulation — these traits were, of course, at the very heart of his scorched-earth outsider campaign; indeed, some of them helped get him elected. But in a real presidency in which he wields unimaginable power, they are nothing short of disastrous.

The *Times* promised more on topics such as "Trump's shocking lack of respect for those fundamental rules and institutions on which our government is based," "[h]is utter lack of regard for truth," and "[h]is scary willingness to repeat alt-right conspiracy theories, racist memes and crackpot, out-of-the mainstream ideas."[65]

THE SYSTEM IS WORKING, OR IS IT?

President Trump is no autocrat—he is being hemmed in by a system of checks and balances, which he finds frustrating. The courts have blocked him on several fronts, the Congress is not his personal rubber stamp, the media (free press) has been a thorn in his side, the Democrats have pushed back, and the bureaucracy seems to have given Trump some trouble in executing what he wants. One could say that the institutions of American government are alive and well, and doing their job. So, did Trump change the presidency, or did the presidency change Trump?

Seemingly driven by a need to prove himself, by deep insecurities and by a narcissistic streak, an unquenchable need for validation, adoration, even love, Trump was not interested in the details of governing and focused on his own aura and identity. He reacts quickly, emotionally, and often with great hostility. Trump lacks the control and self-discipline of a mature leader. He runs the risk of becoming a Saturday Night Live characterization of himself. Thus far, Trump has had to adjust more to the office than he has been able to bend the office to his will.

A BIG PLUS FOR THE PRESIDENT

It took the "nuclear option" on April 6, 2017, when the United States Senate overturned a Senate tradition, which had been standing for more than a century, and confirmed the nomination of Neil M. Gorsuch, President Trump's first Supreme Court nominee. The Senate rules had to be changed in the middle of the game from the 60-vote requirement to a simple majority for confirmation (thus the reference to "the nuclear option"), and this further divided an already deeply divided Senate, but in the end Gorsuch was confirmed.

Gorsuch was confirmed in a 54-45 vote, with only three Democrats—Joe Donnelly of Indiana, Heidi Heitkamp of North Dakota, and Joe Manchin of West Virginia—joining the Republicans in favor of Gorsuch.[66] It was a big win for President Trump.

Tensions Continue

Adding fuel to already-flaming partisan fires, on April 10, 2017, a federal judge in Texas ruled that the Texas voter-identification law, which the Texas legislature passed in 2011 to suppress minority voting, had indeed been deliberately designed to do precisely that—limit Black and Hispanic voters from voting. The Texas law, among the most restrictive in the nation, violated the federal Civil Rights Act, and put more pressure on the federal government to put state electoral procedures under federal oversight.

Tensions with North Korea kept mounting as in response to ongoing missiles testing by the North Koreans, the administration sent a U.S. naval strike group (warships) toward the Korean peninsula. The government of North Korea issued a series of warnings, calling the U.S. move dangerous and provocative, and promised to counter this "reckless act of aggression" with a massive retaliation should the U.S. act militarily against North Korea.

The U.S. kept trying to get China—North Korea's chief sponsor—to intervene and compel their "client state" to pull back on its development of nuclear strike capabilities, but the Chinese—concerned about possible growing U.S. influence in the region—kept propping up the government of North Korea as a buffer against U.S. influence in the region. Also, it is not clear that China, even if it so desired, could force North Korea to back down.

During the campaign, candidate Trump would repeatedly attack President Obama for playing golf when he should have been governing. As one tweet noted, "President Obama is not busy talking to Congress about Syria...he is playing golf...go figure." And he kept up his assault on Obama's golf games with such campaign attacks as "I'm not gonna have time to play golf," and "If I were in the White House, I don't think I'd ever see Turnberry (Trump's golf course) again. I'd just want to stay in the White House and work my ass off."[67]

But as president, Trump sang, and played, a different tune. He played golf about 20 times in his first 100 days, and the cost of Trump family personal travel (paid for by the taxpayers) was, at day 100, on the road to being costlier in his first year as president, than the Obama family racked up in eight years in the White House.[68] As Mr. Trump might say, "go figure."

HUMAN RIGHTS TAKES A HIT AND U.S. PRISONERS ARE FREED

On April 3, 2017, President Trump hosted Egyptian president Abdel Fatah el-Sissi at the White House. El-Sissi's visit marked a reversal of U.S. policy during the Obama presidency as Trump's predecessor refused to invite el-Sissi due to human rights concerns. But Trump saw things differently.

> "I just want to let everybody know, in case there was any doubt, that we are very much behind President el-Sissi...He's done a fantastic job in a very difficult situation. We are very much behind Egypt and the people of Egypt... we have strong backing."[69]

Trump and el-Sissi did not discuss human rights during the visit, signaling a dramatic shift in policy with Trump "systematically dismantling" a forty-year-old bipartisan tradition of U.S. foreign policy.

As Doyle McManus noted:

> Walking away from human rights is a sign of weakness, not strength. It's consistent with Trump's view that the United States is 'a crippled country,' a superpower that can no longer pull its weight. It's a retreat from American exceptionalism; it means we think we no longer have the capability to think much beyond a narrow conception of American interests.[70]

Shortly after Trump hosted el-Sissi in the White House, Egypt released a U.S. charity worker Aya Hijazi, her husband, and four others who were imprisoned in Cairo on charges of child abuse and trafficking. It was a needed victory for an administration hard pressed for good news on the foreign front.

As the World Turns

On April 5, 2017, King Abdullah of Jordan visited the White House, and the following day Chinese President Xi Jinping met Trump in Florida. While the meetings did not yield any major announcements, the outsider Trump used these opportunities to get to know these foreign leaders.

Battles inside the Trump White House continued to plague the president as the vicious internal politics kept going public, making the president appear weak and unable to manage his own team. By early April the battle royale was between Steve Bannon and President Trump's son-in-law Jared Kushner. As a sign of his waning influence, Trump removed Bannon from the National Security Council and sent Kushner on a very public trip to Iraq, in effect replacing Bannon with Kushner as the top policy voice in the White House.

Kushner was also given responsibility for attaining a peace deal between Israel and the Palestinians, heading negotiations with China and Mexico, plus "reinventing government" according to business principles. The Chinese press took to calling Kushner the "princeling."[71]

Bombs in Syria

The ongoing war in Syria pitting the Assad regime against ISIS fighters as well as rebels was a confused mess. Russia and Iran backed Assad; the U.S. didn't. But as Assad weakened, would ISIS rise?

On April 4, 2017, the U.S. accused Syria's president Bashar Assad of using chemical weapons against his own people in a rebel held town of Kahn Sheikhoun of Syria.

Two days later, President Trump issued the order for U.S. Tomahawk cruise missiles to bomb an airfield in Syria in response to Assad's use of poison gas.

> "Assad choked out the lives of helpless men, women and children," Trump said. "Even beautiful babies were cruelly murdered in this very barbaric attack. No child of God should ever suffer such horror. Tonight I ordered a targeted military strike on the airfield in Syria from where the chemical attack was launched," adding "it is in this vital national security interest of the United States to prevent and deter the spread and use of deadly chemical weapons."[72]

The bombing of Syria was a reversal of Trump's hands-off policy and his reluctance to get involved in Syria. Trump's about-face had limited military utility but sent a message. And while administration officials were quick to point out that the attack was a "one-and-done" event, the threat of further U.S. military strikes nonetheless were put on the table.

But the air strikes reversed not only Trump's policy to stay out of the Middle East militarily, it was also a reversal towards the Assad regime itself. Prior to this, the Trump administration repeatedly said they would not support the Obama policy of seeking Assad's removal. Assad's fate, said Secretary of State Rex Tillerson, "will be decided by the Syrian people."[73]

After the attack, the administration went to great lengths to demand that Russia cease its support for Assad.

"I hope Russia is thinking carefully about its continued alliance with Bashar al-Assad, because every time one of these horrific attacks occurs, it draws Russia closer into some level of responsibility," Tillerson said on ABC's "This Week."[74]

Deeper into Russia

Facing intense pressure from both Democrats and Republicans, Devin Nunes, Chairman of the House Intelligence Committee, stepped down as the head of the inquiry. Nunes announced his recusal just minutes before the House Ethics Committee said it was opening a review of whether Nunes broke House rules when he revealed that U.S. intelligence agencies may have picked up some information on Trump associates in relation to the Russia inquiry. Republican House member K. Michael Conaway of Texas took over leadership of the Committee.

As the drama of the House Committee continued, *The Washington Post* reported on a potential bombshell:

> An American executive with ties to Trump and a Russian close to Putin held a secret meeting in a remote location in January, purportedly to establish an unofficial back-channel line of communication between Moscow and the incoming Trump White House. The meeting took place between Erik Prince, founder of security firm Blackwater and brother of education secretary Betsy Devos, and a Putin associate on the Seychelles Islands in the Indian Ocean around January 11, nine days before Trump's inauguration.[75]

If this were true, it would be yet another strand tying Trump and his campaign team closer to the charges of collusion with the Russians. And that was not all. A week later, it was reported that during the campaign, the FBI had obtained a secret FISA (Foreign Intelligence Surveillance Act) order to monitor Donald Trump's adviser on foreign affairs Carter Page for his alleged ties to Russia. *The Washington Post* reported that

> Law enforcement officials obtained the warrant after "convincing a Foreign Intelligence Surveillance Court judge that there was a probable cause to believe Page was acting as an agent of a foreign power, in this case Russia,' our colleagues wrote. Page has not been accused of any crimes, and has repeatedly denied any wrongdoing. Still, news that the FBI obtained a FISA warrant to monitor his communications is significant—it's the clearest evidence so far that

the FBI had reason to believe someone from the Trump campaign was in touch with Russian agents.[76]

Closer and closer; step by step. Would this trail come to an abrupt end, or would it move up the Trump chain of command?

POLICY WHIPLASH

By mid-April, President Trump had done so many 180-degree turns on policy that it was hard to keep up with the changing policies. About-faces abounded: Russia was now a huge irritant and China was our friend —the opposite of the Trump message for over a year; NATO, declared "obsolete" by candidate Trump was "no longer obsolete"; China, whom Trump claimed would be declared a "currency manipulator" now wasn't manipulating currency; "lock her up"—no longer.

As the dust settled on the Trump policy whiplash, analysts began to argue that perhaps the wild, brash Trump of the campaign trail was giving in to the realities of governing, that his shifting positions signaled a reluctant admission that governing in the real world was hard and complex, and that perhaps the seasoned experts might actually have a great deal to contribute. Of course, this irked many Trump voters who like that he snubbed his nose at the establishment and defied conventional answers for a new brand of leadership. Was Trump becoming a card-carrying member of the elite establishment he so often trashed?

While dropping MOAB ("the mother of all bombs") in Afghanistan was vintage Trump (the biggest, the best), the use of force in the region was a grudging admission that perhaps the experts actually knew what they were talking about and should be listened to. Likewise, the limited bombing strike in Syria in response to Assad's use of chemical weapons was measured, limited, prompt, and judicious—everything Trump's campaign rhetoric opposed.[77]

Backpedaling from his isolationist, America First rhetoric, also allowed Trump to recognize the importance of NATO ("it is no longer obsolete") and the need to, at times, bring allies to our side. Even Trump's shift on North Korea marked a move towards the mainstream.

And Yes, Money Matters

While Donald Trump personally financed much of his presidential race, after his election victory, the traditional big-donors scrambled to gain favor—and influence—with the new administration. For example, Las Vegas casino magnate Sheldon G. Adelson, who wants the Trump administration to ban online poker (which competes with his casinos for profits) and move the U.S. Embassy in Israel to Jerusalem, gave a record $5 million to Trump's inaugural committee—the largest gift ever given to a president for the inauguration. For this, Adelson got ready access to the new president and was seated near the Trump family during the inauguration.[78]

Other big-ticket donors who do business with government—especially businesses such as telecommunications, tobacco, and the pharmaceutical industry—were also generous to Trump. Additionally, five NFL team owners gave $1 million each; and the Bank of America, Pfizer, and Dow Chemical each gave $1 million.

The Trump inauguration committee raised a record $107 million, twice as much as any inauguration in history. As inaugural fundraising is largely unregulated, the only restrictions imposed are self-regulations. The George W. Bush Committee capped gifts at $100,000 in his 2001 inauguration, and at $250,000 for the 2005 inauguration. the Barack Obama committee limited gifts to $50,000 and banned gifts from lobbyists and corporations. In 2013 the Obama committee accepted corporate gifts up to $1 million, and individual gifts were capped at $250,000. The Trump committee had no such restrictions.

THE RUSSIA CONNECTION

The investigation into alleged Trump team connections to Russia morphed into a quiet, information-gathering phase. Out of the headlines, the House and Senate committees continued to look into the evidence of collusion, and the three big targets were former Trump campaign manager Paul Manafort, former Trump national security advisor Michael Flynn, and former campaign foreign policy advisor Carter Page. All three, in one way or another, received substantial payments from Russia either directly or indirectly.

The FBI was alerted to some of the potential Trump campaign problems in the summer of 2016, when the bureau obtained a secret FISA court order to monitor Carter Page's communications. This meant that the FBI and Justice Department believed they had—and the FISA court agreed —"probable cause" that a crime was being committed. The crime? Acting as an agent of a foreign government (Russia).[79]

TRANSPARENTLY NONTRANSPARENT

In mid-April, the Trump administration announced that it would end the practice of releasing visitor logs to the White House.[80] So much for open government and transparency. With this act, the administration made it difficult, and in many cases impossible, for the public to know who has access to the White House, who is personally lobbying government officials, and who has the ear of the president.

Trump spokespersons said the logs would not be released so as to 1) protect the privacy of those visiting the White House and 2) for (unspecified) national security purposes. This approach protects Trump but threatens democratic transparency. It is hard to keep the government accountable when we don't know who is meeting with administration officials.

Staff Chaos and Infighting

There seemed to be much chaos the White House. Trump was late in nominating numerous people both to his staff and the agencies, but also to the federal courts. The administration was running on two, not eight cylinders. Understaffed and poorly managed, Team Trump also continued to face serious conflict-of-interest charges as the few new people being brought in came mostly from lobbying firms (thus adding to, not draining the swamp) and industry consultants—the opposite of what Trump promised in the campaign.[81]

On July 21, 2017, White House press secretary Sean Spicer resigned after telling President Trump he vehemently disagreed with his appointment of Anthony Scaramucci, a New York financier, as his new communications director.[82] A week later, reporter Ryan Lizza received a phone call from Scaramucci, asking about who told him about Scaramucci's dinner at the White House with President Trump, the First Lady, Sean Hannity, and the former Fox News executive Bill Shine. Scaramucci threatened to fire anyone who leaked information and then went down his list of suspects. He asked Lizza if it was Reince Priebus.

> "Reince is a fucking paranoid schizophrenic, a paranoiac," Scara-mucci said. He channelled Priebus as he spoke: "'Oh, Bill Shine is coming in. Let me leak the fucking thing and see if I can cock-block these people the way I cock-blocked Scaramucci for six months.'"[83]

About Steve Bannon, Lizza reported that:

> Scaramucci also told me that, unlike other senior officials, he had no interest in media attention. "I'm not Steve Bannon, I'm not trying to suck my own cock," he said, speaking of Trump's chief strategist. "I'm not trying to build my own brand off the fucking strength of the President. I'm here to serve the country."[84]

Most leaders would be very unhappy with Scaramucci's behavior, but what President Trump was reportedly unhappy about was Priebus not fighting back.[85] Such infighting and clearly unhealthy competition was also reportedly encouraged—White House press secretary Sarah Huckabee Sanders said "The president likes that type of competition and encourages it."[86].

A TURN TO FOREIGN POLICY

With little to show in domestic policy, the administration turned to matters abroad in search of policy victories. The administration engaged in tough rhetoric regarding North Korea and Iran, tried to enlist the assistance of China in getting North Korea to halt nuclear testing, and continued to jawbone on trade.

Presidents, as they get rebuffed or frustrated in dealing with Congress on domestic matters, often turn to foreign affairs, an area where they exercise greater independent authority. With fewer internal constraints, presidents feel they have more latitude and power in conducting foreign policy. But foreign policy victories often prove elusive. Sometimes plans backfire and can go wrong. Foreign policy is higher risk but also higher reward.

President Trump does not to seem to have a strategy to guide foreign policy actions. His has been mostly a reactive approach, responding to events yet signaling no strategic cohesion. His response starts with bluster and bellicose rhetoric, moves to aggressive military threats, backing away which suggests a false bravado, then an administration speaking with conflicting, even contradictory voices, followed by a shift to the next problem de jure. For example, as of July 29, 2017, gone was the 'the conciliatory and at times fawning language Trump has used to refer to President Xi, whom he has repeatedly hailed as a "terrific guy" and a "great leader" with whom he enjoys "great chemistry".[87] President Trump tweeted: "I am very disappointed in China. Our foolish past leaders have allowed them to make hundreds of billions of dollars a year in trade, yet..."[88] As Dali Yang, an expert in Chinese politics from the

University of Chicago, noted: "This is the president running his foreign policy by tweeting again."[89]

FROM HANDS OFF TO INTERVENTION

Candidate Trump wanted an "America First" approach that would reduce the U.S. footprint across the globe. His view was that interventions were bad and we should focus on solving our problems at home. But it wasn't long before the world came knocking on America's door, and the president decided to answer.

The threat of a North Korea, headed by Kim Jong-un, armed with nuclear weapons that might soon be able to reach the U.S. homeland, was too dangerous to allow. Trump pressured China to influence North Korea, Vice President Mike Pence toured South Korea and the Pacific constantly issuing public warnings that if China doesn't stop the North Koreans, "we will." Pence added "the era of strategic patience is over."[90] But what to do? Trump boasted about sending "an armada" to the Korean peninsula, but his sabre rattling proved embarrassing when it was revealed that the aircraft carrier *U.S. Carl Vinson* was actually headed in the opposite direction.[91] Bravado, not-so-veiled threats, public proclamations were no replacement for an actual policy, and Trump appeared dazed and confused.

To demonstrate his toughness and punish Syria's troubled dictator Bashar Al-Assad for using chemical weapons, Trump twice bombed Syria—a place where during the campaign Trump said was "none of our business."[92] But Trump's ventures overseas seemed to be reactive. It was unclear what Trump's actual approach on policy was. Improvisational and reactive strikes are one thing, a strategic approach quite another. Was Trump a foreign policy interventionist or hands-off? Was the U.S. the leader of the West or was President Trump leading the U.S. into retreating from global leadership?

THE HIGH COST OF IGNORANCE

If a little knowledge can be a dangerous thing, a whole lot of ignorance can sink the ship of state. Voters knew that candidate Donald J. Trump was, to put it politely, a novice on foreign affairs. But as president his ignorance of the world can come at a high price. A prime example can be seen in President Trump's mishandling of the Korean crises, as well as his misunderstanding of the region's history, politics, and cultural sensitivities.

Tensions between North Korea and South Korea, two countries still technically in a state of war, heated up when President Trump, in his effort to halt the development of North Korea's nuclear weapons program, enlisted the help of China to influence North Korea. In discussions with President Xi Jinping, the Chinese leader gave President Trump a history lesson on Chinese-Korean relations. The problem was that Xi's version of history was "skewed" and that President Trump did not realize this.[93] Trump took the Chinese president's words as true and reliable, and when a few days later Trump parroted Xi's error it caused a South Korean backlash. In an effort to explain his approach to the North-South conflict, Trump told the *Wall Street Journal* that Xi "went into the history of China and Korea."[94] Not North Korea, "Korea." Then Trump added "And you know, you're talking about thousands of years...and many wars. And Korea actually used to be a part of China"[95]—not according to our South Korean allies.

Trump presented the Chinese version of events, angered and insulted our ally, and sparked a strong response from South Korea. A representative of South Korean's Foreign Affairs Ministry Cho June-Hyuck responded with:

> It is a clear historical fact recognized by the international community, which cannot be denied by anyone, that Korea was not a part of China over the past several thousands of years of history of Korea-China relations.[96]

SCRAMBLING FOR A WIN AT THE ELEVENTH HOUR

With day 90 passing and no major legislative victories to point to, the Trump White House began to panic. They desperately went in search of a 100-day prize. They revisited the repeal-and-replace promise on Obamacare, looked again for a tax deal, anything that they might point to on day 100 that could be portrayed as a victory.

The bold promises were not bearing fruit. All the "on day one I will" assurances proved empty promises. This president was stumbling towards day 100 with little to show for it.

THE BIG TRUMP LETDOWN

He promised. "I alone can do it".[97] But at the 100-day mark, the inevitable conclusion is that Trump overpromised and underachieved.

After raising expectations and making bold day-one and 100-day promises, Trump had little to show. And after the 100-day expectations hit snag after snag, Trump retreated, tweeting on April 21, 2017 at 3:50AM:

> No matter how much I accomplish during the ridiculous standard of the first 100 days, & it has been a lot (including S.C.) media will kill.[98]

In terms of Trump's campaign promises and the 100-day assurances of multiple major policy shifts, Trump accomplished very little. No major laws were enacted, he had embarrassing no legislative reform and tax change, and while he continued to talk big, he governed little. Most of Trump's many executive orders are without teeth, merely calling for this agency to revise that policy and review this law. He has few tangible policy changes as a result of such orders. After 100 days, he had very little to show for his efforts.

Table 13. Trump's Track Record.

Wins	Losses	Still Waiting
Gorsuch-Supreme Court	Repeal & Replace	Build a Wall
Required "Nuclear Option"	Travel Ban	Have Mexico Pay for Wall
Out of TPP	Tax Reform	Iran Nuclear Deal
Deportations Up	Financial Scandals	
Executive Orders (mostly symbolic)	Russian Meddling	
	Unfilled Government Posts	

Source. Compiled by author.

In the first 100 days, Trump rushed out a Muslim ban that got reversed in the courts; he had to fire his first national security advisor; he failed at repealing and replacing Obamacare; and his popularity dropped in some polls to the mid-30% range.[99]

President Trump ended his first 100 days with the lowest popularity scores ever recorded. At day 100, President Kennedy had a Gallup approval rating of 83%, President Eisenhower was at 73%, President Reagan at 68%, and President Obama at 65%. On day 100 Donald Trump was at 40%, with some polls showing that he even dropped to the mid-30s.[100]

ANOTHER JUDICIAL SETBACK

The new president's track record with the courts took another hit on April 25 when Judge William H. Orrick of United States District Court placed a nationwide hold on the president's order that would withhold federal funds from "sanctuary cities" that refused to fully cooperate with immigration officials. This was a setback for Trump. As Judge Orrick noted, "The Constitution vests the spending powers in Congress, not the president, so the order cannot constitutionally place new conditions on federal funds."[101]

This was the third time in only the first 100 days that courts had blocked a Trump order. This is unprecedented. Ordinarily, if the courts get involved, it comes late in the process, not this early.

FIRST MEXICO, NOW CANADA!

The United States has been fortunate to have relatively safe borders. With the Atlantic Ocean to the east, the Pacific to the west, and nonthreatening neighbors to our north (Canada) and south (Mexico), the U.S. has not faced hostile entities breathing down our throat. This is a luxury few nations enjoy. So why employ policies designed to jeopardize such a good thing?

First it was attacks against Mexico (they're sending rapists and criminals; we're going to build a wall; Mexico will pay for the wall), and in late April it was a looming trade war with Canada. Our friendly neighbors to the north came under fire from the president over U.S. dairy prices and over the cost of lumber. The president, seeing an easy target for a "get tough on trade stance" imposed a 20–24% tariff on "soft lumber" from Canada.[102] Alienating friends and neighbors is an unusual way to go, especially given the historical importance of having borders that are relatively safe and secure.

A SHUTDOWN?

Was a government shutdown in the cards? It appeared so until President Trump backed away from his demand that money be included to build "the wall." With that out of the way, Democrats and Republicans in Congress seemed poised to pass a temporary spending bill.

Congress members from both parties balked at including funding to build a wall that Mexico, according to Trump, was supposed to pay for. Trump had a choice: back down on the demand or force a government shutdown. Trump caved. It was yet another failure to deliver on a key campaign promise.

On Wednesday, April 26, 2017, the president proposed a massive cut in the corporate tax rate, hoping to drop it from 35% to 15%. No mention was made of how Trump intended to offset the massive loss of tax dollars. The administration rolled out the president's tax plan—which fit on one page—but refused to provide details or guarantee that the changes would be revenue neutral. Was this PR or a serious proposal designed to suggest that the administration was serious about reform?

Trump's one-page tax reform plan, upon closer inspection, appeared to be poorly thought out. It was estimated the plan, if adopted, would 1) increase the deficit by between 3 to 7 trillion dollars over the next decade;[103] 2) and overwhelmingly benefit the wealthy.[104] This deficit increase went against his promises to eliminate national debt,[105] and did not seem to "provide massive tax relief for the middle class" as promised, according to a Forbes report[106] The report also noted that according to the Tax Policy Center, "of the $6.2 trillion in cuts, the richest 1% will enjoy 47% of those cuts, or nearly $3 trillion over ten years. The middle class, however—should we choose to define it as those taxpayers in the wealthiest 20% to 80% of the population—would receive only 20% of the tax cuts *combined*."[107] The report further added: "From a percentage perspective, while the middle class will experience a 1–2% increase in after-tax income, the richest 20% will see a 6.6% rise, while the top 1% will have 14.2% more after-tax income under the Trump plan as compared to current law."[108]

Another broken 100-day promise centered on the North America Free Trade Agreement (NAFTA). As a presidential candidate, Trump promised to tear up the "worst trade deal, maybe ever signed anywhere, but certainly ever signed in this country," but as president, he backed away from that pledge and merely spoke of "renegotiating…"[109] A Bloomberg Businessweek report noted that "Donald Trump has gone squishy by stages on [NAFTA],"[110] and further noted:

many provisions the administration is seeking in a new Nafta were negotiated into the Trans-Pacific Partnership—ironic, since one of Trump's first acts was to pull the U.S. out of it. Among those provisions: unfettered cross-border data flows; regulatory harmonization; stronger labor and environmental standards; and a ban on currency manipulation (which Canada and Mexico don't do anyway). "He's taking Nafta and making it look more like the TPP but with fewer countries," says Todd Tucker, a fellow at the Roosevelt Institute, a think tank in New York.[111]

When asked to identify Trump's 100-day accomplishments, press secretary Sean Spicer cited three successes: a decline in the number of people crossing the U.S.-Mexican border illegally, signing more than thirty executive orders, and the confirmation of Neil Gorsuch to the Supreme Court.

It is true that in the first 100 days, President Trump signed many executive orders—more than any president since the end of World War II. Trump has signed thirty-two executive orders, whereas Obama signed only nineteen, George W. Bush eleven, and Clinton thirteen. Ironically, Trump himself has criticized Obama for issuing executive orders, tweeting "Why is @BarackObama constantly issuing executive orders that are major power grabs of authority?"[112] And while most of Trump's orders called for studies related to enforcement of already-existing laws or regulations, Trump was unable to move Congress to adopt or pass any key legislative victories.

Trump's executive orders have been about undoing, not doing. They repeal previous orders but do not replace them or seek major policy changes. It has been motion over accomplishment. Major changes ran through Congress, and although Trump has Republican majorities in both Houses, he has had no key legislative victories in his first 100 days, with the exception of Neil Gorsuch's being confirmed to the Supreme Court.

When Gorsuch was sworn in on April 10, 2017, it was "the biggest accomplishment of President Donald Trump's early presidency," which

Trump acknowledged was not easy. During his address, he said, "And I got it done in the first 100 days," adding "You think that's easy?"[113]

Shadowing these successes, however, were many other issues, from unfilled key positions to major issues of foreign affairs.

Administratively, Trump was exceedingly slow to nominate people to key government posts. On day 100, many important offices remained unfilled, with more than 500 top posts unfilled, many without even a nominee submitted for the position.[114] In the three months that followed, President Trump continued in his exceedingly slow appointment pace, leaving top positions in state, defense, and other key agencies empty.

On day 100, we also saw how the noose was tightening around Mike Flynn's neck. Members of the House investigating committee were openly talking about how Flynn had "broken the law." The drip-drip-drip of the Russia story just wouldn't stop.

If Trump has lost support from voters in general, his voters—those who made up the 46.1% of voters who chose Trump—have remained supportive of him in his early days as president. The average approval rating for modern presidents at the 100-day mark is 69%. At day 100, Trump hovered at around 40%, roughly 30 points below the average.

UPPING THE ANTE IN NORTH KOREA

As North Korea continued to develop and test nuclear weapons, the U.S. facing a growing threat, shifted gears and upped the pressure on North Korea, hoping to pressure China into getting Kim Jong-un to cease development of these weapons. China complied minimally, and North Korea kept on with its weapons development.

The Trump plan was to talk tough (the president warned that there could be a "major, major conflict" with North Korea[115]) and put diplomatic pressure (Secretary of State Tillerson appealed to the UN and to China to up pressure on North Korea) on Kim Jong-un in hopes they would back down. The United States publicly announced they were not interested in "regime change" in North Korea, hoping Kim Jong-un might feel less threatened and less in need of developing his nuclear capacity.

Kim Jong-un called Trump's bluff (if it were indeed a bluff). On April 28, 2017, North Korea launched yet another ballistic test missile. It was in open defiance to President Trump's threat of "a major, major conflict" with North Korea.

Part of the dilemma facing the U.S. was that they were trying to conduct foreign policy shorthanded. As day 100 approached, more than 200 State Department posts were unfilled, most without even a nominee. It is hard enough to govern with a full team, but to enter the game with half a team can only mean that the administration is not at peak performance.[116]

The opening act of the Trump presidency ended with little of substance to show for it. Trump utterly dominated the media, but he was unable to convert this attention into power. He gave the people "bread and circuses"[117] but little of substance. He was popular with his base, but overall his approval ratings set a record low. Would this be the all-show, no-go presidency or could Trump turn things around?

THE STRETCH RUN

With less than one week remaining for the 100-day standard, the Trump administration needed to pull out more victories to show. Trump pressed Congress to revisit, repeal, and replace; he pushed hard for something to be done on taxes; and he exercised in government shutdown brinksmanship by demanding that Congress include in its temporary funding bill that would prevent on April 27 a government shutdown, that $5 billion be earmarked to begin to "build the wall."

With little to show for the first 100 days, the president held a rally in Harrisburg, Pennsylvania, on April 29, 2017.[118] Although his approval ratings are the lowest of any president in modern times at this point in his presidency, Trump's loyalists have largely remained in support of the president.[119] They turned out for the rally, but Trump's base—if committed to Trump—remained too small to build a genuine governing coalition.

BLAMING OBAMA...AGAIN

It is customary for a newly minted president to blame his predecessor for, well, just about everything, and in this, Donald J. Trump was no exception. However, this became so bad that President Trump actually blamed President Obama for the Flynn fiasco. During the Obama years, Flynn was vetted and given the green light for a high-level job during the Obama presidency.

When Trump took office, he selected Flynn as his national security advisor. Every nominee is supposed to go through a vetting process regardless of who they are or in what positions they had previously served. Team Trump failed to vet Flynn properly, and this sloppy mistake led to Flynn taking one of the top posts in the new Trump administration. But even a cursory vetting should have revealed Flynn's ties to Russia. According to Trump, "General Flynn was given the highest security clearance by the Obama Administration,"[120] but it was later revealed that former acting attorney general Sally Yates had informed the White House counsel on January 26, 2017, that Flynn was possibly compromised in his dealings with Russia because he had lied about the nature of the conversations, and the White House also acknowledged that President Barack Obama had warned Trump not to choose Flynn as national security adviser.[121]

KINDA REPEAL, SORTA REPLACE...OH, FORGET IT!

To try to score a victory for the 100-day standard, President Trump also revisited repealing and replacing Obamacare in hopes of getting Congress to pass something that at least looked like a repeal of Obamacare. But after hours of debate, discussion, and presidential pressure, talks collapsed and Trump was faced with yet another broken promise and failed deal.

The Republicans in Congress voted to repeal Obamacare over fifty times while Obama, a Democrat, was in the White House. But with a Republican president, their efforts failed to produce results.

But where Trump failed to get Congress to act, he still had "the pen," and on day 100, President Trump signed an executive order to relax restrictions on offshore drilling. What was a nightmare for environmentalists was a boom to the oil industry.

"I Thought It Would Be Easier"

As the 100 days came to a close, President Trump made an astonishing admission. Reflecting on his first 100 days, Trump said of the presidency, "I thought it would be easier."[122]

What is one to make of such a statement? What does that say about Donald Trump, the man and the president? Could he really have harbored the illusion that the job would be a breeze for him? That the man who claimed to "know more than the generals" could just step in and govern? As I've written about elsewhere, "being President is rocket science."[123] If it were easy, past presidents would have been much more successful. Governing is hard!

During the campaign, candidate Trump highlighted the 100-day standard as a spotlight illuminating all that he promised to accomplish. But as the importance of the 100-day mark approached, President Trump downplayed the importance of 100 days, calling it "a false standard." Yet, in spite of paltry accomplishments, Trump claimed that "I don't think that there is a presidential period of time in the first 100 days where anyone has done nearly what we've been able to do."[124]

What the First 100 Days Tells Us
About the Trump Presidency

In spite of all the big promises, there were only modest achievements. There was plenty of action but few positive results. The first 100 days reveal a troubled as well as troubling presidency. Governing, as Trump admitted, "is hard."

Arbitrary though the 100-day measurement might be, every new president is judged by this standard, and they know this going in. Comparisons of President Trump to his predecessor on day 100 are not flattering to Trump. While his party controls both Houses of Congress, he is the first president since Jimmy Carter not to sign a major piece of legislation. His approval rating is the lowest at this stage, and his administration is plagued by confusion and infighting. This is decidedly not a good start.

Trump did set the bar rather high by announcing his "contract with the American Voters," in which he listed ten pieces of legislation he would pass by day 100. In the end, this turned out to be high on theatrics but low on performance.

His experience as a businessman hurt more than it helped him. For all his adult life, Trump was the boss, but the boss of a family business. He was not a corporate executive who had to answer to and sometimes obey a board of directors. He was accustomed to having his way.

So much promised, so little achieved. Wheels spinning, getting nowhere. Like a hamster constantly running on a wheel in a cage, Trump moved frantically yet made little progress.

And during the first 100 days, Trump flip-flopped on many of his campaign promises. Does this suggest that Trump is a nonideological pragmatist or a self-centered, self-promoter, interested in "winning" however defined? What, we can still ask, are Trump's core beliefs?

During the campaign, he sold himself as "a winner," painting a dystopian picture of America and asserting the "I alone can fix it." The self-labelled "great dealmaker," however, had a hard time making deals in our hyperpartisan world of fragmented and dispersed powers. Sometimes, Congress or the Courts or the bureaucracy just wouldn't give him his deal.

Plagued by a series of rookie errors and missteps, several scandals, a series of unforced errors and self-inflicted wounds, the first 100 days of the Trump presidency has demonstrated an amateurish approach to governing. Fareed Zakaria's characterization of the Trump administration as a "rocking horse presidency," a lot of back-and-forth motion, but no movement, aptly captures the early stages of the Trump presidency.[125]

According to RealClearPolitics, on Day 100 (April 29, 2017), Trump's approval ratings was 43.1%, which is not that much of a drop from Day 1's approval rating of 44.3%. However, on July 31, 2017, Trump's approval rating had tumbled down to 39.3%.[126]

How bad was it? David Gergen, who served presidents Nixon, Ford, Reagan, and Clinton, said that "this may be the worst 100 days we've ever seen in a president," and Republican strategist Steve Schmidt said that "no administration has ever been off to a worse 100-day start."[127]

It was a rough start for President Trump, but other presidents (e.g., Jimmy Carter, Bill Clinton) got off to rough starts too. Carter never recovered; Clinton did. What did Trump need to do to recover?

In a recorded message, President Trump gave himself high grades for his first 100 days, insisting that he had "just about the most successful in our nation's history."[128]

On the evening of April 29, 2017, Trump's 100th day in office, two events occurred that speak volumes to our understanding of the Trump presidency: the White House Correspondent's dinner and a campaign-style rally held by the president in Harrisburg, Pennsylvania.

Table 14. 100 Days.

Year	President	% Approval	% Disapproval	% No Opinion	Initial Approval	% Change
1953	Dwight D. Eisenhower	73	10	17	68	5
1961	John Kennedy	83	5	12	72	11
1969	Richard Nixon	62	15	23	59	3
1977	Jimmy Carter	63	18	19	66	-3
1981	Ronald Reagan	68	21	11	51	17
1989	George Bush	56	22	22	51	5
1993	William J. Clinton	55	37	8	58	-3
2001	George W. Bush	62	29	9	57	5
2009	Barack Obama	65	29	6	68	-3
2017	Donald Trump	40	55	5	45	-5

Source. The American Presidency Project, Presidential Job Approval Ratings Following the First 100 Days.

The correspondent's dinner is an American tradition. Proceeds from the dinner go to student scholarships. The dinner is an event when the elite of Washington gather to see and be seen, and to engage in humorous give and take between the host, usually a noted comedian, and the president, who tries to give as good as he takes. The evening is much anticipated and often hilarious. The president sits on the dais while from the podium, people take comedic pot shots at him. Then, it is the president's turn. Some presidents demonstrated a real knack for humor (e.g., Obama and Reagan); others know the secret to making people laugh, and this evening the president showed us he could keep a secret.

The exceedingly thin-skinned Donald Trump broke a longstanding presidential tradition and was a no-show for the 103rd White House Correspondents' Dinner. A few years earlier, President Obama launched into a series of jokes directed at Donald Trump, who was in the audience. Trump had been attacking Obama as having not been born in the U.S. (the birther movement). And Obama skewered Trump. Visibly upset, Trump was humiliated by the president and vowed his revenge (and getting elected president and dismantling Obama's legacy is pretty good revenge).

But the event revealed just how fragile was Trump's ego. He could dish it out, verbally assaulting Marco Rubio ("little Marco"), Ted Cruz ("Lyin' Ted") Elizabeth Warren ("Pocahontas"), and Hillary Clinton (Crooked Hillary), but he could not take it. And rather than face his critics, he bailed. He was the first president to skip the dinner in thirty-six years (Ronald Reagan did not attend because he was recovering from an assassination attempt). Trump's no-show was very telling about Trump.

The second noteworthy event of that evening was the rally Trump held in Harrisburg, Pennsylvania to mark his hundredth day on office. Like his inaugural address, it was an insult directed at the political establishment in the U.S. that did not support him and believed he was not worthy of the presidency. In scheduling an alternative event on that evening, Trump was thumbing his nose at the elite, at those who believed that did not deserve to be president.

Trump was not "one of them," and his supporters loved him for attacking the snobs in the elite class who mocked them (Hillary Clinton's "deplorables") and where they lived ("flyover states"). There really were two Americas—Trump represented one, and the Washington D.C. insiders represented the other.

Notes

1. Greg Miller, Ellen Nakashima, and Adam Entous, "Obama's Secret Struggle to Punish Russia for Putin's Election Assault," *Washington Post*, June 23, 2017.
2. Evan Osnos, David Remnick, and Joshua Yaffa, "Active Measures: What Lay Behind Russia's Interference in the 2016 election – and what lies ahead?" *New Yorker.* March 6, 2017.
3. Ashley Parker and David E. Sanger, "Donald Trump Calls on Russia to Find Hillary Clinton's Missing Emails," *New York Times,* July 27, 2016.
4. Andrew Kaczynski, Chris Massie, and Nathan McDermott, "80 Times Trump Talked About Putin," *CNN Politics*, http://www.cnn.com/interactive/2017/03/politics/trump-putin-russia-timeline.
5. Ibid.
6. See Osnos, Remnick, and Yaffa, "Active Measures," 55.
7. Editorial, "Roger Stone Claims, he has: ' Perfeclty Legal Back Channel' to Julian Assange," *The Guardian*, March 5, 2017.
8. Caroline O., Twitter post, March 4, 2017, 7:45 p.m., http://twitter.com/RVAwonk.
9. Roger Stone, Twitter post, March 4, 2017, 7:05 p.m., http://twitter.com/RogerJStoneJr.
10. Donald Trump, Twitter post, March 4, 2017, 3:35 a.m., http://twitter.com/realDonaldTrump.
11. Donald Trump, Twitter post, March 4, 2017, 3:49 a.m., http://twitter.com/realDonaldTrump.
12. Donald Trump, Twitter post, March 4, 2017, 3:52 a.m., http://twitter.com/realDonaldTrump.
13. Donald Trump, Twitter post, March 4, 2017, 4:02 a.m., http://twitter.com/realDonaldTrump.
14. Donald Trump, Twitter post, March 4, 2017, 5:19 a.m., http://twitter.com/realDonaldTrump.
15. Donald Trump, Twitter post, March 4, 2017, 4:02 a.m., http://twitter.com/realDonaldTrump
16. Joel Goldstein, "Trump opponents have rediscovered the 25th Amendment. Here is what you should know about it," The Washington Post, June 7, 2017, https://www.washingtonpost.com/news/monkey-cage/

wp/2017/06/07/5-things-you-should-know-about-the-25th-amendment/
?utm_term=.9682d781b45d.

17. Rebecca Harrington, "James Clapper: 'There was no such wiretap activity mounted against' Trump," *Business Insider*, March 5, 2017.

18. Peter Baker and Steven Erlanger, "Trump Offers No Apology for Claim on British Spying," *New York Times*, March 17, 2017.

19. Ibid.

20. Steven Swinford, "U.S. Makes Formal Apology to Britain After White House Accuses GCHQ of Wiretapping Trump Towers," *The Telegraph*, March 17, 2017.

21. Donald Trump, Twitter post, March 4, 2017, 4:02 a.m., http://twitter.com/realDonaldTrump.

22. Helena Horton, "Kellyanne Conway mocked for 'spy microwaves' claims during interview about Obama 'wire-tapping'," *The Telegraph*, March 13, 2017, http://www.telegraph.co.uk/news/2017/03/13/kellyanne-conway-mocked-spy-microwaves-claims-interview-obama.]

23. *The Week*, "Trump Tones Down Obama Wiretap Claims," March 24, 2017.

24. Editorial, "House Intelligence Chiefs: We Have Seen No Evidence for Trump's Wiretap Claim," *The Guardian*, March 15, 2017.

25. David Remnick, "First as Tragedy," *The New Yorker*, March 20, 2017.

26. Donald Trump, Twitter post, March 7, 2017, 4:04 a.m., http://twitter.com/realDonaldTrump.

27. Philip Rucker, Robert Costa, and Ashley Parker "Inside Trump's Fury: The President Rages at Leaks, Setbacks, and Accusations" *The Washington Post*, March 5, 2017.

28. Evan Halper "Trump Moves to lift Clean Water Rule," *Los Angeles Times*, March 1, 2017, A7.

29. Lucy Pasha-Robinson, "Donald Tusk says Donald Trump Poses Existential Threat to Europe," *Independent*, January 21, 2017.

30. Samuel Osborne, "Germany Elects 'Anti-Trump Candidate as President,'" *Independent*, February 12, 2017.

31. A *Der Spiegel* Editorial, by Klaus Brinkbäumer, "Trump as Nero: Europe Must Defend Itself Against a Dangerous President," *Der Spiegel*, February 5, 2017.

32. Gloria Borger, "Trump Associate Plays Down Twitter Contact with Guccifer 2.0," *CNN Politics*, March 19, 2017.

33. Baker and Erlanger, "Trump Offers No Apology."

34. US House of Representatives Permanent Select Committee on Intelligence (Democrats), Press Release "Intelligence Committee Ranking Member Schiff Opening Statement During Hearing on Russian Active Measures," March 20, 2017, https://democrats-intelligence.house.gov/news/documentsingle.aspx?DocumentID=220.

35. Matthew Rosenberg and Maggie Haberman, "Advisor Admits Twitter Tie to Russians," *The New York Times*, March 12, 2017, A17.

36. Cristiano Lima, "After Health Care Loss, Trump Tweets 'Let ObamaCare Implode,'" *Politico Podcast*, July 28, 2017.

37. Tom Howell Jr., "Trump Limits Reach of Obamacare on 2016 Tax Filings," *The Washington Times*, April 17, 2017.

38. Dan Merica, "Trump Passes the Buck-And How It could Hurt Him Going Forward," *CNN Politics*, July 19, 2017.

39. Steven Rattnew, "Pushing Obamacare Over the Cliff," *The New York Times*, March 28, 2017, A25; and Editorial, "Sabotaging Obamacare Again," *The Los Angeles Times*, March 31, 2017, A8.

40. Andrew Roth, "New Democrats Show Trump Aide Laundered Payments From Party with Moscow Ties, Lawmaker Alleges," *The Washington Post*, March 21, 2017.

41. Madeline Conway, "In awkward exchange, Trump seems to ignore Merkel's handshake request," March, 17, 2017, *POLITICO*, http://www.politico.com/story/2017/03/trump-angela-merkel-no-handshake-236175 ; Editorial, "A Lapdog in a Watchdog Role," *The New York Times*, March 24, 2017, A22.

42. "Germany: Merkel's Bewildering Meeting with Trump," *The Week*, March 31, 2017.

43. John Sicliano, "Mulvaney: Trump Budget Pulls Back From 'Crazy' Climate Stuff," *Washington Examiner*, May 23, 2017.

44. Coral Davenport and Alissa J. Rubin, "Trump Signs Executive Order Unwinding Obama Climate Policies," *New York Times*, March 28, 2017.

45. Evan Halper, "Trump Makes His Mark on Environment," *The Los Angeles Times*, April 30, 2017, A1.

46. Donald Trump, Twitter post, May 4, 2012, 1:13 p.m., http://twitter.com/realDonaldTrump.

47. Donald Trump, Twitter post, November 5, 2012, 8:50 a.m., http://twitter.com/realDonaldTrump.

48. Donald Trump, Twitter post, April 3, 2013, 2:14 a.m., http://twitter.com/realDonaldTrump.

49. Donald Trump, Twitter post, December 6, 2013, 7:13 a.m., http://twitter.com/realDonaldTrump.

50. Donald Trump, Twitter post, December 28, 2013, 4:30 a.m., http://twitter.com/realDonaldTrump.

51. Donald Trump, Twitter post, January 25, 2014, 1:40 p.m., http://twitter.com/realDonaldTrump.

52. Editorial, "President Trump Risks the Planet." *The New York Times,* March 29, 2017, A26.

53. Mark R. Warner, US Senator from the Commonwealth of Virginia, "Sen. Warner's Opening Statement at Senate Intel Committee Hearing on Russian Hacking," January 10, 2017, https://www.warner.senate.gov/public/index.cfm/blog?ID=A1A338E7-6E95-4D9D-82B8-EFBA901821C7.

54. Callum Borchers, "Trump's First 100 Days: An Investigation, and a Revelation on the 'Dossier'," *The Washington Post,* March 29, 2017.

55. Rachel Robert, "Russians Hired 1,000 People to Create Anti-Clinton 'Fake News'," *The Independent* (of London), March 30, 2017.

56. Tom LoBianco, Eugene Scott, and Ashley Killough, "Nunes Apologizes to House Intel Committee," *CNN Politics,* March 23, 2017.

57. Natasha Bertrand, "'This is a bizarre situation: John McCain says Congress no longer has 'credibility' to conduct Trump-Russia probe alone," *Business Insider,* March 22, 2017.

58. "3/31/17: White House Press Briefing" *The White House,* March 31, 2017.

59. Oren Dorell, "Trump's Business Network Reaches Alleged Russian Mobsters," *USA Today,* March 28, 2017.

60. "Partisan Battle Stalls House Russia Probe," *The Week,* April 7, 2017, 5.

61. Ben Brody, "Flynn's Secrete Foreign Ties May Have Broken the Law Chaffetz Says," *Bloomberg Politics,* April 25, 2017.

62. "The World at Large," *The Week,* April 7, 2017, 9.

63. Sam Stein and Dana Liebelson, "Donald Trump Encourages Violence at His Rallies. His Fans are Listening," The Huffington Post, March 10, 2016

64. Aaron Blake, "A Judge rules Trump may have incited violence...And Trump again has his own mouth to blame" *Washington Post,* April 2, 2017.

65. Editorial, "Our Dishonest President," *Los Angeles Times,* April 2, 2017.

66. Ariane deVogue and Dan Berman, "Neil Gorsuch Confirmed to the Supreme Court," *CNN Politics,* April 7, 2017.

67. In point of fact, President Trump has spent far more time golfing than his predecessor. Lauren Carroll and John Kruzel, "Who plays more golf: Donald Trump or Barack Obama? *Politifact,* August 1, 2017.

68. Ibid.

69. Harriet Alexander, Madgy Samaan, and Raf Sanchez, "Donald Trump Welcomes Egypt's President and says he has 'close to him every since the first time we met,'" *The Telegraph*, April 3, 2017.

70. Doyle McManus, "So Much for Human Rights," *The Los Angeles Times*, April 5, 2017. A13.

71. Neil Connor, "Ivanka Trump and Jared Kushner 'invited to visit China,'" *The Telegraph*, June 21, 2017

72. Barbara Starr and Jeremy Diamond, "Trump Launches Military Strike Against Syria," *CNN Politics*, April 7, 2017.

73. Angela Dewan, Euan McKirdy, and Nicole Gaouette, "Putin Meets with Tillerson in Russia as Syria Rift Deepens," *CNN Politics*, April 12, 2017.

74. Rex Tillerson, *ABC This Week*, April 8, 2017.

75. Elise Viebeck, "Trump's First 100 Days: The Expanding Web of Connections Between Trump World and Russia," *The Washington Post*, April 3, 2017.

76. Ibid.

77. Tracy Wilkinson and Brian Bernett, "Trump Foreign Policy Scotch," *The Los Angeles Times*, April 14, 2017, A1.

78. Nicholas Confessore, Nicholas Fandos, and Rachel Shorey, "Vested Donors Gave Millions to Inaugural," *The New York Times*, April 20, 2017, A1.

79. Ellen Nakashima, Devlin Barrett, and Adam Entous, "FBI Obtained FISA Warrant to Monitor Trump Adviser Carter Page," *Washington Post*, April 11, 2017.

80. Julie Hirschfeld Davis, "White House to Keep Its Visitor Logs Secret," *The New York Times*, April 14, 2017, https://www.nytimes.com/2017/04/14/us/politics/visitor-log-white-house-trump.html

81. Eric Lipton, Ben Protess, and Andrew W. Lehren, "Raft of Potential Conflicts in President's Appointees," *The New York Times*, April 16, 2017, A1.

82. Dave Boyer, "Sean Spicer resigns as White House press secretary, calls Scaramucci hire a mistake," *The Washington Times*, July 21, 2017, http://www.washingtontimes.com/news/2017/jul/21/sean-spicer-resigns-as-white-house-press-secretary.

83. Ryan Lizza, "Anthony Scaramucci Called Me to Unload About White House Leakers, Reince Priebus, and Steve Bannon, " The New Yorker, July 27, 2017, http://www.newyorker.com/news/ryan-lizza/anthony-scaramucci-called-me-to-unload-about-white-house-leakers-reince-priebus-and-steve-bannon.

84. Ibid.
85. Sam Levine, "Trump Was Reportedly Upset Reince Priebus Didn't Fight Back Against Anthony Scaramucci," *Huffington Post*, July 29, 2017, http://www.huffingtonpost.com/entry/reince-priebus-anthony-scaramucci_us_597ca1c6e4b02a8434b6b8a6.
86. Sanders, Sarah Huckabee. "Press Briefing by Press Secretary Sarah Huckabee Sanders." *The White House*, July 27, 2017. Accessed July 27, 2017. https://www.whitehouse.gov/the-press-office/2017/07/27/press-briefing-press-secretary-sarah-sanders-7272017-2. See also Sam Levine, "Trump Was Reportedly Upset Reince Priebus Didn't Fight Back Against Anthony Scaramucci," July 29, 2017, http://www.huffingtonpost.com/entry/reince-priebus-anthony-scaramucci_us_597ca1c6e4b02a8434b6b8a6.
87. Tom Phillips, "Donald Trump says China does 'nothing' to thwart North Korea's nuclear quest," *The Guardian*, July 30, 2017, https://www.theguardian.com/us-news/2017/jul/30/donald-trump-says-china-does-nothing-to-thwart-north-koreas-nuclear-quest.
88. Donald Trump, Twitter post, July 29, 2017, 4:29 p.m., http://twitter.com/realDonaldTrump.
89. Phillips, "Donald Trump says China does 'nothing'."
90. James Griffiths and Dana Bash, "US Vice President Pence visits DMZ amid high tensions with North Korea," *CNN Politics*, April 17, 2017.
91. Mark Landler and Eric Schmitt, "Aircraft Carrier Wasn't Sailing to Deter North Korea, as U.S. Suggested," *The New York Times*, April 18, 2017, https://www.nytimes.com/2017/04/18/world/asia/aircraft-carrier-north-korea-carl-vinson.html.
92. Charles Krauthammer, "The Great Reversal-for now," *Washington Post*, April 13, 2017.
93. Samuel Osborne, " Donald Trump Admits Xi Jiping Gives Him a History Lesson on North Korea," *Independent*, April 13, 2017.
94. Samuel Osborne, " Donald Trump Admits Xi Jiping Gives Him a History Lesson on North Korea," *Independent*, April 13, 2017.
95. Ibid.
96. Matt Stiles, "For South Korea, Trump Gaffes Come at a Fraught Time," *The Los Angeles Times*, April 23, 2017, A3.
97. Karen Tumulty and David Nakamura, "Trump vowed, 'I alone can fix it.' But he discovers power has limits," *The Washington Post*, February 6, 2017, https://www.washingtonpost.com/politics/trump-vowed-i-alone-can-fix-it-but-he-discovers-power-has-limits/2017/02/05/6e323320-ebc4-11e6-b4ff-ac2cf509efe5_story.html?utm_term=.a8250aec2ef5.

98. Donald Trump, Twitter post, April 21, 2017, 3:50 a.m., http://twitter. com/realDonaldTrump.

99. Allan Smith and Samantha Lee, "Here's How Trump's 100-day approval rating-the lowest in modern history-compares to recent presidents," *Business Insider*, May 1, 2017.

100. Ibid.

101. Vivian Yee, "Judge Blocks Trump Effort to Withhold Money from Sanctuary Cities," *New York Times*, April 25, 2017.

102. Adam Behsudi, "Why Trump is Starting a Trade War with Canada," *Politico*, April 25, 2017.

103. Wilson Andrews, Kenan Davis, Adam Pearce, and Nadja Popovich, "What Trump's Tax Proposal Will Cost'" *The New York Times*, April 28, 2017, A18.

104. Julie Hirschfield Davis and Patricia Cohen, "Trump's Plan Shifts Trillions to Wealthiest," *The New York Times*, April 28, 2017, A1.

105. Peter Coy, "Trump Promised to Eliminate National Debt in Eight Years. Good Luck With That," *Bloomberg Businessweek*, March 9, 2017, https:// www.bloomberg.com/news/articles/2017-03-09/trump-promised-to- eliminate-national-debt-in-eight-years-good-luck-with-that.

106. Tony Nitti, "Trump's 'Massive' Middle-Class Tax Cuts Are Tiny Compared To Those Promised To The Rich," Forbes.com, March 1, 2017, https://www.forbes.com/sites/anthonynitti/2017/03/01/president- trump-promises-massive-middle-class-tax-cuts-but-will-he-deliver/#1 b42c6886b9e.

107. Ibid.

108. Ibid.

109. Ashley Parker, Phillip Rucker, Damian Paletta, and Karen DeYoung, "'I was all set to terminate': Inside Trump's Sudden Shift on NAFTA," *Washington Post*, April 27, 2017.

110. Peter Coy, Andrew Mayeda, Josh Wingrove, and Eric Martin, "Trump's Modest Proposal for a Nafta Revamp," *Bloomberg Businessweek*, July 20, 2017, https://www.bloomberg.com/news/articles/2017-07-20/trump-s- modest-proposal-for-a-nafta-revamp.

111. Ibid.

112. Donald Trump, Twitter post, July 10, 2012, 10:11 a.m., http://twitter. com/realdonaldtrump.

113. Madeline Conway, "Trump boasts about getting Gorsuch confirmed in first 100 days," *POLITICO*, April 10, 2017, http://www.politico.com/

story/2017/04/neil-gorsuch-supreme-court-swearing-in-donald-trump-237073.

114. Lisa Rein, "Slow Pace of Trump Nominations Leaves Cabinet Agencies 'stuck' in Staffing Limbo," *Washington Post*, April 25, 2017.

115. Gerry Mullany, "Trump Warns That 'Major, Major Conflict' With North Korea Is Possible," *The New York Times*, April 27, 2017, https://www.nytimes.com/2017/04/27/world/asia/trump-north-korea-kim-jong-un.html.

116. Gardiner Harris, "200 State Department Posts Stand Empty, and No Rush to Fill Them," *The New York Times*, April 28, 2017, A 14.

117. Activities or official plans that are intended to keep people happy and to stop them from noticing or complaining about problems.

118. Steve Volk and Mark Berman, "Trump opens 100-day rally assailing media for correspondent's dinner," *Washington Post*, April 29, 2017.

119. Laura King, "Trump Scrambles for a Win," *The Los Angeles Times*, April 24, 2017. A1.

120. Donald Trump, Twitter post, May 8, 2017, 4:57 a.m., http://twitter.com/realdonaldtrump.

121. Glen Kessler, "Trump's pointing of the finger at Obama for failing to vet Flynn," *The Washington Post*, May 9, 2017, https://www.washingtonpost.com/news/fact-checker/wp/2017/05/09/trumps-pointing-of-the-finger-at-obama-for-failing-to-vet-flynn/?utm_term=.3c09198bfcca.

122. Dan Berman, "Trump: I thought it would be easier," *CNN Politics*, April 28, 2017.

123. Michael A. Genovese, *News to a New President* (New York: Oxford University Press, 2008).

124. Mark Z. Barabak, "Like it or Not, It's been 100 Days of Trump in Office," *The Los Angeles Times*, April 29, 2017, A2.

125. Alexandra King, "Zakaria: Trump has done 'hardly anything,'" *CNN Politics*, February 19, 2017.

126. RealClearPolitics, President Trump Job Approval Poll, https://www.realclearpolitics.com/epolls/other/president_trump_job_approval-6179.html.

127. David Gergen, CNN interview, *CNN*, March 24, 2017; and Michael D. Schmear, "For Trump, Missteps May Be Biggest Obstacle to Meeting Policy Goals," *The New York Times*, March 26, 2017, 17.

128. Nikita Vladimirov, "Trump: My first 100 hundred days 'just about the msost successful ever,'" *The Hill*, April 8, 2017.

CHAPTER 9

THE WAY AHEAD

> If this were a dictatorship, it'd be a heck of a lot easier, just so long as I'm the dictator.
>
> —George W. Bush,
> six days after the Supreme Court
> made him president

In a democracy, people tend to get the government they deserve. It remains to be seen just what we got in outsider Donald J. Trump.

In the United States, elections determine who wins political office, not necessarily who gets to wield political power. Power must be won, earned, and taken. In most areas, presidents are dependent on others either to cooperate (e.g., The Senate must confirm a president's Supreme Court nominees) or capitulate (e.g., when Congress "allows" the president to commit U.S. troops to hostilities absent congressional authorization). There are few areas where a president may legitimately act alone.

We've had several historic presidential elections in a row: In 2008, we elected the nation's first African American; in 2016, for the first time, a major party nominated a woman president; also in 2016, we elected the first president with no political or military experience.

Trump got to the White House as an agent of change. He wants to be a transformational leader who makes dramatic changes, disrupts the status quo, and makes America great again. "We keep losing" he would say during the campaign, "we have to win again."

But his road to the White House was also a journey through some of the darker forces in American politics. He made openly racist remarks, which brought white supremacists out of the shadows and legitimized their efforts. He made openly misogynistic statements such as we all heard from the Access Hollywood tape ("I just grab them by the p***y"). He insisted that *he* and only *he* could save America (on his Easter Sunday Tweet he wrote "Another radical Islamic attack...I alone can solve"[1]). He mocked his opponents ("Lyin' Ted, Little Marco, Crooked Hillary"). He disparaged our electoral process ("It is rigged," adding that if he did not win he might not accept the outcome of the election[2]). And he displayed the qualities of a narcissist ("I know more than the generals"[3]).

Donald Trump is not the first such figure in American history, but he is the first to be elected president. Huey Long, Joseph McCarthy, and others appealed to the darker forces within us, but in the end, their anger and hatred were rejected. Trump's anger and hatred were rewarded. In fact, it carried him to the White House.

Now the question is, *can he govern?* Getting elected is one thing, governing quite another. What got him to the White House might not work in the White House.

Upon entering office, Donald Trump enjoyed what is the most important ingredient for presidential success: his party controlled both houses of Congress. But his election victory gave him little political capital, his experience in government was nonexistent, and he was an intentionally divisive figure.

A Businessman In the White House

Trump's outsider status is often touted by Trump supporters; they believe that because he is a successful businessman, he can bring the skills of running a large business to running the government. But are the skills and experiences of a businessman—however successful—truly transferable to governing?

Let us proceed by first asking, *just what does a president have to do?* Perhaps the best way to answer that question in the context of the race for the presidency is to treat the selection of a new president as one would any other job opening; by putting together a "want ad" for the job. It would look something like this:

> WANTED: A chief executive of a large multidimensional organization that is directly responsible for more than 320 million people. The successful applicant should have substantial executive/managerial experience, be of the highest character, have a proven track-record of success, must be able to work well with others and be able to bargain, compromise, and build coalitions and consensus. The occupant of this job will have very limited power to accomplish the very high expectations placed upon him/her. Long hours (12-hour days will be the norm for entire time in office). Must be very dignified as job entails numerous ceremonial duties. Should have experience in the following fields: national security, economics, health care, crisis management, education, immigration, fighting terrorism, diplomacy, environmental management, building a democracy, working with an independent and very powerful Board of Directors (we call them Congress), wide experience in public speaking. Some background in the military would be helpful but not necessary. Must be a high-energy, thick-skinned person who can take constant criticism as he/she and their family live in a 24/7 fishbowl with virtually no privacy. Performance evaluations occur every day, often several times each day, and are circulated across the globe. Any blemish on one's record will be blown out of proportion. Must also have a winning personality, exhibit strength and resolve where necessary, but be able to compromise most of the time. Be willing to order thousands of

your employees to their possible death, and be willing to kill an undetermined number of our organizations competitors. Should be a people person. The applicant will have to get elected by an angry and demanding electorate, roughly half of whom will hate him/her from day one. Entry fee to apply is over $1 billion. Poor people, middle-class workers, and those unable or unwilling to raise this money should not apply. Note: The job interview will take three years, and you will hardly be able to see your family for those three years. If the applicant, and/or the applicant's spouse, family, and associates have any "skeletons" in their closet, these will be exposed on national media. Working environment is generally pleasant enough, but the pay is not commensurate with what one might expect. A good deal of travel (in high style) will be required. Housing is included, along with round-the-clock assistance to attend to the successful applicant's every need.[4]

To fill this job, we put a number of self-selected people through a rigorous job interview: the campaign. In this extended job interview, we get to see certain characteristics of the applicant on display, and judge whether person X fits the demands of the job. Also, we would want to see "letters of recommendation" from people whom we respect and who might know how qualified person X is for the job. We might also ask how well people with X's background have done when they were given the job. Finally, we have to match skills and temperament with the job at hand and make a determination.

By this standard, how has Trump fared? First, his campaign was high on glamour and bombast, but short on policy. He has proven to be an attractive personality able to draw attention and votes. He might fail the character test because of his constant attacks on rivals as "dumb," "dull," "low energy" a "liar" a "loser"; open mocking of the disabled; announcements that he'd like to "punch someone in the face"; declarations of wanting to round up and deport 11 million people living illegally in the U.S., build a wall that someone else (Mexico) is supposed to pay for, kill the families of terrorists, bring back torture, including waterboarding and much worse; and demeaning the military service war heroes like John McCain.

Virtually no person with knowledge of the presidency and politics endorsed Trump. His letters of recommendation were thin and troubling. He is a very successful businessman, but the only other true businessman to get to the White House is Herbert Hoover, widely seen as an unsuccessful president.

Finally, is Trump a good match for the demands of the job? That, of course, is for the voters to decide. In that, this choice says about as much about the state of the Republican Party as it does about Trump.

Is being a successful businessman similar to being a successful president? The jobs do share some characteristics (running a large organization, appealing to the public's taste), but overall there is a very thin link between a successful businessperson and a successful president.

Moreover, Trump ran a *family business*, and did not have to deal with a board, stockholders, or rivals for these positions.

First, in business the goal is very clear: make money. In politics, the goal is contested territory. Is the goal to further justice? Equality? Individual Rights? Opportunity? Liberty? Security? And when we must choose one over the other (e.g., giving up some of our rights for more security), how do we decide? On what basis?

Second, in business there is a command/hierarchy model of leadership that is nothing like the persuade/fragmentation model in government. The president of a corporation can order underlings to act, and act they will. A president has no such power. He must seek compliance from others who do not owe their jobs to him. And rather than there being a clear hierarchy of authority, our political system is fragmented and separated, with multiple veto points over which a president has very limited influence. It is a very frustrating job, and how well one handles setbacks goes a long way in telling us about the fit of temperament to task.

Third, a corporate executive can hire and fire almost at will. Presidents can't fire members of Congress, or Supreme Court Justices. And members of Congress and the Court believe that they should be making the decisions as much as the president. However, it should be noted that the Trump administration has, in less than half a year, witnessed many high-profile exits (either fired by Trump or resignations), such as acting attorney general Sally Yates, national security advisor Michael Flynn, FBI director James Comey, director of the Office of Government Ethics Walter M. Shaub Jr., White House press secretary Sean Spicer, and White House chief-of-staff Reince Priebus.[5] To some, this might further signal a White House in disorder; to Trump supporters, this could reinforce their perception of his good business acumen—getting rid of people who are not performing.

Fourth, business is a one branch operation, whereas government is a three-branch operation. In government power is shared, dispersed, and overlapping. In response to House Speaker Paul Ryan's questioning him about Trump's tepid denunciation of the racist David Duke, Trump responded, "Paul Ryan. I don't know him well, but I'm sure I'm going to get along great with him. And if I don't, he's going to have to pay a big price, OK?"[6] That does not bode well for relations with the Congress.

Finally, a corporate leader is largely out of the public eye, while a president is the center of constant attention in the 24/7 intrusive news cycle (something Trump seems to enjoy). A president and the presidential family are put under a microscope, and if there is but a single small blemish on any family member, it will become the topic of national conversation, even ridicule. And for Trump, running a family business meant no board of directors to answer to, and no institutional check-and-balances on the exercise of power—all very different from running the White House.

From Liberal to Illiberal Democracy

Governing is a specialized task. All the great thinkers from Plato, to Machiavelli, to Erasmus believed so, and we should too. It requires skill, experience, knowledge, character, vision, temperament and, most of all, sound judgment. Is Trump truly qualified?

Donald J. Trump represents a distinctly American version of illiberal democracy.[7] We have had our would-be populist demagogues in our past, but none has ever gotten close to becoming president. Donald Trump is thus an American first!

His brash, bombastic, attack style; his bold promises and manifest lack of knowledge; his rapid-fire insults and misogynistic utterances; his racist rants and bullying ways—they all make him a unique and compelling figure.

Trump won the presidency when no one in their right mind thought it possible. He beat sixteen more experienced and more politically accomplished rivals to gain the Republican Party nomination for president; then he beat a seasoned professional in the race to the White House. Trump achieved the near impossible. It is indeed a remarkable accomplishment.

And yet, Trump won—in part—by appealing to our fears, our anger, our prejudices—that which is worst in all of us. It is no accident that the Ku Klux Klan celebrated Trump's victory—they see him as a kindred spirit. And while Trump has denounced such groups, white supremacists hail him as one of their own.

With Trump at the fore, the hate groups began coming out of the shadows. His harsh, and at times hateful, messages directed at Mexicans, women, and Muslims made him a magnet for hate groups across America. Whether he meant to or not, such hate groups saw Trump as validation for their prejudices.

Ironically, Donald Trump represents what our founders most feared: a strong leader enflaming the passions of the people leading to a form of mobocracy. American conservatives have been warning since World War II of government overreach and how governments suffocate liberty. But liberty can be lost not only from the top down but also from the bottom up. Alexis de Tocqueville among others, warned that the people in a democracy—excited, angry, ruled by their passions—could just as easily ride roughshod over the very institutions established to preserve their freedom.[8] The unleashing of popular passions—to Alexander Hamilton and other founders—could lead to tyranny just as easily as a strongman riding to power...only now that tyrant rode to power on the shoulders of the people.

The United States was founded on the basis of principles we call *liberal democracy*. This is a form of—but not pure, direct—democracy that embraces the rule of law, limited government, universal adult suffrage, checks on power with representative government, and a rights-based system with free and fair elections, with a constitution and the separation of government powers.

Examples of liberal democracies are the United States, Great Britain, and Canada. The point of liberal democracy was to both tame the state and give it a warrant to use limited powers granted by the people. No one has argued that liberal democracies are efficient—they are not, but that is the point. They are designed to limit, not liberate, governmental power.

Illiberal democracy is another form of democracy (although some do not see it as democratic). In it, elections are held to choose leaders, power is not separated but is concentrated in the hands of the elected leader. This translates into the people electing a strongman who governs the people without the confining forces of checks and balances or separated powers. The people elect a leader and that leader has the power to govern largely on his own.[9]

Examples of illiberal democracies are Russia, Poland, the Philippines, and Turkey. These electorally based systems confer real power to their elected leaders with little of the red tape and checks imposed by liberal democracies. Illiberal governments do not so much limit power as liberate power.

But giving government so much power opens the door to tyranny and the abuse of power. Thus, if liberal democracies seem able to do too little, illiberal democracies may have the capacity to do too much.

At the end of the Cold War (1989) and with the collapse of the Soviet Union, a number of Soviet client states—Ukraine, Poland, Romania, for example—moved to democracies. It was a time when both democratic political systems and market economic systems dominated the landscape. So thoroughly did the West crush communism that the influential analyst Francis Fukuyama wrote a widely read book entitled *The End of History*. It celebrated the West's victory by announcing that the conflicts that plagued us in the past were over with the total victory of liberal democracy!

Of course, Fukuyama was wrong. Cleavages and conflicts—north versus south, the West versus terrorism—continued to plague the world, and rather than witnessing liberal democracy take the victory lap, these liberal democratic systems soon became—to many—the problem that had to be solved.

The critique was that liberal democracies were too slow to move, too captured by societal elites, unable to perform up to the demands of the public, and unable to solve society's problems. They appeared weak in the face of globalization, hyperchange, and economic stagnation.

On the defensive, liberal governments faced assault largely from the political (sometimes authoritarian) right. The perceived failures of liberal democracies opened a door for the rise of illiberal democracies which held the promise of "getting things done."

As liberal democracies came increasingly to be seen as the enemy, illiberal democracies came to be seen as the solution. A strong government had the capacity to succeed, whereas weak governments were bound to fail.

Today, across the globe illiberal tendencies are on the rise and liberal democracies are on the defensive. The perceived failure of liberal democracies has led to anger and frustration on the part of citizens impatient for the government to govern effectively. Putin in Russia, Orbán in Hungary, Duterte in the Philippines, Erdogan in Turkey, as well as the rise of hard right and neo-Nazi parties in France (Marine Le Pen), Germany (Frauke Petry of the AFD) and elsewhere, are all serious challenges to the liberal democracies they hope to replace.

The American system of government is not built for speed; it is built for deliberation, bargaining, and compromise. Today, voters find this frustrating and unacceptable. We want results, and we want them now!

The promise of Donald J. Trump (Make America Great Again) must be measured against the threat of Donald J. Trump (illiberal tendencies).[10] Can he make our system work, or will he try to destroy the system? Will he work to improve the lot of all Americans, or will he do this for only a select few? Will he divest from the many conflicts of interest that plague him, or will he thumb his nose at legality and propriety? Will he make America great again, or will he be a threat to the republic?

As one suspicious of both Trump's message and methods, I face the uncertain future with a bit more trepidation than usual. I sincerely hope he becomes a great president because if he is great for America, he will also be great for me. My hope is that he succeeds at improving our nation for all its people, that he grows the economy and spreads the benefits widely, that he makes America safer and stronger, and that he heals the wounds of hatred, racism, and sexism. It is a big job. May he be a big enough man to do it.

Many see Trump's ultimate goal being developed under the tutelage of Steve Bannon—the dismantling of the "deep state" better known as the administrative state that consists of career bureaucrats and career intelligence and law enforcement officials. Bannon, Trump's top strategist, has publicly stated that his goal was the "deconstruction" of the administrative state, which he calls the fourth branch of government.[11]

Trump is, by style and temperament, a disruptive force. Steve Bannon's alt-right ideology gives form and content to Trump's personal style. Donald Trump likes being the hammer; Steve Bannon supplies the nails.

As nations such as Turkey, the Philippines, Hungary, Poland move towards what Alexis de Tocqueville warned was the "tyranny of the majority"[12] where electoral victories grant virtually unchecked powers to leaders, and minority interests have few rights and little recourse of courts or other agencies to protect them from official power, the United States may run the risk of sliding into illiberalism.

A healthy democracy embraces debate, recognizes multiple and competing centers of power, employs counter-institutions to check power, and uses countervailing weights to bring about balance and equilibrium. In this sense, the Trump challenge to liberal democracy has been met— and not quite successfully—with pushback and the assertion of authority of other branches, agencies, and actors. The "system"—at least thus far in his presidency—did its job.

THE TRUMP PARADOX

One of the key paradoxes of the American presidency is that the qualities needed to get elected might not be constructive in trying to govern.[13] But Donald Trump is a different sort of president. Might his oversized ego, his excessive need to feel loved and respected, his thin-skinned sensitivity, and his over-the-top anger actually be assets instead of liabilities?

Do the inner needs of Trump make him hungrier to succeed? Do they make him more likely to fight for what he wants and needs? Do they intensify his efforts? And if he puts these motivations toward the service of the people, and not just of himself, might he be more likely to put America first, to Make America Great Again?

There is an old French saying, "Happy people do not make history."[14] Leaders are often people who are angry with the status quo; they are driven to change things. They might even be a bit prickly. But this propels them to leap into battle. Happy people are content with the status quo; they are less inclined to upend the system that has produced their happiness. Thus, might Donald Trump's personal demons drive him to succeed, hopefully for the betterment of the nation?

THE ROAD AHEAD

With little to show for the first 100 days of his administration, along with ongoing staff chaos and turmoil and a confused and shifting agenda, what might the coming years of a Trump presidency bring?

Two political problems that could bring Trump down are Russia and conflicts of interest. Investigations into Russian meddling (and Trump associates colluding) in the 2016 presidential election could erode trust in Trump, or worse, find a "smoking gun" that does Trump in. Even more likely, the ongoing problems with Trump (and family) financial conflicts of interest and violations of the emoluments clause of the U.S. Constitution put the president just one step short of impeachment. Either of those problems could blow up in Trump's face. And Trump's often-repeated defense (the people know who I was and elected me[15]) rings hollow and most assuredly does not give Trump an irreversible "get-out-of-jail-free" card.

Will Trump learn? Will he grow? And did Trump change the presidency, or did the presidency change Trump? The early indications suggest that Trump, satisfied that "being Trump" got him this far sees no need to change now. Let Trump be Trump.

Is the problem Trump's governing style or Trump himself? Some believe that Trump is his own worst enemy—that his narcissism and high self-destructive tweeting, to overconfidence, to bullying, to overestimating (and overstating) his own prowess, to his thin-skinned sensitivity, to his occasional disconnect from reality ("I won the popular vote"), Trump—if he falls—will probably fall from self-inflicted wounds.

The journalist and public intellectual Fareed Zakaria, writing about what Trump's 100 days have taught us, noted:

> We have watched the sheer incompetence of Trump's first 100 days —orders that can't through courts, bills that collapse in Congress, agencies that remain understaffed, ceaseless infighting within the White House and the constant flip-flops. It turns out that running a family-owned real estate franchising operation is not really the same as presiding over the executive branch of the U.S.[16]

One thing the early days of the Trump presidency revealed is that the agents of liberal democracy were still capable of pushing back against aggressive presidential leadership. Congress (even one controlled by the Republicans), the courts, the media, the bureaucracy, and the public, all at various times, when called upon to put a halt to presidential transgressions, rose up and demonstrated that ours is a system of three, not one, branch of government, with fragmented power spread across a wide range of political players. Liberal democracy may be facing a stiff challenge, but as of now, its strength—even its wisdom—is still very much with us.

Donald Trump, in his short time as president, has been a norm-busting, disruptive force in American politics. He has challenged the status quo and tried to upend a few political sacred cows. The forces of the system have pushed back, leading to confrontations, roadblocks, and a good deal of presidential frustration. The professional class of politicians, against whom Trump railed in his inaugural address and elsewhere, did not retreat quietly in the face of Trump's assault. Have we witnessed the first shots fired in what will be a cultural war and political chaos in America? Have the first 100 days been a prelude of a larger battle to come? Can Trump take on the establishment—what Steve Bannon and others call the "deep state"—or are the forces of the status quo, the establishment, too entrenched to be upended?

Winston Churchill once said of Russia, something that applies equally to Donald Trump, "It is a riddle, wrapped in a mystery, inside an enigma."

Or is it simpler than that? Is what you see what you get? Is his disruptive behavior one that is with purpose, or merely disruption for the sake of disruption? Is he the savior of our republic ("I alone can do it"), or is he the chief threat to it?

And what has our brief time with Donald Trump as president revealed about Donald Trump, the man? Is he the spoiled man-child, self-absorbed and narcissistic, or the brave defender of the forgotten Americans? Is he fighting for American values, or a threat to those values? Is Trump being disruptive for a deeper purpose, or just to be disruptive? Does Trump "get it" or is he merely playing a TV reality show role on "governing with the stars?" Is he at all mindful of the damage he is doing, or is that the point?

Donald Trump does not seem temperamentally predisposed to function within the confines of a system of separation-of-powers, where power is fragmented into three different branches of government. Accustomed to being the autocrat within a family business, Trump could not abide by the pushback and roadblocks in a checks-and-balances system. In this sense, he jumped into the deep end of the pool before learning how to swim. Will he drown or learn to swim? Ours is a three—not one—branch government. It is hard to imagine Donald Trump working well with branches that will on occasion put the brakes on his efforts. This will result in a great deal of frustration on Donald Trump's part, and that will likely lead to open conflict between the branches. Such conflict ultimately leads to deadlock, divisiveness, and failed government.

Notes

1. Aaron Blake, "19 things Donald Trump knows better than anyone else." The Washington Post, October 4, 2016, https://www.washingtonpost.com/news/the-fix/wp/2016/10/04/17-issues-that-donald-trump-knows-better-than-anyone-else-according-to-donald-trump/?utm_term=.5d18 8fce374b.
2. Ibid.
3. Ibid.
4. This was previously published in Genovese, *The Trumping of American Politics.*
5. Jeremy Berke, "Here are all the casualties of the Trump administration so far," *Business Insider,* July 28, 2017, http://www.businessinsider.com/who-has-trump-fired-so-far-james-comey-sean-spicer-michael-flynn-2 017-7/#reince-priebus-1.
6. Ian Schwartz, "Trump: Paul Ryan 'will pay a big price' if he doesn't get along," *RealClear Politics,* March 1, 2016.
7. Fareed Zakaria, "America's democracy has become illiberal," *The Washington Post,* December 29, 2016, https://www.washingtonpost.com/opinions/america-is-becoming-a-land-of-less-liberty/2016/12/29/2a9174 4c-ce09-11e6-a747-d03044780a02_story.html?utm_term=.241bced34078.
8. Alexis de Tocqueville, *Democracy in America* (New York: Bantan Classics, 2000).
9. Fareed Zakaria, *The Future of Freedom: Illiberal Democracy at Home and Abroad* (New York: Norton, 2007.
10. See Timothy Snyder, *On Tyranny: Twenty Lessons From the Twentieth Century* (New York: Tim Duggan, 2017).
11. Massimo Calabresi, "Inside Donald Trump's War Against the State," *Time Magazine,* March 20, 2017.
12. Alexis de Tocqueville, *Democracy in America,* edited and translated by Harvey Claflin Mansfield, and Delba Winthrop (Chicago: University of Chicago Press; 2000). This is true, but ironically, Trump does not have majority support in the country or among voters, though he does have majorities in Congress.
13. Thomas E. Cronin, Michael A. Genovese, and Meena Bose, *The Paradoxes of the American Presidency,* 5th edition (New York: Oxford University Press, 2017).

14. French folktale believed to be from the 16th century.
15. Margaret Hartmann, "Trump on business conflicts: you knew who you were voting for," *New York Magazine*, November 22, 2016.
16. Fareed's Global Briefing, *CNN*, April 28, 2017.

POSTSCRIPT

In the post-100-day period, things went from bad, to worse, to disastrous for President Trump. His popularity plummeted, his agenda stalled, a House committee, a Senate committee and a special prosecutor were on the trail of Trump corruption, as of mid-June the Muslim travel ban was still stalled, a trip to the Middle East and Europe produced mock derision aimed at Trump for his curtsy to the Saudi leader, and a series of disastrous meetings with our allies (who were treated as adversaries by Trump), outrage as Trump pulled the U.S. out of the Paris climate accord (the U.S., Syria, and Nicaragua were the only nations who refused to be a part of the accord, with more than190 nations in favor of the Paris deal), and the list goes on.

Crisis after crisis has marked the Trump presidency, to the point that it is no longer a question of the crisis du jour, but the crisis of the moment. This is because the White House operates on chaos, distraction, and disruption. This is a White House at war with itself. Take, for an example, Anthony Scaramucci, who was fired as White House communications director after only ten days, reportedly because of his foul-mouthed rant to a reporter.[1] While some might argue that firing Scaramucci is a good move and shows how Trump is quick to right wrongs, others might argue that hiring Scaramucci in the first place demonstrates flawed judgment. And yet, on the day Scaramucci was fired, Trump tweeted in the midst of all the chaos: "No WH chaos!"[2] and that it was "A great day at the White House!"[3]

There are many problems that need to be addressed, but Trump does not seem to be able to take responsibility. For example, he blamed Reince Priebus and replaced him with John Kelly as chief of staff. Kelly is an excellent choice because he will bring order, hierarchy, and discipline to the White House staff—one of his first orders was to ask Scaramucci to leave, which signals a good start[4]—but the real question is whether he can bring order, hierarchy, and discipline to President Trump. Trump has shown that he can tear down but he is not able to build up, at least so far.

As far as health care is concerned, the table is set for a bipartisan deal but is not encouraging. There are two problems: the Democrats and the Republicans. The Democrats have built their whole approach to resisting any GOP efforts, but they have failed the American people because they have not offered any alternatives. The Republicans have failed us because they cannot come up with an alternative plan that is widely acceptable. President Trump has said that we should just let Obamacare implode. This would be grossly irresponsible because millions of Americans would suffer. A president cannot control the challenges that he faces but he must nevertheless deal with them. To walk away and let the problem implode is grossly irresponsible. Trump's response has been "If ObamaCare is hurting people, & it is, why shouldn't it hurt the insurance companies & why should Congress not be paying what public pays?"[5] While the idea that spreading the damage all around to the insurance companies and Congress would force a change, the damage done to millions of Americans as we wait for this could be irreversible. Lives are literally at stake. Surely, the president should take the lead in trying to broker a bipartisan deal. After all, he wrote *The Art of the Deal.*

On the international front, the problem from hell is North Korea and its nuclear missiles. As North Korea launched its second successful missile launch, we face a situation of two volatile leaders—Trump and Kim Jong-un. The way out of this mess, which the military has already brought up, is the Iran nuclear model. Although it is an imperfect solution, it will help move things forward. Even though it is what the generals and analysts are recommending, Trump is very opposed to doing anything like the Iran nuclear deal because of its flaws. This boils down to an issue of sacrificing the good for the perfect. How Trump handles North Korea is one of the biggest tests of his presidency.

Related to this is Trump's encouragement of South Korea and Japan building their own nuclear weapons, but there is no question that the world is better off with fewer nuclearized countries. There are many problems with proliferation, from weapons getting into the wrong hands or potential catastrophic accidents. So, the fewer nuclear powers there are, the better for the world. To encourage the nuclearization of the Pacific is a crisis waiting to happen.

On July 31, 2017, Trump declared that "Highest Stock Market EVER, best economic numbers in years, unemployment lowest in 17 years, wages raising, border secure, S.C.: No WH chaos!"[6] President Trump kept tweeting, kept being the brash person he was during the campaign and first 100 days. Did Trump *learn*, did he *grow* into the office? Clearly not.

Trump is Trump, and continues to be; even if it profits him to change, he refuses. Used to bullying and pressuring others, used to getting his way in the Trump family business, now, as president, Trump believes he can bully Congress, the courts, the media, the intelligence agencies, and even our allies and adversaries. The president, however, is facing serious (and expected) pushback from members of Congress who are not dependent on Trump for their positions; judges who have safe, lifetime appointments; a free press; a determined set of professionals in the intelligence agencies; and allies who fear that Trump is not a reliable friend. At the same time, there are adversaries who know that the way to Trump's heart is with excessive flattery.

By mid-June, D.C. insiders began discussing impeachment in their conversations about Trump. Less than six months into his presidency, the possibility of impeaching Trump became an issue of discussion. Two members of Congress (unsurprisingly, both Democrats, Al Green of Texas and Brad Sherman of California) announced that they were in the process of drafting impeachment resolutions. If to most observers, this seemed premature, this was nonetheless a sign of just how much trouble President Trump was in.[7]

Donald Trump, the outsider, defiantly marched into Washington to "drain the swamp," oust the establishment that had mocked him, unravel the "deep state." He would, he promised, bring about a revolution in America in which the cancerous, selfish establishment elites would be replaced by Trump as tribune of "the people."

But the biggest thing blocking this revolution was Trump himself. He shook things up; he was a disruptive force, but the reality that what gets torn down must be built up is becoming very stark. This was perhaps why Trump appointed John Kelly as chief of staff whose "absence of partisan stripes" makes Kelly a valuable asset as "Trump, who campaigned promising to be a dealmaking president, is eager for his chief of staff to have an open dialogue with Democratic leaders and to try to build bipartisan coalitions this fall on tax policy and infrastructure spending, especially as tensions with recalcitrant Republicans rise."[8]

A large agenda remained unfulfilled. If most doubted that President Trump could achieve his goals, many still hoped that somehow *we* could continue to make America greater.

Notes

1. Abby Phillip and Damian Paletta, "Anthony Scaramucci removed as White House communications director," *The Washington Post*, July 31, https://www.washingtonpost.com/news/post-politics/wp/2017/07/31/anthony-scaramucci-removed-as-white-house-communications-director/?utm_term=.cdf8f35bae66.
2. Donald Trump, Twitter post, July 31, 2017, 5:28 a.m., http://twitter.com/realdonaldtrump.
3. Donald Trump, Twitter post, July 31, 2017, 3:19 p.m., http://twitter.com/realdonaldtrump.
4. Jennifer Rubin, "Scaramucci's firing means John Kelly is off to a good start," *The Washington Post*, July 31, 2017, https://www.washingtonpost.com/blogs/right-turn/wp/2017/07/31/scaramuccis-firing-means-john-kelly-is-off-to-a-good-start/?utm_term=.848b6b769f42.
5. Donald Trump, Twitter post, July 31, 2017, 5:16 a.m., http://twitter.com/realdonaldtrump.
6. Donald Trump, Twitter post, July 31, 2017, 5:28 a.m., http://twitter.com/realdonaldtrump.
7. See Editorial, "The Impeachment Zone," *The Los Angeles Times*, June 11, 2017; and Lawrence H. Tritle, "Trump Must Be Impeached: Here's Why," *The Washington Post*, May 13, 2017.
8. Robert Costa and Philip Rucker, "Even in North Korea crisis, retired general John Kelly is an apolitical force in a White House divided by ideology," *The Washington Post*, August 9, 2017, https://www.washingtonpost.com/politics/john-kelly-is-an-apolitical-force-in-a-white-house-divided-by-ideology/2017/08/08/6a14cd4a-7c4a-11e7-9d08-b79f191668ed_story.html?utm_term=.addd7e829df0.

Selected Bibliography

By Donald J. Trump

Trump, Donald J., and Tony Schwartz. *Trump: The Art of the Deal.* London: Arrow Books, 2016.

Trump, Donald, and Charles Leerhsen. *Trump: Surviving at the Top.* New York: Random House, 1990.

Trump, Donald, and Charles Leerhsen. *Trump: The Art of Survival.* New York, N.Y.: Warner Books, 1990.

Trump, Donald J, and Kate Bohner. *Trump: The Art of the Comeback.* New York: Times Books, 1997.

Trump, Donald, and Dave Shiflett. *The America We Deserve.* Los Angeles: Renaissance Books, 2000.

Trump, Donald, Meredith McIver, and Donald Trump. *Trump: How to Get Rich; and; Think Like a Billionaire.* New York: Random House, 2004.

Trump, Donald J. *The Way to the Top: The Best Business Advice I Ever Received.* New York: Crown Publishers, 2004.

Trump, Donald. *How to Build a Fortune: Your Plan for Success from the World's Most Famous Businessman.* Trump University, 2005.

Trump, Donald, and Robert T. Kiyosaki. *Why We Want You To Be Rich: Two Men-One Message.* Scottsdale: Plata Publishing, LLC., 2015.

Trump, Donald, Bill Zanker, and Donald Trump. *Think Big: Make It Happen in Business and Life.* New York: Morrow Avon, 2012.

Trump, Donald, and Meredith McIver. *Trump 101: The Way to Success.* Hoboken: John Wiley & Sons Incorporated, 2007.

Trump, Donald, and Meredith McIver. Trump Never Give Up: How I Turned My Biggest Challenges into Success. Hoboken: Wiley, 2013.

Trump, Donald, and Meredith McIver. Think Like a Champion: An Informal Education in Business and Life. Philadelphia: Running Press, 2013.

Trump, Donald, and Robert T. Kiyosaki. Midas Touch: Why Some Entrepreneurs Get Rich-- and Why Most Don't. Scottsdale: Plata Publishing, 2012.

Trump, Donald J. Time to Get Tough: Make America Great Again. Washington DC: Regnery Publishing, 2011.

Trump, Donald. Great Again: How to Fix Our Crippled America. New York: Threshold Editions, 2016.

About Donald J Trump

Barrett, Wayne. Trump: The Deals and the Downfall. New York: HarperCollins, 1992.

Blair, Gwenda. Donald Trump: The Candidate. New York: Simon & Schuster, 2007.

Coulter, Ann H. In Trump We Trust: E Pluribus Awesome! New York: Sentinel, 2016.

D'Antonio, Michael. Never Enough: Donald Trump and the Pursuit of Success. New York: Thomas Dunne Books, St. Martin's Press, 2016.

Hurt, Harry. Lost Tycoon: The Many Lives of Donald J. Trump. Brattleboro: Echo Point Books & Media, 2016.

Katz, Jackson. Man Enough?: Donald Trump, Hillary Clinton, and the Politics of Presidential Masculinity. Northampton: Interlink Books, 2016.

Kranish, Michael, and Marc Fisher. Trump Revealed: An American Journey of Ambition, Ego, Money and Power. London: Simon & Schuster UK Ltd., 2017.

Lord, Jeffrey. What America Needs: The Case for Trump. Washington DC: Regnery Publishing, 2016.

O'Brien, Timothy L. TrumpNation: The Art of Being The Donald. New York: Grand Central Publishing, 2016.

O'Donnell, John R. *Trumped!: The Inside Story of the Real Donald Trump - His Cunning Rise and Spectacular Fall.* New York: Pocket Books, 1993.

Ross, George H. *Trump-Style Negotiation: Powerful Strategies and Tactics for Mastering Every Deal.* Hoboken: Wiley, 2013.

Schlafly, Phyllis, Ed Martin, and Brett M. Decker. *The Conservative Case for Trump.* Washington DC: Regnery Publishing, 2016.

Slater, Robert. *No Such Thing as Over-Exposure: Inside the Life and Celebrity of Donald Trump.* Upper Saddle River: Prentice Hall, 2005.

Stone, Roger J. *The Making of the President 2016: How Donald Trump Orchestrated a Revolution.* New York: Skyhorse Publishing, 2017.

Taibbi, Matt, and Victor Juhasz. *Insane Clown President: Dispatches from the 2016 Circus.* New York: Spiegel & Grau, 2017.

Tuccille, Jerome. *Trump: The Saga of America's Most Powerful Real Estate Baron.* Washington, DC: Beard Books, 2004.

Williamson, Kevin D. *Case Against Trump.* New York: Encounter Books, 2015.

Wooten, Sara McIntosh. *Donald Trump: From Real Estate to Reality TV.* Berkeley Heights, NJ: Enslow Publishers, 2009.

INDEX

CPSIA information can be obtained
at www.ICGtesting.com
Printed in the USA
LVHW040006160819
627876LV00002B/216

9 781604 979886